The Golden Chersonese and the Way Thither (Travels in Malaysia)

The Golden Chersonese and the Way Thither (Travels in Malaysia)

Victorian Travelogue Series (Annotated)

Isabella Lucy Bird

Cedar Lake Classics

Copyright © 2023 by Cedar Lake Classics

This is a proofread and newly designed edition of a public domain work.

CONTENTS

PREFACE	ix
INTRODUCTORY CHAPTER	xiii
Letter I	1
Letter II	7
Letter III	13
Letter IV	22
Letter IV Continued	34
Letter IV Concluded	46
Letter V	51
Letter VI	57
Letter VII	69
Letter VIII	81
Letter IX	86
Letter X	100

CONTENTS

A CHAPTER ON SUNGEI UJONG | 111

Letter XI | 118

Letter XII | 125

Letter XIII | 137

A CHAPTER ON SELANGOR* | 157

Letter XIV | 163

Letter XIV | Continued 172

Letter XV | 182

Letter XVI | 188

Letter XVII | 196

A CHAPTER ON PERAK | 205

Letter XVIII | 216

Letter XIX | 230

Letter XX | 234

Letter XX | Continued 247

Letter XX | Concluded 260

Letter XXI | 276

CONTENTS

Letter XXII | 284

Letter XXIII | 299

APPENDIX A: RESIDENTS | 303
APPENDIX B: SLAVERY IN THE MALAY STATES | 305
APPENDIX C: TWO LETTERS | 313
ABOUT ISABELLA LUCY BIRD | 319
BOOKS BY ISABELLA LUCY BIRD | 323

PREFACE

In presenting to the public the last installment of my travels in the Far East, in 1879, I desire to offer, both to my readers and critics, my grateful acknowledgments for the kindness with which my letters from Japan were received, and to ask for an equally kind and lenient estimate of my present volume, which has been prepared for publication under the heavy shadow of the loss of the beloved and only sister to whom the letters of which it consists were written, and whose able and careful criticism, as well as loving interest, accompanied my former volumes through the press.

It is by her wish that this book has received the title of the "Golden Chersonese," a slightly ambitious one; and I must at once explain that my letters treat of only its western portion, for the very sufficient reason that the interior is unexplored by Europeans, half of it being actually so little known that the latest map gives only the position of its coast-line. I hope, however, that my book will be accepted as an honest attempt to make a popular contribution to the sum of knowledge of a beautiful and little-traveled region, with which the majority of educated people are so little acquainted that it is constantly confounded with the Malay Archipelago, but which is practically under British rule, and is probable destined to afford increasing employment to British capital and enterprise.

The introductory chapter, and the explanatory chapters on Sungei Ujong, Selangor and Perak, contain information of a rather more solid character than is given in my sketches of travel, and are intended to make the letters more intelligible and useful.* The map by Mr. Daly is the result of the most recent surveys, and is published here by permission

PREFACE

of the Royal Geographical Society. [*These chapters are based upon sundry reports and other official papers, and I have largely drawn upon those storehouses of accurate and valuable information, Newbold's "British Settlements in Malacca," and Crawfurd's "Dictionary of the Indian Islands."]

As I traveled under official auspices, and was entertained at the houses of officials everywhere, I feel it to be due to my entertainers to say that I have carefully abstained from giving their views on any subjects on which they may have uttered them in the ease of friendly intercourse, except in two or three trivial instances, in which I have quoted them as my authorities. The opinions expressed are wholly my own, whether right or wrong, and I accept the fullest responsibility for them.

For the sketchy personal descriptions which are here and there given, I am sure of genial forgiveness from my friends in the Malay Peninsula, and from them also I doubt not that I shall receive the most kindly allowance, if, in spite of carefulness, I have fallen into mistakes.

In writing to my sister my first aim was accuracy, and my next to make her see what I saw; but beside the remarkably contradictory statements of the few resident Europeans and my own observations, I had little to help me, and realized every day how much truth there is in the dictum of Socrates—"The body is a hindrance to acquiring knowledge, and sight and hearing are not to be trusted."* [*Phaedo of Plato. Chapter x.]

This volume is mainly composed of my actual letters, unaltered, except by various omissions and some corrections as to matters of fact. The interest of my visits to the prison and execution ground of Canton, and of my glimpses of Anamese villages, may, I hope, be in some degree communicated to my readers, even though Canton and Saigon are on the beaten track of travelers.

I am quite aware that "Letters" which have not received any literary dress are not altogether satisfactory either to author or reader, for the author sacrifices artistic arrangement and literary merit, and the reader is apt to find himself involved among repetitions, and a multiplicity of minor details, treated in a fashion which he is inclined to term "slipshod;" but, on the whole, I think that descriptions written on the spot, even with their disadvantages, are the best mode of making the reader travel with the traveler, and share his first impressions in their original vividness. With these explanatory remarks I add my little volume to the ever-growing library of the literature of travel.

I. L. B.
FEBRUARY, 1883

INTRODUCTORY CHAPTER

The Aurea Chersonesus—The Conquest of Malacca—The Straits Settlements—The Configuration of the Peninsula—A Terra Incognita—The Monsoons—Products of the Peninsula—The Great Vampire—Beasts and Reptiles—Malignant and Harmless Insects—Land and Water Birds—Traditions of Malay Immigration—Wild and Civilized Races —Kafirs—The Samangs and Orang-outang—Characteristics of the Jakuns—Babas and Sinkehs—The Malay Physiognomy—Language and Literature—Malay Poetry and Music—Malay Astronomy—Education and Law—Malay Sports—Domestic Habits—Weapons—Slavery and Debt Bondage—Government—"No Information"

Canton and Saigon, and whatever else is comprised in the second half of my title, are on one of the best beaten tracks of travelers, and need no introductory remarks.

But the Golden Chersonese is still somewhat of a terra incognita; there is no point on its mainland at which European steamers call, and the usual conception of it is as a vast and malarious equatorial jungle, sparsely peopled by a race of semi-civilized and treacherous Mohammedans. In fact, it is as little known to most people as it was to myself before I visited it; and as reliable information concerning it exists mainly in valuable volumes now out of print, or scattered through blue books and the Transactions of the Asiatic Society of Singapore, I make no apology for prefacing my letters from the Malay Peninsula with as many brief preliminary statements as shall serve to make them intelligible, requesting those of my readers who are familiar with the subject to skip this chapter altogether.

INTRODUCTORY CHAPTER

The Aurea Chersonesus of Ptolemy, the "Golden Chersonese" of Milton, the Malay Peninsula of our day, has no legitimate claim to an ancient history. The controversy respecting the identity of its Mount Ophir with the Ophir of Solomon has been "threshed out" without much result, and the supposed allusion to the Malacca Straits by Pliny is too vague to be interesting.

The region may be said to have been rediscovered in 1513 by the Portuguese, and the first definite statement concerning it appears to be in a letter from Emanuel, King of Portugal, to the Pope. In the antique and exaggerated language of the day, he relates that his general, the famous Albuquerque, after surprising conquests in India, had sailed to the Aurea Chersonesus, called by its inhabitants Malacca. He had captured the city of Malacca, sacked it, slaughtered the Moors (Mohammedans) who defended it, destroyed its twenty-five thousand houses abounding in gold, pearls, precious stones, and spices, and on its site had built a fortress with walls fifteen feet thick, out of the ruins of its mosques. The king, who fought upon an elephant, was badly wounded and fled. Further, on hearing of the victory, the King of Siam, from whom Malacca had been "usurped by the Moors," sent to the conqueror a cup of gold, a carbuncle, and a sword inlaid with gold. This conquest was vaunted of as a great triumph of the Cross over the Crescent, and as its result, by the year 1600 nearly the whole commerce of the Straits had fallen into the hands of the Portuguese.

Of the remaining "Moorish", or Malay kingdoms, Acheen, in Sumatra, was the most powerful, so powerful, indeed, that its king was able to besiege the great stronghold of Malacca more than once with a fleet, according to the annalist, of "more than five hundred sail, one hundred of which were of greater size than any then constructed in Europe, and the warriors or mariners that it bore amounted to sixty thousand, commanded by the king in person." The first mention of Johore, or Jhor, and Perak occurs about the same time, Perak being represented as a very powerful and wealthy State.

INTRODUCTORY CHAPTER

The Portuguese, by their persevering and relentless religious crusade against the Mohammedans, converted all the States which were adjacent to their conquests into enemies, and by 1641 their empire in the Straits was seized upon by the Dutch, who, not being troubled by much religious earnestness, got on very well with the Malay Princes, and succeeded in making advantageous commercial treaties with them.

A curious but fairly accurate map of the coasts of the Peninsula was prepared in Paris in 1668 to accompany the narrative of the French envoy to the Court of Siam, but neither the mainland nor the adjacent islands attracted any interest in this country till the East India Company acquired Pinang in 1775, Province Wellesley in 1798, Singapore in 1823, and Malacca in 1824. These small but important colonies were consolidated in 1867 into one Government under the Crown, and are now known as the Straits Settlements, and prized as among the most valuable of our possessions in the Far East. Though these settlements are merely small islands or narrow strips of territory on the coast, their population, by the census of 1881, exceeded four hundred and twenty-two thousand souls, and in 1880 their exports and imports amounted to 32,353,000 pounds!

Besides these little bits of British territory scattered along a coast-line nearly four hundred miles in length, there are, on the west side of the Peninsula, the native States of Kedah, Perak, Selangor, and Sungei Ujong, the last three of which are under British "protection;" and on the east are Patani, Kelantan, Tringganu, and Pahang; the southern extremity being occupied by the State of Johore. The interior, which is scarcely at all known, contains toward its centre the Negri Sembilan, a confederation of eight (formerly nine) small States. The population of the native States of the Peninsula is not accurately known, but, inclusive of a few wild tribes and the Chinese immigrants, it is estimated at three hundred and ten thousand; which gives under nine inhabitants to the square mile, the population of the British settlements being about four hundred and twenty to the square mile.

INTRODUCTORY CHAPTER

The total length of the Peninsula is eight hundred miles, and its breadth varies from sixty to one hundred and fifty miles. It runs down from lat. 13 degrees 50' N. to 1 degree 41' N. The northern part, forming the Isthmus of Kraw, which it is proposed to pierce for a ship canal, runs nearly due north and south for one hundred and forty miles, and is inhabited by a mixed race, mainly Siamese, called by the Malays Sansam. This Isthmus is under the rule of Siam, which is its northern boundary; and the northern and eastern States of Kedah, Patani, Kelantan, Pahang, and Tringganu, are more or less tributary to this ambitious empire, which at intervals has exacted a golden rose, the token of vassalage, from every State in the Peninsula. Except at the point where the Isthmus of Kraw joins Siam, the Peninsula is surrounded by the sea to the east by the China Sea and the Gulf of Siam, and to the south and west by the Straits of Malacca and the Bay of Bengal. The area of the mainland is conjectured to be the same as that of Britain, but the region occupied by the Malays does not exceed sixty-one thousand one hundred and fifty square miles, and is about half the size of Java.

Its configuration is not very well known, but a granitic mountain chain, rising in Perak to ascertained heights of eight thousand feet, runs down its whole length near the centre, with extensive outlying spurs, and alluvial plains on both sides densely covered with jungle, as are also the mountains. There are no traces of volcanic formation, though thermal springs exist in Malacca. The rivers are numerous, but with one exception small, and are seldom navigable beyond the reach of the tides, except by flat-bottomed boats. It is believed that there are scarcely any lakes.

The general formation is granitic, overlaid by sandstone, laterite or clay ironstone, and to the north by limestone. Iron ores are found everywhere, and are so little regarded for their metallic contents that, though containing, according to Mr. Logan, a skillful geologist, sixty percent of pure metal, they are used in Singapore for macadamizing the roads! Gold has been obtained in all ages, and formerly in considerable quantities, but the annual yield does not now exceed nineteen thousand ounces. The vastest tin fields in the world are found in the western Malay States, and hitherto the produce has been "stream tin" only, the metal not having been traced to its veins in the rock.

The map, the result of recent surveys by Mr. Daly, and published in 1882 by the Royal Geographical Society, shows that there is a vast extent, more than half of the Malay Peninsula, unexplored. Its most laborious explorer confesses that "of the internal government, geography, mineral products, and geology of these regions, we do not know anything," and, he adds, that "even in this nineteenth century, a country rich in its resources, and important through its contiguity to our British possessions, is still a closed volume." "If we let the needle in, the thread is sure to follow" (meaning that if they let an Englishman pass through their territories, British annexation would be the natural sequence), was the reason given to Mr. Daly for turning him back from the States of the Negri Sembilan.

The climate is singularly healthy for Europeans as well as natives, although both hot and moist, as may be expected from being so close to the equator. Besides, the Peninsula is very nearly an insular region; it is densely covered with evergreen forests, and few parts of it are more than fifty miles from the sea. There are no diseases of climate except marsh fevers, which assail Europeans if they camp out at night on low, swampy grounds.

In 5 degrees 15' N., about the latitude of the northern boundary of Perak, at the sea-level the mean annual temperature is nearly 80 degrees, with a range of 20 degrees; at Malacca in 2 degrees 14' N. it is 80 degrees, with a range of 15 degrees; and at Singapore, in lat. 1 degree 17', it is 82 degrees, with a range of 24 degrees. Though the climate is undeniably a "hot" one, the heat, tempered by alternating land and sea breezes, is seldom oppressive except just before rain, and the thermometer never attains anything approaching those torrid temperatures which are registered in India, Japan, the United States, and other parts of the temperate zones.

INTRODUCTORY CHAPTER

The rainfall is not excessive, averaging about one hundred and ten inches annually, and there is no regular rainy season. In fact it rains in moderation all the year round. Three days seldom pass without refreshing showers, and if there are ten rainless days together, a rare phenomenon, people begin to talk of "the drought." Practically the year is divided into two parts by the "monsoons."* The monsoon is not a storm, as many people suppose, from a vague association of the word "typhoon," but a steady wind blowing, in the case of the Malay Peninsula, for six months from the north-east, bringing down the Chinamen in their junks, and for six months from the southwest, bringing traders from Arabia and India. The climate is the pleasantest during the north-east monsoon, which lasts from October to April. It is during the south-west monsoon that the heavier rains, accompanied by electrical disturbances, occur. The central mountain range protects the Peninsula alternately from both monsoons, the high Sumatran mountains protecting its west side from the south-west winds. The east side is exposed for six months to a modified north-east monsoon. Everywhere else throughout the almost changeless year, steadily alternating land and sea breezes with gentle variable winds and calms prevail, interrupted occasionally on the west coast during the "summer" by squalls from the south-west, which last for one or two hours, and are known as "Sumatrans." Hurricanes and earthquakes are unknown. Drenching dews fall on clear nights. [*This word is recognized as a corruption by Portuguese and British tongues of the Arabic word "musim," "season."]

The Peninsula is a gorgeous tropic land, and, with its bounteous rainfall and sunshine, brings forth many of the most highly prized productions of the tropics, with some that are peculiar to itself. Its botany is as yet very imperfectly known. Some of its forest trees are very valuable as timber, and others produce hard-veined woods which take a high polish. Rattans, Malacca canes, and gutta are well known as among its forest products; gutta, with its extensive economical uses, having been used only for Malay horsewhips and knife-handles previous to 1843. The wild nutmeg is indigenous, and the nutmeg of commerce and the clove have been introduced and thrive. Pepper and some other spices flourish, and the soil with but a little cultivation produces rice wet and dry, tapioca, gambier, sugar-cane, coffee, yams, sweet potatoes, cocoa, sago, cotton, tea, cinchona, india rubber, and indigo. Still it is doubtful whether a soil can be called fertile which is incapable of producing the best kinds of cereals. European vegetables are on the whole a dismal failure. Conservatism in diet must be given up by Europeans; the yam, edible arum, and sweet potato must take the place of the "Irish potato," and water-melons and cucumbers that of our peas, beans, artichokes, cabbages, and broccoli. The Chinese raise coarse radishes and lettuce, and possibly the higher grounds may some day be turned into market gardens. The fruits, however, are innumerable, as well as wholesome and delicious. Among them the durion is the most esteemed by the natives, and the mangosteen by Europeans.

The fauna of the Peninsula is most remarkable and abundant; indeed, much of its forest-covered interior is inhabited by wild beasts alone, and gigantic pachyderms, looking like monsters of an earlier age, roam unmolested over vast tracts of country. Among this thick-skinned family are the elephant, the one-horned rhinoceros, the Malayan tapir, and the wild hog; the last held in abomination by the Malays, but constituting the chief animal food of some of the wild tribes.

A small bear with a wistful face represents the Plantigrade family. The Quadrumana are very numerous. There are nine monkeys, one, if not two apes, and a lemur or sloth, which screens its eyes from the light.

Of the Digitigrada there are the otter or water-dog, the musang and climbing musang, the civet cat, the royal tiger, the spotted black tiger, in whose glossy raven-black coat the characteristic markings are seen in certain lights; the tiger cat, the leopard, the Java cat, and four or five others. Many of these feline animals abound.

Among the ruminants are four species of deer, two smaller than a hare, and one as large as an elk; a wild goat similar to the Sumatran antelope; the domestic goat, a mean little beast; the buffalo, a great, nearly hairless, gray or pink beast, bigger than the buffalo of China and India; a short-legged domestic ox, and two wild oxen or bisons, which are rare.

The bat family is not numerous. The vampire flies high, in great flocks, and is very destructive to fruit. This frugiverous bat, known popularly as the "flying fox," is a very interesting-looking animal, and is actually eaten by the people of Ternate. At the height of the fruit season, thousands of these creatures cross from Sumatra to the mainland, a distance never less than forty miles. Their strength of wing is enormous. I saw one captured in the steamer Nevada, forty-five miles from the Navigators, with wings measuring, when extended, nearly five feet across. These are formed of a jet black membrane, and have a highly polished claw at the extremity of each. The feet consist of five polished black claws, with which the bat hangs on, head downward, to the forest trees. His body is about twice the size of that of a very large rat, black and furry underneath, and with red foxy fur on the head and neck. He has a pointed face, a very black nose, and prominent black eyes, with a remorseless expression in them. An edible bat of vagrant habits is also found.

Ponies are imported from Sumatra, and a few horses from Australia, but the latter do not thrive.

The domestic cat always looks as if half his tail had been taken off in a trap. The domestic dog is the Asiatic, not the European dog, a leggy, ugly, vagrant, uncared-for fellow, furnishing a useful simile and little more.

Weasels, squirrels, polecats, porcupines, and other small animals exist in numbers, and the mermaid, of the genus Halicore, connects the inhabitants of the land and water. This Duyong, described as a creature seven or eight feet long, with a head like that of an elephant deprived of its proboscis, and the body and tail of a fish, frequents the Sumatran and Malayan shores, and its flesh is held in great estimation at the tables of sultans and rajahs. Besides these (and the list is long enough) there are many small beasts.

INTRODUCTORY CHAPTER

The reptiles are unhappily very numerous. Crawfurd mentions forty species of snakes, including the python and the cobra. Alligators in great numbers infest the tidal waters of the rivers. Iguanas and lizards of several species, marsh-frogs, and green tree-frogs abound. The land-leeches are a great pest. Scorpions and centipedes are abundant. There are many varieties of ants, among them a formidable-looking black creature nearly two inches long, a large red ant, whose bite is like a bad pinch from forceps, and which is the chief source of formic acid, and the termes, or white ant, most destructive to timber.

The carpenter beetle is also found, an industrious insect, which riddles the timber of any building in which he effects a lodgment, and is as destructive as dry rot. There are bees and wasps, and hornets of large size, and a much-dreaded insect, possibly not yet classified, said to be peculiar to the Peninsula, which inflicts so severe a wound as to make a strong man utter a cry of agony. But of all the pests the mosquitoes are the worst. A resident may spend some time in the country and know nothing from experience of scorpions, centipedes, land-leeches, and soldier ants, but he cannot escape from the mosquito, the curse of these well-watered tropic regions. In addition to the night mosquito, there is a striped variety of large size, known as the "tiger mosquito," much to be feared, for it pursues its bloodthirsty work in the daytime.

Among the harmless insects may be mentioned the cicada, which fills the forest with its cheery din, the green grasshopper, spiders, and flies of several species, dragon-flies of large size and brilliant coloring, and butterflies and moths of surpassing beauty, which delight in the hot, moist, jungle openings, and even surpass the flowers in the glory and variety of their hues. Among them the atlas moth is found, measuring from eight to ten inches across its wings. The leaf insects are also fascinating, and the fire-flies in a mangrove swamp on a dark, still night, moving in gentle undulations, or flashing into coruscations after brief intervals of quiescence, are inconceivably beautiful.

The birds of the Peninsula are many and beautiful. Sun-birds rival the flashing colors of the humming-birds in the jungle openings; kingfishers of large size and brilliant blue plumage make the river banks gay; shrieking paroquets with coral-colored beaks and tender green feathers, abound in the forests; great, heavy-billed hornbills hop cumbrously from branch to branch, rivaling in their awkward gait the rhinoceros hornbills; the Javanese peacock, with its gorgeous tail and neck covered with iridescent green feathers instead of blue ones, moves majestically along the jungle tracks, together with the ocellated pheasant, the handsome and high-couraged jungle cock, and the glorious Argus pheasant, a bird of twilight and night, with "a hundred eyes" on each feather of its stately tail.

According to Mr. Newbold, two birds of paradise (Paradisea regia and Paradisea gularis) are natives of the Peninsula,* and among other bright-winged creatures are the glorious crimson-feathered pergam, the penciled pheasant, the peacock pheasant, the blue pheasant partridge, the mina, and the dial bird, with an endless variety of parrots, lories, green-feathered pigeons of various sizes, and wood-peckers. Besides these there are falcons, owls, or "spectre birds," sweet-voiced butcher birds, storks, fly-catchers, and doves, and the swallow which builds the gelatinous edible nest, which is the foundation of the expensive luxury "Bird's Nest Soup," frequents the verdant islands on the coast. [*Mr. Newbold is ordinarily so careful and accurate that it is almost presumptuous to hint that in this particular case he may not have been able to verify the statements of the natives by actual observation.]

Nor are our own water birds wanting. There are bitterns, rails, wild-duck, teal, snipes; the common, gray, and whistling plover; green, black, and red quails; and the sport on the plains and reedy marshes, and along the banks of rivers, is most excellent.

Turtles abound off the coast, and tortoises, one variety with a hard shell, and the other with a soft one and a rapid movement, are found in swampy places. The river fish are neither abundant nor much esteemed; but the sea furnishes much of the food of both Malays and Chinese, and the dried and salted fish prepared on the coast is considered very good.

INTRODUCTORY CHAPTER

At European tables in the settlements the red mullet, a highly prized fish, the pomfret, considered more delicious than the turbot, and the tungeree, with cray-fish, crabs, prawns, and shrimps, are usually seen. The tongue-fish, something like a sole, the gray mullet, the hammer-headed shark, and various fish, with vivid scarlet and yellow stripes alternating with black, are eaten, along with cockles, "razor shells," and king-crabs. The lover of fishy beauty is abundantly gratified by the multitudes of fish of brilliant colors, together with large medusae, which dart or glide through the sunlit waters among the coral-groves, where every coral spray is gemmed with zoophytes, whose rainbow-tinted arms sway with the undulations of the water, and where sea-snakes writhe themselves away into the recesses of coral caves.

Nature is so imposing, so magnificent, and so prolific on the Malay Peninsula, that one naturally gives man the secondary place which I have assigned to him in this chapter. The whole population of the Golden Chersonese, a region as large as Great Britain, is not more than three-quarters of a million, and less than a half of this is Malay. Neither great wars, nor an ancient history, nor a valuable literature, nor stately ruins, nor barbaric splendors, attract scholars or sight-seers to the Peninsula.

The Malays are not the Aborigines of this singular spit of land, and, they are its colonists rather than its conquerors. Their histories, which are chiefly traditional, state that the extremity of the Peninsula was peopled by a Malay emigration from Sumatra about the middle of the twelfth century, and that the descendants of these colonists settled Malacca and other places on the coast about a century later. Tradition refers the peopling of the interior States to another and later migration from Sumatra, with a chief at its head, who, with all his followers, married Aboriginal wives; the Aboriginal tribes retreating into the jungles and mountains as the Malays spread themselves over the region now known as the States of the Negri Sembilan. The conquest or colonization of the Malay Peninsula by the Malays is not, however, properly speaking, matter of history, and the origin of the Malay race and its early history are only matters of more or less reasonable hypothesis. It is fair, however, to presume that Sumatra was the ancient seat of the race, and the wonderful valley of Menangkabau, surrounded by mountains ten thousand feet in height, that of its earliest civilization. The only Malay "colonial" kingdoms on the Peninsula which ever attained any importance were those of Malacca and Johore, and even their reliable history begins with the arrival of the Portuguese. The conversion of the Sumatra Malays to Mohammedanism arose mainly out of their commercial intercourse with Arabia; it was slow, not violent, and is supposed to have begun in the thirteenth century.

A population of "Wild Tribes," variously estimated at from eight thousand to eleven thousand souls, is still found in the Peninsula, and even if research should eventually prove them not to be its Aborigines, they are, without doubt, the same races which were found inhabiting it by the earliest Malay colonists.

These are frequently called by the Malays "Orang Benua," or "men of the country," but they are likewise called "Orang-outang," the name which we apply to the big ape of Borneo. The accompanying engraving represents very faithfully the "Orang-outang" of the interior. The few accounts given of the wild tribes vary considerably, but apparently they may be divided into two classes, the Samangs, or Oriental Negroes or Negritos and the Orang Benua, frequently called Jakuns, and in Perak Sakei. By the Malays they are called indiscriminately Kafirs or infidels, and are interesting to them only in so far as they can use them for bearing burdens, clearing jungle, procuring gutta, and in child-stealing, an abominable Malay custom, which, it is hoped, has received its death-blow in Perak at least.

The Samangs are about the same height as the Malays, but their hair, instead of being lank and straight like theirs, is short and curly, though not woolly like that of the African negro, and their complexions, or rather skins, are of a dark brown, nearly black. Their noses, it is said, incline to be flat, their foreheads recede, and their lips are thick. They live in rude and easily removable huts made of leaves and branches, subsist on jungle birds, beasts, roots, and fruits, and wear a scanty covering made from the inner bark of a species of Artocarpus. They are expert hunters, and have most ingenious methods of capturing both the elephant and the "recluse rhinoceros." They are divided into tribes, which are ruled by chiefs on the patriarchal system. Of their customs and beliefs, if they have any, almost nothing is known. They are singularly shy, and shun intercourse with men of other races. It has been supposed that they worship the sun.

The Orang Benua or Orang-outang, frequently called Sakeis or Jakuns, consist of various tribes with different names, thinly scattered among the forests of the chain of mountains which runs down the middle of the Peninsula from Kedah to Point Romania.* In appearance and color they greatly resemble the Malays, and there is a very strong general resemblance between their dialects and pure Malayan. They have remarkably bright and expressive eyes, with nothing Mongolian about their internal angles, and the forehead is low rather than receding. The mouth is wide and the lips are large, the lower part of the face projects, the nose is small, the nostrils are divergent, and the cheek bones are prominent. The hair is black, but it often looks rusty or tawny from exposure to the sun, against which it is their only protection. It is very abundant and long, and usually matted and curly, but not woolly. They have broad chests and very sturdy muscular limbs. They are, however, much shorter in stature than the Malays, the men in some of the tribes rarely exceeding four feet eight inches in height, and the women four feet four. Their clothing consists of a bark cloth waist-cloth. Some of the tribes live in huts of the most primitive description supported on posts, while others, often spoken of as the "tree people," build wigwams on platforms, mainly supported by the forking branches of trees, at a height of from twenty to thirty feet. These wild people, says Mr. Daly, lead a gregarious life, rarely remaining long in one place for fear of their wives and children being kidnapped by the Malays. They fly at the approach of strangers. As a rule, their life is nomadic, and they live by hunting, fishing, and on jungle fruits. They are divided into tribes governed by elders. They reverence the sun, but have no form of

INTRODUCTORY CHAPTER

worship, and are believed to be destitute of even the most rudimentary ideas of religion. Their weapon is the sumpitan, a blow-gun, from which poisoned arrows are expelled. They have no ceremonies at birth, marriage, or death. They are monogamists, and, according to Mr. Syers, extremely affectionate. One of their strongest emotions is fear, and their timidity is so great that they frequently leave the gutta which they have collected at the foot of the tree, not daring to encounter the trader from whom they expect some articles in exchange; while the fear of ridicule, according to Mr. Maxwell, keeps them far from the haunts of the Malays. [*I was so fortunate as to see two adult male Jakuns and one female, but my information respecting them is derived chiefly from Mr. Syers, Superintendent of Police in Selangor, and from Mr. Maxwell, the Assistant-Resident in Perak.]

The Rayet, or Orang Laut, "subjects," or men of the sea, inhabit the coast and the small islets off the coast, erecting temporary sheds when they go ashore to build boats, mend nets, or collect gum dammar and wood oil, but usually living in their boats. They differ little from the Malays, who, however, they look down upon as an inferior race, except that they are darker and more uncouth looking. They have no religious (!) beliefs but in the influence of evil spirits, to whom at times they perform a few propitiatory rites. Many of them become Mohammedans. They live almost entirely upon fish. They are altogether restless and impatient of control, but, unlike some savages, are passionately fond of music, and are most ingenious in handicrafts, specially in boat-building.

The Chinese in the Peninsula and on the small islands of Singapore and Pinang are estimated at two hundred and forty thousand, and their numbers are rapidly increasing, owing to direct immigration from China. It is by their capital, industry, and enterprise that the resources of the Peninsula are being developed. The date of their arrival is unknown, but the Portuguese found them at Malacca more than three centuries ago. They have been settled in Pinang and Singapore for ninety-three and sixty-three years respectively; but except that they have given up the barbarous custom of crushing the feet of girls, they are, in customs, dress, and habits, the exact counterparts of the Chinese of Canton or Amoy. Many of them have become converts to Christianity, but this has not led to the discarding of their queues or national costume. The Chinese who are born in the Straits are called Babas. The immigrant Chinese, who are called Sinkehs, are much despised by the Babas, who glory specially in being British-born subjects. The Chinese promise to be in some sort the commercial rulers of the Straits.

The Malays proper inhabit the Malay Peninsula, and almost all the coast regions of Borneo and Sumatra. They all speak more or less purely the Malay language; they are all Mohammedans, and they all write in the Arabic character. Their color is a lightish, olive-tinted, reddish brown. Their hair is invariably black, straight, and coarse, and their faces and bodies are nearly hairless. They have broad and slightly flat faces, with high cheek bones; wide mouths, with broad and shapely lips, well formed chins, low foreheads, black eyes, oblique, but not nearly so much so as those of the Chinese, and smallish noses, with broad and very open nostrils. They vary little in their height, which is below that of the average European. Their frames are lithe and robust, their chests are broad, their hands are small and refined, and their feet are thick and short. The men are not handsome, and the women are decidedly ugly. Both sexes look old very early.

The Malays undoubtedly must be numbered among civilized peoples. They live in houses which are more or less tasteful and secluded. They are well clothed in garments of both native and foreign manufacture; they are a settled and agricultural people; they are skilful in some of the arts, specially in the working of gold and the damascening of krises; the upper classes are to some extent educated; they have a literature, even though it be an imported one, and they have possessed for centuries systems of government and codes of land and maritime laws which, in theory at least, show a considerable degree of enlightenment.

Their religion, laws, customs, and morals are bound up together. They are strict Mussulmen, but among the uneducated especially they mix up their own traditions and superstitions with the Koran. The pilgrimage to Mecca is the universal object of Malay ambition. They practice relic worship, keep the fast of Ramadhan, wear rosaries of beads, observe the hours of prayer with their foreheads on the earth, provide for the "religious welfare" of their villages, circumcise their children, offer buffaloes in sacrifice at the religious ceremonies connected with births and marriages, build mosques everywhere, regard Mecca as the holy city, and the Koran, as expounded by Arab teachers, as the rule of faith and practice.

Much learning has been expended upon the origin of Malayan, but it has not been reliably traced beyond the ancient empire of Menangkabau in Sumatra. Mohammedanism undoubtedly brought with it a large introduction of Arabic words, and the language itself is written in the Arabic character. It has been estimated by that most painstaking and learned scholar, Mr. Crawfurd, that one hundred parts of modern Malayan are composed of twenty-seven parts of primitive Malayan, fifty of Polynesian, sixteen of Sanskrit, five of Arabic, and two of adventitious words, the Arabic predominating in all literature relating to religion. Malay is the lingua franca of the Straits Settlements, and in the seaports a number of Portuguese and Dutch words have been incorporated with it.

The Malays can hardly be said to have an indigenous literature, for it is almost entirely derived from Persia, Siam, Arabia, and Java. Arabic is their sacred language. They have, however, a celebrated historic Malay romance called the Hang Tuah, parts of which are frequently recited in their villages after sunset prayers by their village raconteurs, and some Arabic and Hindu romances stand high in popular favor. Their historians all wrote after the Mohammedan era, and their histories are said to contain little that is trustworthy; each State also has a local history preserved with superstitious care and kept from common eyes, but these contain little but the genealogies of their chiefs. They have one Malay historical composition, dated 1021 A.H., which treats of the founding of the Malay empire of Menangkabau in Sumatra, and comes down to the founding of the empire of Johore and the conquest of Malacca by

Albuquerque in 1511. This has been thought worthy of translation by Dr. Leyden.

Their ethical books consist mainly of axioms principally derived from Arabic and Persian sources. Their religious works are borrowed from the Arabs. The Koran, of course, stands first, then comes a collection of prayers, and next a guide to the religious duties required from Mussulmen. Then there are books containing selections from Arabic religious works, with learned commentaries upon them by a Malay Hadji. It is to be noticed that the Malays present a compact front against Christianity, and have successfully resisted all missionary enterprise.

They have a good deal of poetry, principally of an amorous kind, characterized, it is said, by great simplicity, natural and pleasing metaphor, and extremely soft and melodious rhyme. They sing their poems to certain popular airs, which are committed to memory. Malay music, though plaintive and less excruciating than Chinese and Japanese, is very monotonous and dirge-like, and not pleasing to a European ear. The pentatonic scale is employed. The violin stands first among musical instruments in their estimation. They have also the guitar, the flageolet, the aeolian flute, a bamboo in which holes are cut, which produce musical sounds when acted upon by the wind, and both metallic and wooden gongs.

They have no written system of common arithmetic, and are totally unacquainted with its higher branches. Their numerals above one thousand are borrowed from the Hindus, and their manner of counting is the same as that of the Ainos of Yezo.

Their theory of medicine is derived from Arabia, and abounds in mystery and superstition. They regard man as composed of four elements and four essences, and assimilate his constitution and passions to the twelve signs of the zodiac, the seven planets, etc., exaggerating the mysterious sympathy between man and external nature. The successful practice of the hakim or doctor must be based on the principle of "preserving the balance of power" among the four elements, which is chiefly effected by moderation in eating.

INTRODUCTORY CHAPTER

They know nothing of astronomy, except of some meagre ideas derived through the Arabs from the Ptolemaic system, and Mr. Newbold, after most painstaking research, failed to discover any regular treatise on astronomy, though Arabic and Hindu tracts on interpretations of dreams, horoscopes, spells, propitious and unpropitious moments, auguries, talismans, love philters, medicinal magic and recipes for the destruction of people at a distance, are numerous. They acknowledge the solar year, but adopt the lunar, and reckon the months in three different ways, dividing them, however, into weeks of seven days, marking them by the return of the Mohammedan Sabbath. They suppose the world to be an oval body revolving on its axis four times within a year, with the sun, a circular body of fire, moving round it. The majority of the people still believe that eclipses are caused by the sun or moon being devoured by a serpent, and they lament loudly during their continuance. The popular modes of measuring distance are ingenious, but, to a stranger at least, misleading. Thus Mr. Daly, in attempting to reach the interior States, received these replies to his inquiries about distance—"As far as a gunshot may be heard from this particular hill;" "If you wash your head before starting it will not be dry before you reach the place," etc. They also measure distances by the day's walk, and by the number of times it is necessary to chew betel between two places. The hours are denoted by terms not literally accurate. Cockcrowing is daybreak, 1 P.M., and midnight; 9 A.M., Lepas Baja, is the time when the buffaloes, which cannot work when the sun is high, are relieved from the plough; Tetabawe is 6 P.M., the word signifying the cry of a bird which is silent till after sunset. The Malay day begins at sunset.

They are still maritime in their habits, and very competent practical sailors and boat-builders; but though for centuries they divided with the Arabs the carrying trade between Eastern and Western Asia, and though a mongrel Malay is the nautical language of nearly all the peoples from New Guinea to the Tenasserim coast, the Malays knew little of the science of navigation. They timed their voyages by the constant monsoons, and in sailing from island to island coasted the Asiatic shores, trusting, when for a short time out of sight of land, not to the compass, though they were acquainted with it, but to known rocks, glimpses of headlands, the direction of the wind, and their observation of the Pleiades.

They have no knowledge of geography, architecture, painting, sculpture, or even mechanics; they no longer make translations from the Arabic or create fiction, and the old translations of works on law, ethics, and science are now scarcely studied. Education among them is at a very low ebb; but the State of Kedah is beginning to awake to its advantages. Where schools exist the instruction consists mainly in teaching the children to repeat, in a tongue which they do not understand, certain passages from the Koran and some set prayers.

As to law, Sir Stamford Raffles observed in a formal despatch, "Nothing has tended more decidedly to the deterioration of the Malay character than the want of a well-defined and generally acknowledged system of law." There are numerous legal compilations, however, and nearly every State has a code of its own to a certain extent; there are maritime and land codes, besides "customs" bad and good, which override the written law; while in Perak, Selangor, and Sungei Ujong an ill understood adaptation of some portions of British law further complicates matters. "The glorious uncertainty" of law is nowhere more fully exemplified than on this Peninsula. It is from the Golden Island, the parent Empire of Menangkabau, that the Malays profess to derive both their criminal and civil law, their tribal system, their rules for the division of land by boundary marks, and the manner of government as adapted for sovereigns and their ministers. The existence of the various legal compilations has led to much controversy and even bloodshed between zealots for the letter of the Koran on one side, and the advocates of ancient custom on the other. Among the reasons which have led to the migration of Malays from the native states into the Straits Settlements, not the least powerful is the equality of rights before English law, and the security given by it to property of every kind. In the Malay country itself, occupied by Malays and the Chinese associated with them, there are four Malays to the square mile, whilst under the British flag some one hundred and twenty-five Malays to the square mile have taken refuge and sought protection for their industry under our law!

Cock-fighting, which has attained to the dignity of a literature of its own, is the popular Malay sport; but the grand sport is a tiger and buffalo fight, reserved for rare occasions, however, on account of its expense. Cock-fighting is a source of gigantic gambling and desperate feuds. The birds, which fight in full feather and with sharpened steel spurs, are very courageous, and die rather than give in. Wrestling among young men and tossing the wicker ball, are favorite amusements. There are professional dancing girls, but dancing as a social amusement is naturally regarded with disfavor. Children have various games peculiar to themselves, which are abandoned as childish things at a given age. Riddles and enigmas occupy a good deal of time among the higher classes. Chess also occupies much time, but it is much to be feared that the vice of gambling stimulated by the Chinese, who have introduced both cards and dice, is taking the place of more innocent pastimes.

The Malays, like other Mohammedans, practice polygamy. They are very jealous, and their women are veiled and to a certain extent secluded; but they are affectionate, and among the lower classes there is a good deal of domesticity. Their houses are described in the following letters. The food of the poorer classes consists mainly of rice and salt-fish, curries of both, maize, sugar-cane, bananas, and jungle fruits, cocoa-nut milk being used in the preparation of food as well as for a beverage. As luxuries they chew betelnut and smoke tobacco, and although intoxicants are forbidden, they tap the toddy palm and drink of its easily fermented juice. Where metal finds its way into domestic utensils it is usually in the form of tin water-bottles and ewers. Every native possesses a sweeping broom, sleeping mats, coarse or fine, and bamboo or grass baskets. Most families use an iron pan for cooking, with a half cocoa-nut shell for a ladle. A large nut shell filled with palm-oil, and containing a pith wick, is the ordinary Malay lamp. Among the poor, fresh leaves serve as plates and dishes, but the chiefs possess china.

The Malay weapons consist of the celebrated kris, with its flame-shaped wavy blade; the sword, regarded, however, more as an ornament; the parang, which is both knife and weapon; the steel-headed spear, which cost us so many lives in the Perak war; matchlocks, blunderbusses, and lelahs, long heavy brass guns used for the defense of the stockades behind which the Malays usually fight. They make their own gunpowder, and use cartridges made of cane.

The Malays, like the Japanese, have a most rigid epistolary etiquette, and set forms for letter writing. Letters must consist of six parts, and are so highly elaborate that the scribes who indite them are almost looked upon as litterateurs. There is an etiquette of envelopes and wafers, the number and color of which vary with the relative positions of the correspondents, and any error in these details is regarded as an insult. Etiquette in general is elaborate and rigid, and ignorant breaches of it on the part of Europeans have occasionally cost them their lives.

The systems of government in the Malay States vary in detail, but on the whole may be regarded as absolute despotisms, modified by certain rights, of which no rulers in a Mohammedan country can absolutely deprive the ruled, and by the assertion of the individual rights of chiefs. Sultans, rajahs, maharajahs, datus, etc., under ordinary circumstances have been and still are in most of the unprotected States unable to control the chiefs under them, who have independently levied taxes and blackmail till the harassed cultivators came scarcely to care to possess property which might at any time be seized. Forced labor for a quarter of the laboring year was obligatory on all males, besides military service when called upon.

Slavery and debt bondage exist in all the native States; except in Selangor and Sungei Ujong, where it has recently been abolished, as it is hoped it will be in Perak. The slaves of the reigning princes were very easily acquired, for a prince had only to send a messenger bearing a sword or kris to a house, and the parents were obliged to give up any one of their children without delay or question. In debt slavery, which prevails more or less among all classes, and has done a great deal to degrade the women of the Peninsula, a man owing a trifling debt incurred through extravagance, misfortune or gambling, can be seized by his creditor; when he, his wife, and children, including those who may afterwards be born, and probably their descendants, become slaves.

In most of the States the reigning prince has regular officers under him, chief among whom are the Bandahara or treasurer, who is the first minister, chief executive officer, and ruler over the peasantry, and the Tumongong or chief magistrate. Usually the throne is hereditary, but while the succession in some States is in the male line, in others it is in the female, a sister's son being the heir; and there are instances in which the chiefs have elected a sultan or rajah. The *theory* of government does not contain anything inherently vicious, and is well adapted to Malay circumstances. Whatever is evil in practice is rather contrary to the theory than in accordance with it. The States undoubtedly have fallen, in many ways, into evil case; the privileged few, consisting of rajahs and their numerous kindred and children, oppressing the unprivileged many, living in idleness on what is wrung from their toil. The Malay sovereigns in most cases have come to be little more than the feudal heads of bodies of insubordinate chiefs, while even the headmen of the villages take upon themselves to levy taxes and administer a sort of justice. Nomadic cultivation, dislike of systematic labor, and general insecurity as to the boundaries and tenure of land, have further impoverished the common people, while Islamism exercises its usual freezing and retarding influence, producing the fatal isolation which to weak peoples is slow decay.

When Sir A. Clarke was appointed Governor of the Straits Settlements in 1873 he went to the Curator of the Geographical Society's library in quest of maps and information of any kind about the country to which he was going, but was told by that courteous functionary that there was absolutely no information of the slightest value in their archives. Since then the protectorate which we have acquired over three of the native States and the war in Perak have mended matters somewhat; but Mr. Daly, on appearing in May last before the same Society

INTRODUCTORY CHAPTER

with the map which is the result of his partial survey, regrets that we have of half of the Peninsula "only the position of the coast-line!" Of the States washed by the China Sea scarcely anything is known, and the eastern and central interior offer a wide field for the explorer.

The letters which follow those written from China and Saigon relate to the British settlements in the Straits of Malacca, and to the native States of Perak, Selangor, and Sungei Ujong, which, since 1874, have passed under British "protection." The preceding brief sketch is necessarily a very imperfect one, as to most of my questions addressed on the spot and since to the best informed people, the answer has been, "No information." The only satisfaction that I have in these preliminary pages is, that they place the reader in a better position than I was in when I landed at Malacca. To a part of this beautiful but little known region I propose to conduct my readers, venturing to hope for their patient interest in my journeyings over the bright waters of the Malacca Straits and in the jungles of the Golden Chersonese.

I. L. B.

Letter I

The Steamer Volga—Days of Darkness—First View of Hong Kong—Hong Kong on Fire—Apathy of the Houseless—The Fire Breaks Out Again—An Eclipse of Gayety

S.S. "VOLGA," CHINA SEA, Christmas Eve, 1878.

The snowy dome of Fujisan, reddening in the sunrise, rose above the violet woodlands of Mississippi Bay as we steamed out of Yokohama harbor on the 19th, and three days later I saw the last of Japan—a rugged coast, lashed by a wintry sea.

THE PALACE, VICTORIA, HONG KONG, December 27.

Of the voyage to Hong Kong little need be said. The Volga is a miserable steamer, with no place to sit in, and nothing to sit on but the benches by the dinner-table in the dismal saloon. The master, a worthy man, so far as I ever saw of him, was Goth, Vandal, Hun, Visigoth, all in one. The ship was damp, dark, dirty, old, and cold. She was not warmed by steam, and the fire could not be lighted because of a smoky chimney. There were no lamps, and the sparse candles were obviously grudged. The stewards were dirty and desponding, the serving inhospitable, the cooking dirty and greasy, the food scanty, the table-linen frowsy. There were four French and two Japanese male passengers, who sat at meals in top-coats, comforters, and hats. I had a large cabin, the salon des dames, and the undivided attention of a very competent, but completely desponding stewardess. Being debarred from the deck by incessant showers of spray, sleet, and snow, and the cold of mid-winter being unbearable in the dark, damp saloon, I went to bed at four for the first two days. On the third it blew half a gale, with a short violent sea, and this heavy weather lasted till we reached Hong Kong, five days afterward. During those cold, dark, noisy days, when even the stewards could scarcely keep their feet, I suffered so much in my spine from the violent movements of the ship that I did not leave my cabin; and besides being unable to read, write, or work, owing to the darkness, I was obliged to hold on by day and night to avoid being much hurt by the rolling, my berth being athwart ships; consequently, that week, which I had relied upon for "overtaking" large arrears of writing and sewing, was so much lost out of life—irrecoverably and shamefully lost, I felt—as each dismal day, dawned and died without sunrise or sunset, on the dark and stormy Pacific. No one, it seemed, knew any more English than "Yes" and "No;" and as the ship knocked French out of my memory, I had not even the resource of talking with the stewardess, who told me on the last day of our imprisonment that she was "triste, triste," and "one mass of bruises!"

In this same gale, but on a dry day, we came close up with the mainland of Eastern Asia. Coasts usually disappoint. This one exceeded all my expectations; and besides, it was the coast of Asia, the mysterious continent which has been my dream from childhood—bare, lofty, rocky, basaltic; islands of naked rock separated by narrow channels, majestic, perpendicular cliffs, a desolate uninhabited region, lashed by a heavy sea, with visions of swirling mists, shrieking sea-birds, and Chinese high-sterned fishing-boats with treble-reefed, three-cornered brown sails, appearing on the tops of surges, at once to vanish. Soon we were among mountainous islands; and then, by a narrow and picturesque channel, entered the outer harbor, with the scorched and arid peaks of Hong Kong on one side; and on the other the yet redder and rockier mainland, without a tree or trace of cultivation, or even of habitation, except here and there a few stone huts clustering round inlets, in which boats were lying. We were within the tropic of Cancer, but still the cold, coarse bluster continued, so that it was barely possible to see China except in snatches from behind the deck-house.

Turning through another channel, we abruptly entered the inner harbor, and sailed into the summer, blue sky, blue water, a summer sun, and a cool breeze, while a tender veil of blue haze softened the outlines of the flushed mountains. Victoria, which is the capital of the British colony of the island of Hong Kong, and which colloquially is called Hong Kong, looked magnificent, suggesting Gibraltar, but far, far finer, its peak eighteen hundred feet in height—a giant among lesser peaks, rising abruptly from the sea above the great granite city which clusters upon its lower declivities, looking out from dense greenery and tropical gardens, and the deep shade of palms and bananas, the lines of many of its streets traced in foliage, all contrasting with the scorched red soil and barren crags which were its universal aspect before we acquired it in 1843. A forest of masts above the town betoken its commercial importance, and "P. and O." and Messageries Maritimes steamers, ships of war of all nations, low-hulled, big-masted clippers, store and hospital ships, and a great fishing fleet lay at anchor in the harbor. The English and Romish cathedrals, the Episcopal Palace, with St. Paul's College, great high blocks of commercial buildings, huge sugar factories, great barracks in terraces, battery above battery, Government House, and massive stone wharves, came rapidly into view, and over all, its rich folds spreading out fully on the breeze, floated the English flag.

But dense volumes of smoke rolling and eddying, and covering with their black folds the lower slopes and the town itself made a surprising spectacle, and even as we anchored came off the rapid tolling of bells, the roll of drums, and the murmur of a "city at unrest." No one met me. A few Chinese boats came off, and then a steam launch with the M. M. agent in an obvious flurry. I asked him how to get ashore, and he replied, "It's no use going ashore, the town's half burned, and burning still; there's not a bed at any hotel for love or money, and we are going to make up beds here." However, through the politeness of the mail agent, I did go ashore in the launch, but we had to climb through and over at least eight tiers of boats, crammed with refugees, mainly women and children, and piled up with all sorts of household goods, whole and broken, which had been thrown into them promiscuously to save them. "The palace of the English bishop," they said, was still untouched; so, escaping from an indescribable hubbub, I got into a bamboo chair, with two long poles which rested on the shoulders of two lean coolies, who carried me to my destination at a swinging pace through streets as steep as those of Varenna. Streets choked up with household goods and the costly contents of shops, treasured books and nick-nacks lying on the dusty pavements, with beds, pictures, clothing, mirrors, goods of all sorts; Chinamen dragging their possessions to the hills; Chinawomen, some of them with hoofs rather than feet, carrying their children on their backs and under their arms; officers, black with smoke, working at the hose like firemen; parties of troops marching as steadily as on parade, or keeping guard in perilous places; Mr. Pope Henessey, the Governor, ubiquitous in a chair with four scarlet bearers; men belonging to the insurance companies running about with drawn swords; the miscellaneous population running hither and thither; loud and frequent explosions; heavy crashes as of tottering walls, and, above all, the loud bell of the Romish cathedral tolling rapidly, calling to work or prayer, made a scene of intense excitement; while utterly unmoved, in grand Oriental calm (or apathy), with the waves of tumult breaking round their feet, stood Sikh sentries, majestic men, with swarthy faces and great, crimson turbans. Through the encumbered streets and up grand flights of stairs my bearers brought me to these picturesque grounds, which were covered over with furniture and goods of all descriptions brought hither for safety, and Chinese families camping out among them. Indeed, the Bishop and Mrs. Burdon had not only thrown open their beautiful grounds to these poor people, but had accommodated some Chinese families in rooms in the palace under their own. The apathy or calm of the Chinese women as they sat houseless amidst their possessions was very striking. In the broad, covered corridor which runs round the palace everything the Burdons most value was lying ready for instantaneous removal, and I was warned not to unpack or take off my traveling dress. The Bishop and I at once went down to the fire, which was got under, and saw the wreck of the city and the houseless people camping out among the things they had saved. Fire was still burning or smouldering everywhere, high walls were falling, hose were playing on mountains of smouldering timber, whole streets were blocked with masses of fallen brick and stone, charred telegraph poles and fused wires were lying about, with half burned ledgers and half burned everything. The colored population exceeds one hundred and fifty-two thousand souls, and only those who know the Babel which an eastern crowd is capable of making under ordinary circumstances can imagine what the deafening din of human tongues was under these very extraordinary ones. In the prison, which was threatened by the flames, were over eight hundred ruffians of all nations, and it was held by one hundred soldiers with ten rounds of ammunition each, prepared to convey the criminals to a place of safety and to shoot any who attempted to escape. The dread of these miscreants, which was everywhere expressed, is not unreasonable, for the position of Victoria, and the freedom and protection afforded by our laws, together with the present Governor's known sympathies with colored people, have attracted here thousands of the scum of Canton and other Chinese cities, to say nothing of a mass of European and Asiatic ruffianism, much of which is at all times percolating through the magnificent Victoria prison.

On returning, I was just beginning to unpack when the flames burst out again. It was luridly grand in the twilight, the tongues of flame lapping up house after house, the jets of flame loaded with blazing fragments, the explosions, each one succeeded by a burst of flame, carrying high into the air all sorts of projectiles, beams and rafters paraffine soaked, strewing them over the doomed city, the leaping flames coming nearer and nearer, the great volumes of smoke, spark-laden, rolling toward us, all mingling with a din indescribable. Burning fragments shortly fell on the window-sills, and as the wind was very strong and setting this way, there seemed so little prospect of the palace being saved that important papers were sent to the cathedral and several of the refugees fled with their things to the hills. At that moment the wind changed, and the great drift of flame and smoke was carried in a comparatively harmless direction, the fire was got well in hand the second time, the official quarter was saved, and before 10 P.M. we were able for the first time since my arrival at mid-day to sit down to food.

Most people seem much upset as well from personal peril as from sympathy, and all parties and picnics for two days were given up. Even the newspapers did not come out this morning, the types of one of them being in this garden. The city is now patrolled night and day by strong parties of marines and Sikhs, for both the disposition to loot and the facilities for looting are very great.

I. L. B.

Letter II

A Delightful Climate—Imprisoned Fever Germs—"Pidjun" English— Hong Kong Harbor—Prosperity of Hong Kong—Rampageous Criminal Classes—Circumspice!

THE PALACE, VICTORIA, December 29.

I like and admire Victoria. It is so pleasant to come in from the dark, misty, coarse, loud-tongued Pacific, and the December colorlessness of Japan to bright blue waters crisped by a perpetual north wind—to the flaming hills of the Asian mainland, which are red in the early morning, redder in the glow of noon, and pass away in the glorious sunsets through ruby and vermilion into an amethyst haze, deepening into the purple of a tropic night, when the vast expanse of sky which is seen from this high elevation is literally one blaze of stars. Though they are by no means to be seen in perfection, there are here many things that I love,—bananas, poinsettias, papayas, tree-ferns, dendrobiums, dracenas, the scarlet passion-flower, the spurious banyan, date, sago, and traveler's palms, and numberless other trees and shrubs, children of the burning sun of the tropics, carefully watered and tended, but exotics after all.

It is a most delightful winter climate. There has not been any rain for three months, nor will there be any for two more; the sky is cloudless, the air dry and very bracing. It is cold enough at night for fires, and autumn clothing can be worn all the day long, for though the sun is bright and warm, the shade temperature does not rise above 65 degrees, and exercise is easy and pleasant. At night, even at a considerable height, the lowest temperature is 40 degrees. It is impossible to praise the climate too highly, with its bright sky, cool dry air, and five months of rainlessness; but I should write very differently if I came here four months later, when the mercury ranges from 80 degrees to 90 degrees both by day and night, and the cloudy sky rests ever on the summits of the island peaks, and everything is moist, and the rain comes down continually in torrents, rising in hot vapors when the sun shines, and people become limp and miserable, and their possessions limp and moldy, and insect life revels, and human existence spent in a vapor bath becomes burdensome. But the city is healthy to those who live temperately. It has, however, a remarkable peculiarity. Standing in and on rock, one fancies that fever would not be one of its maladies, but the rock itself seems to have imprisoned fever germs in some past age, for whenever it is quarried or cut into for foundations, or is disturbed in any way, fever immediately breaks out.

Victoria is a beautiful city. It reminds me of Genoa, but that most of its streets are so steep as to be impassable for wheeled vehicles, and some of them are merely grand flights of stairs, arched over by dense foliaged trees, so as to look like some tropical, colored, deep colonnades. It has covered green balconies with festoons of creepers, lofty houses, streets narrow enough to exclude much of the sun, people and costumes of all nations, processions of Portuguese priests and nuns; and all its many-colored life is seen to full advantage under this blue sky and brilliant sun.

This house is magnificently situated, and very large and airy. Part is the Episcopal Palace, and the rest St. Paul's College, of which Bishop Burdon is warden. The mountainous grounds are beautiful, and the entrance blazes with poinsettias. There are no female servants, but Chinese men perform all the domestic service satisfactorily. I learn that for a Chinese servant to appear without his skull-cap is rude, but to appear with his pig-tail wound round his head instead of pendent, is a gross insult! The "Pidjun English" is revolting, and the most dignified persons demean themselves by speaking it. The word "pidjun" appears to refer generally to business. "My pidjun" is undoubtedly "my work."

How the whole English-speaking community, without distinction of rank, has come to communicate with the Chinese in this baby talk is extraordinary.

If you order a fire you say something like this: "Fire makee, chop, chop, here, makee fire number one," chop being quick, and number one good, or "first-class." If a servant tells you that some one has called he says, "One piecey manee here speak missey," and if one asks who he is, he very likely answers, "No sabe," or else, "Number one, tink," by which he implies that the visitor is, in his opinion, a gentleman. After the courteous, kindly Japanese, the Chinese seem indifferent, rough and disagreeable, except the well-to-do merchants in the shops, who are bland, complacent, and courteous. Their rude stare and the way they hustle you in the streets and shout their "pidjun" English at you is not attractive. Then they have an ugly habit of speaking of us as barbarian or foreign devils. Since I knew the word I have heard it several times in the streets, and Bishop Burdon says that before his servants found out that he knew Chinese, they were always speaking of him and Mrs. Burdon by this very ugly name.

[Victoria is, or should be, well known, so I will not describe its cliques, its boundless hospitalities, its extravagances in living, its quarrels, its gayeties, its picnics, balls, regattas, races, dinner parties, lawn tennis parties, amateur theatricals, afternoon teas, and all its other modes of creating a whirl which passes for pleasure or occupation. Rather, I would write of some of the facts concerning this very remarkable settlement, which is on its way to being the most important British colony in the Far East.

Moored to England by the electric cable, and replete with all the magnificent enterprises and luxuries of English civilization, with a population of one hundred and sixty thousand, of which only seven thousand, including soldiers and sailors, are white, and possessing the most imposing city of the East on its shores, the colony is only forty years old; the island of Hong Kong having been ceded to England in 1841, while its charter only bears the date of 1843. The island, which is about eleven miles long, from two to five broad, and with an area of about twenty-nine square miles, is one of a number situated off the south-eastern coast of China at the mouth of the Canton river, ninety miles from Canton. It is one of the many "thieves' islands," and one of the first necessities of the administration was to clear out the hordes of sea and river pirates which infested its very intricate neighborhood. It lies just within the tropic of Cancer in lat. 22 degrees N. and long. 114 degrees E. The Ly-ee-moon Pass, the narrow strait which separates it from the Chinese mainland, is only half a mile wide. Kowloon, on the mainland, an arid peninsula, on which some of the Hong Kongese have been attempting to create a suburb, was ceded to England in 1861. The whole island of Hong Kong is picturesque. The magnificent harbor, which has an area of ten square miles, is surrounded by fantastic, broken mountains from three thousand to four thousand feet high, and the magnificent city of Victoria extends for four miles along its southern shore, with its six thousand houses of stone and brick and the princely mansions and roomy bungalows of its merchants and officials scrambling up the steep sides of the Peak, the highest point of the island, carrying verdure and shade with them. Damp as its summer is, the average rainfall scarcely exceeds seventy-eight inches, but it is hotter than Singapore in the hot season, though the latter is under eighty miles from the Equator.

The causes by which this little island, which produces nothing, has risen into first-rate importance among our colonies are, that Victoria, with its magnificent harbor, is a factory for our Chinese commerce and offers unrivaled facilities for the military and naval forces which are necessary for the protection not only of that commerce but of our interests in the far East. It is hardly too much to say that it is the naval and commercial terminus of the Suez Canal. Will it be believed that the amount of British and foreign tonnage annually entering and leaving the port averages two millions of tons? and that the number of native vessels trading to it is about fifty-two thousand, raising the total ascertained tonnage to upward of three millions and a half, or half a million tons in excess of Singapore? To this must be added thousands of smaller native boats of every build and rig trading to Hong Kong, not only from the Chinese coasts and rivers, but from Siam, Japan, and Cochin China. Besides the "P. and O.," the Messageries Maritimes, the Pacific Mail Company, the Eastern and Australian Mail Company, the Japanese "Mitsu Bichi" Mail Company, etc., all regular mail lines, it has a number of lines of steamers trading to England, America, and Germany, with local lines both Chinese and English, and lines of fine sailing clippers, which, however, are gradually falling into disuse, owing to the dangerous navigation of the China seas, and the increasing demand for speed.

Victorian firms have almost the entire control of the tea and silk trade, and Victoria is the centre of the trade in opium, sugar, flour, salt, earthenware, oil, amber, cotton, and cotton goods, sandal-wood, ivory, betel, vegetables, live stock, granite, and much else. The much abused term "emporium of commerce" may most correctly be applied to it.

It has five docks, three slips, and every requisite for making extensive repairs for ships of war and merchantmen.

It has telegraphic communication with the whole civilized world, and its trade is kept thereby in a continual fever.

It has a large garrison, for which it pays to England 20,000 pounds a year. Were it not for this force, its six hundred and fifty policemen, of whom only one hundred and ten are Europeans, might not be able to overawe even as much as they do the rowdy and ruffianly elements of its heterogeneous population. As it is, the wealthier foreign residents, for the security of their property, are obliged to supplement the services of the public caretakers by employing private watchmen, who patrol their grounds at night. It must be admitted that the criminal classes are very rampageous in Victoria, whether from undue and unwise leniency in the treatment of crime, or whether from the extraordinary mass of criminals to which our flag affords security is not for a stranger to say, though the general clamor raised when I visited the great Chinese prison in Canton, "I wish I were in your prison in Hong Kong," and my own visit to the Victoria prison, render the former suspicion at least permissible.

Hong Kong possesses the usual establishment of a Crown Colony, and the government is administered by a Governor, aided by a Legislative

Council, of which he is the President, and which is composed of the Chief Justice, the Colonial Secretary, the Attorney-General, the Treasurer, and four unofficial members, nominated by the Crown on the Governor's recommendation.

The enormous preponderance of the mixed Oriental population is a source of some difficulty, and it is not easy by our laws to punish and destroy a peculiarly hateful form of slavery which is recognized by Chinese custom, and which has attained gigantic proportions in Victoria. There is an immense preponderance of the masculine element, nearly six to one among the Europeans, and among the Orientals the men are nearly two and a half times as numerous as the women.

As Victoria is a free port, it is impossible to estimate the value of its imports and exports, but its harbor, full of huge merchantmen, and craft of all nations, its busy wharves, its crowd of lighters loading and unloading by day and night, its thronged streets and handsome shops, its huge warehouses, packed with tea, silk, and all the costly products of the East, and its hillsides terraced with the luxurious houses of its merchants, all say, "Circumspice, these are better than statistics!"]

I. L. B.

Letter III

The S.S. Kin Kiang—First View of Canton—The Island of Shameen—England in Canton—The Tartar City—Drains and Barricades—Canton at Night—Street Picturesqueness—Ghastly Gifts—Oriental Enchantments—The Examination Hall

S.S. "KIN KIANG," December 30.

You will remember that it is not very long since a piratical party of Chinese, shipping as steerage passengers on board one of these Hong Kong river steamers, massacred the officers and captured the boat. On board this great, white, deck-above-deck American steamer there is but one European passenger beside myself, but there are four hundred and fifty second-class passengers, Chinamen, with the exception of a few Parsees, all handsomely dressed, nearly all smoking, and sitting or lying over the saloon deck up to the saloon doors. In the steerage there are fifteen hundred Chinese steerage passengers, all men. The Chinese are a noisy people, their language is inharmonious, and the lower class male voices, at least, are harsh and coarse. The fifteen hundred men seem to be all shouting at once, and the din which comes up through the hatchways is fearful. This noisy mass of humanity is practically imprisoned below, for there is a heavy iron grating securely padlocked over each exit, and a European, "armed to the teeth," stands by each, ready to shoot the first man who attempts to force it. In this saloon there is a stand of six rifles with bayonets, and four revolvers, and, as we started, a man carefully took the sheaths off the bayonets, and loaded the firearms with ball cartridge.

ISABELLA LUCY BIRD

Canton, January 1, 1879.

The Canton River for the ninety miles up here has nothing interesting about it. Soon after leaving Hong Kong the country becomes nearly a dead level, mainly rice-swamps varied by patches of bananas, with their great fronds torn to tatters by the prevailing strong breeze. A very high pagoda marks Whampoa, once a prosperous port, but now, like Macao, nearly deserted. An hour after disgorging three boat loads of Chinamen at Whampoa, we arrived at the beginning of Canton, but it took more than half an hour of cautious threading of our way among junks, sampans, house-boats, and slipper-boats, before we moored to the crowded and shabby wharf. If my expectations of Canton had been much raised they would certainly have been disappointed, for the city stands on a perfectly level site, and has no marked features within or around it except the broad and bridgeless tidal river which sweeps through it at a rapid rate. In the distance are the White-Cloud hills, which were painted softly in amethyst on a tender green sky, and nearer are some rocky hills, which are red at all hours of daylight. Boats and masts conceal the view of the city from the river to a great extent, but even when from a vantage ground it is seen spread out below, it is so densely packed, its streets are so narrow, and its open spaces so few, that one almost doubts whether the million and a half of people attributed to it are really crowded within the narrow area. From the river, and indeed from any point of view, Canton is less imposing even than Tokiyo. Few objects rise above the monotonous level, and the few are unimpressive. There are two or three pagodas looking like shot towers. There is a double-towered Romish cathedral of great size, not yet finished. There is the "Nine-storied pagoda." But in truth the most prominent objects from the river are the "godowns" of the pawnbrokers, lofty, square towers of gray brick which dominate the city, play a very important part in its social economy, and are very far removed from those establishments with the trinity of gilded balls, which hide themselves shamefacedly away in our English by-streets. At one part of the riverside there are some substantial looking foreign houses among trees, on the site of the foreign factories of former days, but they and indeed all else are hidden by a crowd of boats, a town of boats, a floating suburb. Indeed, boats are my earliest and strongest impressions of what on my arrival I was hasty enough to think a mean city. It is not only along the sides of the broad Pearl river, but along the network of innumerable canals and creeks which communicate with it, that they are found.

These boats, the first marvel of a marvelous city, have come between me and my landing. When the steamer had disgorged her two thousand passengers, Mr. Mackrill Smith, whose guest I am, brought me in a bamboo chair, carried by two coolies, through a covered and crowded street of merchandise six feet wide, to Shameen, the island in the river on which the foreigners reside; most of the missionary community, however, living in the buildings on the site of the old factory farther down.

I am now domiciled on Shameen, a reclaimed mud flat, in the beautiful house belonging to the firm of Jardine, Matheson & Co. This island, which has on the one side the swift flowing Canton river, with its ever shifting life, has on the other a canal, on which an enormous population lives in house boats, moored stem and stern, without any space between them. A stone bridge with an iron gate gives access into one of the best parts of Canton, commercially speaking; but all the business connected with tea, silk, and other productions, which is carried on by such renowned firms as Jardine, Matheson & Co., the Dents, the Deacons, and others, is transacted in these handsome dwellings of stone or brick, each standing in its tropical garden, with a wall or ornamental railing or bamboo hedge surrounding it, but without any outward sign of commerce at all. The settlement, insular and exclusive, hears little and knows less of the crowded Chinese city at its gates. It reproduces English life as far as possible, and adds a boundless hospitality of its own, receiving all strangers who are in any way accredited, and many who are not. A high sea-wall with a broad concrete walk, shaded by banyan trees, runs round it, a distance of a mile and a quarter. It is quite flat and covered with carefully kept grass, intersected with concrete walks and banyan avenues, the tropical gardens of the rich merchants giving variety and color.

The community at present consists of forty-five people—English, French, and German. The establishment of the electric telegraph has not only favored business, but has enabled some of the senior partners of the old firms to return home, leaving very junior partners or senior clerks here, who receive their instructions from England. Consequently, in some of these large family dwellings there are only young men "keeping bach." There are a pretty English church, a club bungalow, a book club, lawn tennis and croquet grounds, and a small hall used for dancing, lectures and amateur theatricals. No wheeled vehicle larger than a perambulator ever disturbs the quiet. People who go into the city are carried in chairs, or drop down the river in their luxurious covered boats, but for exercise they mostly walk on the bund, and play croquet or lawn tennis. In this glorious weather the island is very charming. It is possible to spend the whole year here, as the tidal breezes modify the moist heat of summer; but the English children look pale and languid even now.

Canton, January 4.

If I were to describe Canton, and had time for it, my letters would soon swell to the size of Archdeacon Gray's quaint and fascinating book, "Walks in Canton;" but I have no time, and must content myself with brief sketches of two or three things which have greatly interested me, and of the arrangement and management of the city; putting the last first, if I am able "to make head or tail of it," and to cram its leading features into a letter.

Viewing Canton from the "five-storied pagoda," or from the dignified elevation of a pawn tower, it is apparent that it is surrounded by a high wall, beyond which here and there are suburban villages, some wealthy and wood-embosomed, others mean and mangy. The river divides it from a very populous and important suburb. Within the city lies the kernel of the whole, the Tartar city, occupied by the garrison and a military colony numbering about twenty thousand persons. This interesting area is walled round, and contains the residence of the Tartar General, and the consulates of the great European Powers. It is well wooded and less closely built than the rest of Canton. Descending from any elevation one finds oneself at once involved at any and every point in a maze of narrow, crowded streets of high brick and stone houses, mostly from five to eight feet wide. These streets are covered in at the height of the house roofs by screens of canvas matting, or thin boards, which afford a pleasant shade, and at the same time let the sunbeams glance and trickle among the long, pendent signboards and banners which swing aloft, and upon the busy, many-colored, jostling throng below.

Every street is paved with large slabs of granite, and under each of the massive foot-ways (for carriage-ways there are none) there is a drain for carrying off the rain-water, which is then conveyed into six large culverts, from them into four creeks which intersect the city, and thence into the river. These large drains are supervised by the "prefect," who is bound by an ancient law to have them thoroughly cleansed every autumn, while each of the small drains is cleansed by the orders and at the expense of the "vestry" of the street under which it passes. This ancient sanitary law, like many other of the admirable laws of this empire, is said to be by no means punctiliously carried out; and that Canton is a very healthy city, and that pestilences of any kind rarely gain a footing in it, may be attributed rather to the excellent plan of sending out the garbage of the city daily to fertilize the gardens and fields of the neighborhood, than to the vigilance of the municipal authorities.

There are heavy and ancient gates or barricades which enclose each street, and which are locked at night, only to be opened by favor of the watchmen who guard them. Their closing brings to an end the busy street life, and at 10 P.M. Canton, cut up into small sections, barred out from each other, is like a city of the dead. Each gate watchman is appointed and paid by the "vestry" of the street in which he keeps guard. They wear uniform, but are miserable dilapidated-looking creatures, and I have twice seen one fast asleep. In the principal streets night watchmen are stationed in watch-towers, which consist of small mat huts, placed on scaffolds raised far above the house-tops, on bamboo poles bound together with strong cords. These men are on the look-out for armed bands of robbers, but specially for fire. They are provided with tom-toms and small gongs on which to proclaim the hours of the night, but, should fire arise, a loud, rapid, and incessant beating of the gong gives the alarm to all the elevated brotherhood in turn, who at the same time, by concerted signals, inform the citizens below of the ward and street in which the fire has originated. In each principal street there is a very large well, covered with granite slabs, with its exact position denoted on a granite slab on the adjoining wall. These wells, which are abundant reservoirs, are never opened except in case of fire.

Besides these watchmen, eleven hundred military constabulary are answerable for the good order of the "new city" and its suburbs, and a thousand more, called the Governor's brigade, garrison the outer gates in the city wall and several interior guard-houses, all the inner gates being garrisoned by Tartar troops. Canton is divided into thirty-six wards, under twelve officers in summer, but in winter, as now, when burglars are supposed to be more on the alert, this number is increased. Each officer having soldiers under him traverses at intervals during the night every street under his jurisdiction, and these armed followers, whether to intimidate criminals or to show their vigilance, are in the habit of discharging their old-fashioned matchlocks and gingalls as they patrol. In consequence of so many precautions, which are carried out very thoroughly, fires and burglaries are much minimized, and the proverb "as safe as Canton" appears to have a substantial foundation. The barricaded streets at night have an eerie solemnity about them. One night, my present hostess, Mrs. H., and I prowled through some of them quite unattended, on our way back from a friend's dwelling, roused up the watchmen to unlock and unbar the gates, saw no other people astir, went down one of the water streets, hailed a boat, and were deposited close to the door of our own abode about midnight; such an event being quite of common occurrence in this quarter.

In the streets the roofs of the houses and shops are rarely, if ever, regular, nor are the houses themselves arranged in a direct line, This queer effect results from queer causes. Every Chinese house is built on the principles of geomancy, which do not admit of straight lines, and were these to be disregarded the astrologers and soothsayers under whose auspices all houses are erected, predict fearful evils to the impious builders. There are few open spaces in Canton, and these are decorated, not with statues, but with monumental arches of brick, red sandstone, or gray granite, which are put up as memorials of virtuous men and women, learned or aged men, and specially dutiful sons or daughters. Such memorials are erected by citizens, and, in some cases, by Imperial sanction or decree.

The public buildings and temples, though they bear magnificent names, are extremely ugly, and are the subjects of slow but manifest decay, while the streets of shops exceed in picturesqueness everything I have ever seen. Much of this is given by the perpendicular sign boards, fixed or hanging, upon which are painted on an appropriate background immense Chinese characters in gold, vermilion, or black. Two or three of these belong to each shop, and set forth its name and the nature of the goods which are to be purchased at it. The effect of these boards as the sun's rays fall upon them here and there is fascinating. The interiors of the shops are lofty, glass lamps hang from the ceilings and large lanterns above every door, and both are painted in bright colors, with the characters signifying happiness, or with birds, butterflies, flowers, or landscapes. The shop wall which faces the door invariably has upon it a gigantic fresco or portrait of the tutelary god of the building, or a sheet of red paper on which the characters forming his name are placed, or the character Shan, which implies all gods, and these and the altars below are seen from the street. There is a recess outside each shop, and at dusk the joss-sticks burning in these fill the city with the fragrance of incense.

As there are streets of shops and trades, so there are streets of dwelling-houses, but even the finest of these present a miserable appearance to the passers-by, for all one can see is a lofty and dimly-lighted stone vestibule, furnished with carved ebony chairs with marble seats and backs, and not infrequently with gigantic coffins placed on end, the gift of pious juniors to their seniors! A porter stands in this vestibule ready to open the lofty triple gate which admits to the courtyard of the interior. Many Chinese mansions contain six or seven courtyards, each with its colonnade, drawing, dining, and reception rooms, and at the back of all there is a flower garden adorned with rockeries, fish-ponds, dwarf trees, and miniature pagodas and bridges.

The streets in which the poor dwell are formed of low, small, dark, and dirty houses, of two or three rooms each. The streets of dwellings are as mean and ugly as those of shops are brilliant and picturesque.

This is a meagre outline of what may be called the anatomy of this ancient city, which dates from the fourth century B.C., when it was walled only by a stockade of bamboo and mud, but was known by the name of "the martial city of the south," changed later into "the city of rams." At this date it has probably greater importance than it ever had, and no city but London impresses me so much with the idea of solid wealth and increasing prosperity.

My admiration and amazement never cease. I grudge the hours that I am obliged to spend in sleep; a week has gone like half a day, each hour heightening my impressions of the fascination and interest of Canton, and of the singular force and importance of the Chinese. Canton is intoxicating from its picturesqueness, color, novelty and movement. To-day I have been carried eighteen miles through and round it, reveling the whole time in its enchantments, and drinking for the first time of that water of which it may truly be said that who so drinks "shall thirst again"—true Orientalism. As we sat at mid-day at the five-storied pagoda, which from a corner of the outer wall overlooks the Tartar city, and ever since, through this crowded week, I have wished that the sun would stand still in the cloudless sky, and let me dream of gorgeous sunlight, light without heat, of narrow lanes rich in color, of the glints of sunlight on embroideries and cloth of gold, resplendent even in the darkness, of hurrying and colored crowds in the shadow, with the blue sky in narrow strips high above, of gorgeous marriage processions, and the "voice of the bridegroom and the voice of the bride," of glittering trains of mandarins, of funeral processions, with the wail of hired mourners clad in sackcloth and ashes, of the Tartar city with its pagodas, of the hills of graves, great cities of the dead outside the walls, fiery-red under the tropic blue, of the "potter's field" with its pools of blood and sacks of heads, and crosses for crucifixion, now, as on Calvary, symbolical of shame alone, of the wonderful river life, and all the busy, crowded, costumed hurry of the streets, where blue banners hanging here and there show that in those houses death has stilled some busy brains forevermore. And I should like to tell you of the Buddhist and Confucian temples; of the monastery garden, which is the original of the famous "Willow Pattern;" of the great Free Dispensary which is to rival that of the Medical Mission; of the asylums for lepers, foundlings, the blind, aged men and aged women, dating from the fourteenth to the seventeenth centuries, originally well conceived and noble institutions, but reduced into inefficiency and degradation by the greed and corruption of generations of officials; of the "Beggars' Square" and beggars' customs; of the trades, and of the shops with their splendors; of the Examination Hall with its streets numbering eleven thousand six hundred and seventy-three cells for the candidates for the literary honors which are the only road to office and distinction in China, but Canton deserves a volume, and Archdeacon Gray has written one!

I. L. B.

Letter IV

"Faithful unto Death"—"Foreign Devils"—Junks and Boats—Chinese Luxury—Canton Afloat—An Al Fresco Lunch-Light and Color—A Mundane Disappointment—Street Sights and Sounds—Street Costume—Food and Restaurants—A Marriage Procession—Temples and Worship—Crippled Feet

REV. B. C. HENRY'S, CANTON, January 6.

In the week in which I have been here I have given myself up to ceaseless sight-seeing. Almost the first sight that I saw on arriving in this quarter, which is in Canton itself, was a number of Christian refugees, old men, women, and children, who, having fled from a bloody persecution which is being waged against Christianity about ninety miles from Canton, are receiving shelter in the compound of the German mission. It was late in the evening, and these poor refugees, who had sacrificed much for their faith and had undergone great terror, were singing hymns, and reading and worshipping in Chinese. In the place from which they came a Christian of wealth wished to build a church, and last week he was proceeding to do so, when the heathen, instigated by the district mandarin, seized upon him and four other Christians, and when he would neither say the word nor make the obeisance which is regarded as equivalent to denying Christ, they wrapped him in cotton wadding soaked in oil, tied him to a cross, and burned him, no extremity of torture availing to shake his constancy. They cut off the arms and legs of the four other persons, tied crosses to the trunks, and then burned them. This deed, done so near Canton, has caused great horror among the foreigners both here and at Hong Kong, and the deepest sympathy is felt both with the converts and the missionary priests. In the sympathy with the heroism and sufferings of those who have been "faithful unto death," all the Protestant missionaries join heartily, as in the belief that these victims are reckoned among "the noble army of martyrs." It is estimated that there are seven hundred and fifty thousand Romish Christians in China, many of them of the third or fourth generation of Christians, and in some places far in the interior there are whole villages of them. The Portuguese and French missionary priests who devote themselves for life to this work, dress, eat, and live as Chinamen, and are credited with great devotion.

It is most interesting to be brought by the spectacle of these poor refugees so near to the glory and the woe of martyrdom, and to hear that the martyr spirit can still make men "obedient unto death, even the death of the cross." A placard was posted up some time ago calling for a general massacre of the native Christians on Christmas Day. It attributes every vice to the "Foreign Devils," and says that, "to preserve the peace and purity of Chinese Society, those whom they have corrupted must be cut off." One phrase of this placard is, "The wickedness of these foreign devils is so great that even pigs and dogs would refuse to eat their flesh!"

Mr. and Mrs. Henry speak Chinese, and are both fearless, and familiar with the phases of Canton life. Of all the places I have seen, Canton is the most overwhelmingly interesting, fascinating, and startling. "See Canton and die," I would almost say, and yet I can give no idea of all that has taken such a strong hold of me. I should now be quite content to see only the manifold street life, with its crowds, processions, and din, and the strange and ever-shifting water life, altogether distinct from the land life. The rice-paper pictures give a very good idea of the forms and colors of the boats, but the thousands of them, and the rate at which they are propelled, are altogether indescribable, either by pen or pencil.

There are junks with big eyes on either side of the stem, "without which they could not see their way,"* and with open bows with two six-pounders grinning through them. Along the sides there are ten guns, and at the lofty, square, quaint, broad, carved stern, two more. This heavy armament is carried nominally for protection against pirates, but its chief use is for the production of those stunning noises which Chinamen delight in on all occasions. In these helpless and unwieldy-looking vessels which are sailed with an amount of noise and apparent confusion which is absolutely shocking to anyone used to our strict nautical discipline, the rudder projects astern six feet and more, the masts are single poles, the large sails of fine matting; and what with their antique shape, rich coloring, lattice work and carving, they are the most picturesque craft afloat. Then there are "passage boats" from the whole interior network of rivers and canals, each district having its special rig and build, recognizable at once by the initiated. These sail when they can, and when they can't are propelled by large sweeps, each of which is worked by six men who stand on a platform outside. These boats are always heavily laden, crowded with passengers and "armed to the teeth" as a protection against river pirates, and they carry crews of from thirty-five to fifty men.

> [*These eyes are really charms, but the above is the explanation given to "griffins."]

At some distance below Shameen there are moored tiers of large, two-storied house boats, with entrance doors seven feet high, always open, and doorways of rich wood carving, through which the interiors can be seen with their richly decorated altars, innumerable colored lamps, chairs, and settees of carved ebony with white marble let into the seats and backs, embroidered silk hangings, gilded mirrors and cornices, and all the extravagances of Chinese luxury. Many of them have gardens on their roofs. These are called "flower boats," and are of noisy and evil reputation. Then there are tiers of three-roomed, comfortable house boats to let to people who make their homes on the water in summer to avoid the heat. "Marriage boats," green and gold, with much wood carving and flags, and auspicious emblems of all kinds; river junks, with their large eyes and carved and castellated sterns lying moored in treble rows; duck boats, with their noisy inmates; florists' boats, with platforms of growing plants for sale; two-storied boats or barges, with glass sides, floating hotels, in which evening entertainments are given with much light and noise; restaurant boats, much gilded, from which proceeds an incessant beating of gongs; washing boats, market boats, floating shops, which supply the floating population with all marketable commodities; country boats of fantastic form coming down on every wind and tide; and, queerest of all, "slipper boats," looking absurdly like big shoes, which are propelled in and out among all the heavier craft by standing in the stern.

One of the most marvelous features of Canton is the city of house boats, floating and stationary, in which about a quarter of a million people live, and it may with truth be added are born and die. This population is quite distinct in race from the land population of Canton, which looks down upon it as a pariah and alien caste. These house boats, some of which have a single bamboo circular roof, others two roofs of different heights, and which include several thousand of the marvelous "slipper boats," lie in tiers along the river sides, and packed closely stem and stern along the canals, forming bustling and picturesque water streets. Many of the boats moored on the canals are floating shops, and do a brisk trade, one end of the boat being the shop, the other the dwelling-house. As the "slipper boats" are only from fifteen to twenty feet long, it may be imagined, as their breadth is strictly proportionate, that the accommodation for a family is rather circumscribed, yet such a boat is not only the home of a married pair and their children, but of the eldest son with his wife and children, and not unfrequently of grandparents also! The bamboo roofs slide in a sort of telescope fashion, and the whole interior space can be inclosed and divided. The bow of the boat, whether large or small, is always the family joss house; and the water is starred at night with the dull, melancholy glimmer, fainter, though redder than a glow-worm's light, of thousands of burning joss-sticks, making the air heavy with the odor of incense. Unlike the houses of the poor on shore, the house boats are models of cleanliness, and space is utilized and economized by adaptations more ingenious than those of a tiny yacht. These boats, which form neat rooms with matted seats by day, turn into beds at night, and the children have separate "rooms." The men go on shore during the day and do laborer's work, but the women seldom land, are devoted to "housewifely" duties, and besides are to be seen at all hours of day and night flying over the water, plying for hire at the landings, and ferrying goods and passengers, as strong as men, and clean, comely, and pleasant-looking; one at the stern and one at the bow, sending the floating home along with skilled and sturdy strokes. They are splendid boat-women, and not vociferous. These women don't bandage their feet.

Their dress is dark brown or blue cotton, and consists of wide trousers and a short, loose, sleeved upper garment up to the throat. The feet are big and bare, the hair is neat and drawn back from the face into a stiff roll or chignon, and they all wear jade-stone earrings. You see a woman cooking or sewing in most housewifely style in one of these "slipper boats;" but if you hail it, she is plying the heavy oar in one moment, and as likely as not with a wise-looking baby on her back, supported by a square piece of scarlet cloth embroidered in gold and blue silks. Not one of this river population has yet received Christianity. Very little indeed is known about them and their customs, but it is said that their morals are low, and that when infanticide was less discouraged than it is now, the river was the convenient grave of many of their newly-born female children. I spent most of one afternoon alone in one of these boats, diving into all canals and traversing water streets, hanging on to junks and "passage boats," and enjoying the variety of river life to the full.

On another day I was carried eighteen miles through Canton on a chair by four coolies, Mr. Smith and his brother walking the whole distance—a great testimony to the invigorating influences of the winter climate. As to locomotion, one must either walk or be carried. A human being is not a heavy weight for the coolies, but it is distressing to see that the shoulders of very many of them are suffering from bony tumors, arising from the pressure of the poles. We lunched in the open air upon a stone table under a banyan-tree at the "Five-storied Pagoda" which forms the north-east corner of the great wall of Canton, from which we looked down upon the singular vestiges of the nearly forgotten Tartar conquest, the walled inner city of the Tartar conquerors, containing the Tartar garrison, the Yamun (official residence) of the Tartar governor, the houses of the foreign consuls, and the unmixed Tartar population. The streets of this foreign kernel of Canton are narrow and dirty, with mean, low houses with tiled roofs nearly flat, and small courtyards, more like the houses of Western than Eastern Asia. These Tartars do not differ much in physiognomy from the Chinese. They are somewhat uglier, their stature is shorter, and the women always wear three rings in their ears. I saw more women in a single street in one day in the Tartar city than I have seen altogether in the rest of Canton.

The view from that corner of the wall (to my thinking) is beautiful, the flaming red pagoda with its many roofs; the singularly picturesque ancient gray wall, all ups and downs, watch-towers, and strongholds, the Tartar city below, with the "flowery pagoda," the mosques, the bright foliage of the banyan, and the feathery grace of the bamboo; outside the wall the White-Cloud hills, and nearer ranges burrowed everywhere for the dead, their red and pink and orange hues harmonized by a thin blue veil, softening without obscuring, all lying in the glory of the tropic winter noon-light without heat, color without glare. Vanish all memories of grays and pale greens before this vividness, this wealth of light and color! Color is at once music and vitality, and after long deprivation I revel in it. This wall is a fine old structure, about twenty feet wide and as many high, with a broad pavement on which to walk, and a high platform on the outside, with a battlement pierced for marksmen. It is hardly ever level for ten yards, but follows the inequalities of the ground, and has picturesque towers which occur frequently. It is everywhere draped with ferns, which do not help to keep it in repair. The "Five-storied Pagoda" which flames in red at one of its angles, is a striking feature in the view. As we sat on stone seats by stone tables in what might be called its shadow, under the cloudless heaven, with the pure Orientalism of the Tartar city spread out at our feet, that unimaginable Orientalism which takes one captive at once, and, like the first sight of a palm or a banana, satisfies a longing of which one had not previously been conscious, a mundane disappointment was severely felt. We had been, as the Americans say, "exercising" for five hours in the bracing air, and I had long been conscious of a craving for solid food which no Orientalism could satisfy; and our dismay was great not only to find that the cook had put up lunch for two when there were three hungry persons, but that the chicken was so underdone that we could not eat it, and as we were not starving enough to go and feed at a cat and dog or any other Chinese restaurant, my hosts at least, who had not learned that bananas are sustenance for men as well as "food for gods," were famished. As we ate "clem pie" or "dined with Duke Humphrey," two water buffaloes, dark gray ungainly forms, with little more hair than elephants, recurved horns, and muzzles like deer, watched us closely, until a Tartar drove them off. Such beasts, which stand in the water and plaster themselves with mud like elephants, are the cows and draught oxen of China. Two nice Chinese boys sat by us, and Mr. Smith practiced Chinese upon them, till a man came out angrily and took them away, using many words, of which we only understood "Barbarian Devils." The Cantonese are not rude, however. A foreign lady can walk alone without being actually molested, though as a rule Chinese women are not seen in the streets. I have certainly seen half a million men, and not more than ninety women, and those only of the poorest class. The middle and upper class women never go out except in closed palanquins with screened windows, and are nearly as much secluded as the women of India.

Passing through the Tartar city and some streets of aristocratic dullness, inhabited by wealthy merchants, we spent some hours in the mercantile quarter; which is practically one vast market or bazaar, thronged with masculine humanity from morning till night. Eight feet is the width of the widest street but one, and between the passers-by, the loungers, the people standing at stalls eating, or drinking tea, and the itinerant venders of goods, it is one long push. Then, as you are elbowing your feeble self among the big men, who are made truly monstrous by their many wadded garments of silk and brocade, you are terrified by a loud yell, and being ignominiously hustled out of the way, you become aware that the crowd has yielded place to a procession, consisting of several men in red, followed by a handsome closed palanquin, borne by four, six, or eight bearers in red liveries, in which reclines a stout, magnificently dressed mandarin, utterly oblivious of his inferiors, the representative of high caste feeling all the world over, either reading or absorbed, never taking any notice of the crowds and glitter which I find so fascinating. More men in red, and then the crowd closes up again, to be again divided by a plebeian chair like mine, or by pariahs running with a coffin fifteen feet long, shaped like the trunk of a tree, or by coolies carrying burdens slung on bamboo poles, uttering deafening cries, or by a marriage procession with songs and music, or by a funeral procession with weeping and wailing, succeeding each other incessantly. All the people in the streets are shouting at the top of their voices, the chair and baggage coolies are yelling, and to complete the bewildering din the beggars at every corner are demanding charity by striking two gongs together.

Color riots in these narrow streets, with their high houses with projecting upper stories, much carved and gilded, their deeply projecting roofs or eaves tiled with shells cut into panes, which let the light softly through, while a sky of deep bright blue fills up the narrow slit between. Then in the shadow below, which is fitfully lighted by the sunbeams, hanging from all the second stories at every possible interval of height, each house having at least two, are the richly painted boards of which I wrote before, from six to ten feet long, some black, some heavily gilded, a few orange, but the majority red and perfectly plain, except for the characters several inches long down the middle of each, gold on the red and black, and black on the gold and orange—these, with banners, festoons, and the bright blue draperies which for a hundred days indicate mourning in a house, form together a spectacle of street picturesqueness such as my eyes have never before beheld. Then all the crowd is in costume, and such costume! The prevailing color for the robe is bright blue. Even the coolies put on such a one when not working, and all above the coolies wear them in rich, ribbed silk, lined with silk of a darker shade. Over this a sleeveless jacket of rich dark blue or puce brocade, plain or quilted, is worn; the trousers, of which little is seen, being of brocade or satin. The stockings are white, and the shoes, which are on thick, white, canoe-shaped soles, are of black satin. The cap, which is always worn, and quite on the back of the head, is of black satin, and the pigtail, or plait of hair and purse silk mixed, hangs down nearly to the bottom of the robe. Then the most splendid furs are worn, and any number of quilted silk and brocade garments, one above another. And these big, prosperous-looking men, who are so richly dressed, are only the shopkeepers and the lower class of merchants. The mandarins and the rich merchants seldom put their feet to the ground.

The shops just now are filled with all sorts of brilliant and enticing things in anticipation of the great festival of the New Year, which begins on the 21st. At the New Year they are all closed, and the rich merchants vie with each other in keeping them so; those whose shops are closed the longest, sometimes even for two months, gaining a great reputation for wealth thereby. Streets are given up to shops of one kind. Thus there is the "Jade-Stone Street," entirely given up to the making and sale of jade-stone jewelry, which is very costly, a single bracelet of the finest stone and workmanship costing 600 pounds. There is a whole street devoted to the sale of coffins; several in which nothing is sold but furniture, from common folding tables up to the costliest settees, bedsteads, and chairs of massive ebony carving; chinaware streets, book and engraving streets, streets of silk shops, streets of workers in brass, silver, and gold, who perform their delicate manipulations before your eyes; streets of second-hand clothing, where gorgeous embroideries in silk and gold can be bought for almost nothing; and so on, every street blazing with colors, splendid with costume, and abounding with wealth and variety.

We went to a "dog and cat restaurant," where a number of richly dressed men were eating of savory dishes made from the flesh of these animals. There are thousands of butchers' and fishmongers' shops in Canton. At the former there are always hundreds of split and salted ducks hanging on lines, and pigs of various sizes roasted whole, or sold in joints raw; and kids and buffalo beef, and numbers of dogs and cats, which, though skinned, have the tails on to show what they are. I had some of the gelatinous "birds'-nest" soup, without knowing what it was. It is excellent; but as these nests are brought from Sumatra and are very costly, it is only a luxury of the rich. The fish shops and stalls are legion, but the fish looks sickening, as it is always cut into slices and covered with blood. The boiled chrysalis of a species of silkworm is exposed for sale as a great delicacy, and so are certain kinds of hairless, fleshy caterpillars.

In our peregrinations we came upon a Yamun, with its vestibule hung with scarlet, the marriage color as well as the official color. Within the door the "wedding garments" were hanging for the wedding guests, scarlet silk crepe, richly embroidered. Some time later the bridal procession swept through the streets, adding a new glory to the color and movement. First marched a troop of men in scarlet, carrying scarlet banners, each one emblazoned with the literary degrees of the bride's father and grandfather. Then came ten heavily gilded, carved, and decorated pavilions, containing the marriage presents, borne on poles on the shoulders of servants; and after them the bride, carried in a locked palanquin to the bridegroom's house, completely shrouded, the palanquin one mass of decoration in gold and blue enamel, the carving fully six inches deep; and the procession was closed by a crowd of men in scarlet, carrying the bridegroom's literary degrees, with banners, and instruments of music. It is the China of a thousand years ago, unaltered by foreign contact.

There are many beggars, and a "Beggars' Square," and the beggars have a "king," and a regular guild, with an entrance fee of 1 pound. The shopkeepers are obliged by law to give them a certain sum, and on the occasion of a marriage or any other festivity, the giver sends a fee to the "king," on the understanding that he keeps his lieges from bothering the guests. They make a fearful noise with their two gongs. There is one on the Shameen bridge who has a callosity like a horn on his forehead, with which he strikes the pavement and produces an audible thump.

After the cleanliness, beauty, and good repair of the Japanese temples, those of Canton impress me as being very repulsive. In Japan the people preserve their temples for their exquisite beauty, and there are a great many sincere Buddhists; but China is irreligious; a nation of atheists or agnostics, or slaves of impious superstitions. In an extended tramp among temples I have not seen a single male worshiper or a thing to please the eye. The Confucian temples, to which mandarinism resorts on certain days to bow before the Confucian tablets, are now closed, and their courts are overgrown with weeds. The Buddhist temples are hideous, both outside and inside, built of a crumbling red brick, with very dirty brick floors, and the idols are frightful and tawdry. We went to several which have large monasteries attached to them, with great untidy gardens, with ponds for sacred fish and sacred tortoises, and houses for sacred pigs, whose sacredness is shown by their monstrous obesity. In the garden of the Temple of Longevity, the scene of the "Willow Pattern," dirty and degraded priests, in spite of a liberal douceur to one of them, set upon us, clamoring *kum-sha*, attempting at the same time to shut us in, and the two gentlemen were obliged to use force for our extrication. In the court of the "Temple of Horrors," which is surrounded by a number of grated cells containing life-sized figures of painted wood, undergoing at the hands of other figures such hell-torments as are decreed for certain offences, there is perpetually a crowd of fortune-tellers, and numbers of gaming tables always thronged with men and boys. Each temple has an accretion of smaller temples or shrines round it, but most, on ordinary occasions, are deserted, and all are neglected and dirty. Where we saw worshipers they were always women, some of whom looked very earnest, as they were worshiping for sick children, or to obtain boys, or to insure the fidelity of their husbands. "Worship" consists in many prostrations, in the offering of many joss-sticks, and in burning large squares of gilded paper, this being supposed to be the only way in which gold can reach either gods or ancestors. One or two of the smaller temples were thronged by women of the poorest class, whose earnest faces were very touching. Idolatry is always pathetic. It is not, however, idol worship which sits like a nightmare on China, and crushes atheists, agnostics, and heathens alike, but ancestral worship, and the tyranny of the astrologers and geomancers.

I like the faces of the lower orders of Chinese women. They are both strong and kind, and it is pleasant to see women not deformed in any way, but clothed completely in a dress which allows perfect freedom of action. The small-footed women are rarely seen out of doors; but the sewing-woman at Mrs. Smith's has crippled feet, and I have got her shoes, which are too small for the English baby of four months old! The butler's little daughter, aged seven, is having her feet "bandaged" for the first time, and is in torture, but bears it bravely in the hope of "getting a rich husband." The sole of the shoe of a properly diminished foot is about two inches and a half long, but the mother of this suffering infant says, with a quiet air of truth and triumph, that Chinese women suffer less in the process of being crippled than foreign women do from wearing corsets! To these Eastern women the notion of deforming the figure for the sake of appearance only is unintelligible and repulsive. The crippling of the feet has another motive.

I. L. B.

Letter IV

Continued

Outside the Naam-Hoi Prison—The Punishment of the Cangue—Crime and Misery—A Birthday Banquet—"Prisoners and Captives"—Prison Mortality—Cruelties and Iniquities—The Porch of the Mandarin—The Judgment-Seat—The Precincts of the Judgment-Seat—An Aged Claimant—Instruments of Punishment—The Question by Torture

Yesterday, after visiting the streets devoted to jade-stone workers, jewelers, saddlers, dealers in musical instruments, and furriers, we turned aside from the street called Sze-P'aai-Lau, into a small, dirty square, on one side of which is a brick wall, with a large composite quadruped upon it in black paint, and on the other the open entrance gate of the Yamun, or official residence of the mandarin whose jurisdiction extends over about half Canton, and who is called the Naam-Hoi magistrate. Both sides of the road passing through this square, and especially the open space in front of the gate which leads into the courtyard of the Yamun, were crowded with unshaven, ragged, forlorn, dirty wretches, heavily fettered round their ankles, and with long heavy chains padlocked round their necks, attached, some to large stones with holes in the centre, others to short thick bars of iron. Two or three, into whose legs the ankle fetters had cut deep raw grooves, were lying in a heap on a ragged mat in the corner; some were sitting on stones, but most were standing or shifting their position uneasily, dragging their weighty fetters about, making a jarring and dismal clank with every movement.

These unfortunates are daily exposed thus to the scorn and contempt of the passers-by as a punishment for small thefts. Of those who were seated on stones or who were kneeling attempting to support themselves on their hands, most wore square wooden collars of considerable size, weighing thirty pounds each, round their necks. These cangues are so constructed that it is impossible for their wearers to raise their hands to their mouths for the purpose of feeding themselves, and it seemed to be a choice pastime for small boys to tantalize these criminals by placing food tied to the end of sticks just within reach of their mouths, and then suddenly withdrawing them. Apart from the weight of their fetters, and of the cangue in which they are thus pilloried, these men suffer much from hunger and thirst. They are thus punished for petty larcenies. Surely "the way of transgressors is hard."

The bearers set me down at the gate of the Yamun among the festering wretches dragging the heavy weights, the filthy and noisy beggars, the gamblers, the fortune-tellers, the messengers of justice, and the countless hangers-on of the prison and judgment-seat of the Naam-Hoi magistrate, and passing through a part of the courtyard, and down a short, narrow passage, enclosed by a door of rough wooden uprights, above which is a tiger's head, with staring eyes and extended jaws, we reached the inner entrance, close to which is a much blackened altar of incense foul with the ashes of innumerable joss-sticks, and above it an equally blackened and much worn figure of a tiger in granite. To this beast, which is regarded by the Chinese as possessing virtue, and is the tutelary guardian of Chinese prisons, the jailers offer incense and worship night and day, with the object of securing its aid and vigilance on their behalf.

Close to the altar were the jailers' rooms, dark, dirty, and inconceivably forlorn. Two of the jailers were lying on their beds smoking opium. There we met the head jailer, of all Chinamen that I have seen the most repulsive in appearance, manner, and dress; for his long costume of frayed and patched brown silk looked as if it had not been taken off for a year; the lean, brown hands which clutched the prison keys with an instinctive grip were dirty, and the nails long and hooked like claws, and the face, worse, I thought, than that of any of the criminal horde, and scored with lines of grip and greed, was saturated with opium smoke. This wretch pays for his place, and in a few years will retire with a fortune, gains arising from bribes wrung from prisoners and their friends by threats and torture, and by defrauding them daily of a part of their allowance of rice.

The prison, as far as I can learn, consists mainly of six wards, each with four large apartments, the walls of these wards abutting upon each other, and forming a parallelogram, outside of which is a narrow, paved pathway, on which the gates of the wards open, and which has on its outer side the high boundary wall of the prison. This jailer, this fiend—made such by the customs of his country—took us down a passage, and unlocking a wooden grating turned us into one of the aforesaid "wards," a roughly paved courtyard about fifty feet long by twenty-four broad, and remained standing in the doorway jangling his keys.

If crime, vice, despair, suffering, filth and cruelty can make a hell on earth, this is one. Over its dismal gateway may well be written, "Whoso enters here leaves hope behind."

This ward is divided into four "apartments," each one having a high wall at the back. The sides next the court are formed of a double row of strong wooden bars, black from age and dirt, which reach from the floor to the roof, and let in light and air through the chinks between them. The interiors of these cribs or cattle-pens are roughly paved with slabs of granite, slimy with accumulations of dirt. In the middle and round the sides are stout platforms of laths, forming a coarse, black gridiron, on which the prisoners sit and sleep.

In each ward there is a shrine of a deity who is supposed to have the power of melting the wicked into contrition, and to this accursed mockery, on his birthday, the prisoners are compelled to give a feast, which is provided by the jailer out of his peculations from their daily allowances. No water is allowed for washing, and the tubs containing the allowance of foul drinking water are placed close to those which are provided for the accumulation of night soil, etc., the contents of which are only removed once a fortnight. Two pounds of rice is the daily allowance of each prisoner, but this is reduced to about one by the greed of the jailer.

As we entered the yard, fifty or sixty men swarmed out from the dark doorways which led into their dens, all heavily chained, with long, coarse, matted hair hanging in wisps, or standing on end round their death-like faces, in filthy rags, with emaciated forms caked with dirt, and bearing marks of the torture; and nearly all with sore eyes, swelled and bleeding lips, skin diseases, and putrefying sores. These surrounded us closely, and as, not without a shudder, I passed through them and entered one of their dens, they pressed upon us, blocking out the light, uttering discordant cries, and clamoring with one voice, *kum-sha*, i.e., backsheesh, looking more like demons than living men, as abject and depraved as crime, despair, and cruelty can make them.

Within, the blackness, the filth, the vermin, the stench, overpowering even in this cool weather, the rubbish of rags and potsherds, cannot be described. Here in semi-starvation and misery, with nameless cruelties practised upon them without restraint, festering in one depraved mass, are the tried and untried, the condemned, the guilty and innocent (?), the murderer and pirate, the debtor and petty thief, all huddled together, without hope of exit except to the adjacent judgment-seat, with its horrors of "the question by torture," or to the "field of blood" not far away. On earth can there be seen a spectacle more hideous than these abject wretches, with their heavy fetters eating into the flesh of their necks and ankles (if on their wasted skeletons, covered with vermin and running sores, there is any flesh left), their thick matted, bristly, black hair—contrasting with the shaven heads of the free—the long, broken claws on their fingers and toes, the hungry look in their emaciated faces, and their clamorous cry, *kum-sha! kum-sha!* They thronged round us clattering their chains, one man saying that they had so little rice that they had to "drink the foul water to fill themselves;" another shrieked, "Would I were in your prison in Hong Kong," and this was chorused by many voices saying, "In your prison at Hong Kong they have fish and vegetables, and more rice than they can eat, and baths, and beds to sleep on; good, good is the prison of your Queen!" but higher swelled the cry of *kum-sha*, and as we could not give alms among several hundred, we eluded them, though with difficulty, and, as we squeezed through the narrow door, execrations followed us, and high above the heavy clank of the fetters and the general din rose the cry, "Foreign Devils" (Fan-Kwai), as we passed out into sunshine and liberty, and the key was turned upon them and their misery.

We went into three other large wards, foul with horror, and seething with misery, and into a smaller one, nearly as bad, where fifteen women were incarcerated, some of them with infants devoured by cutaneous diseases. Several of them said that they are there for kidnapping, but others are hostages for criminal relations who have not yet been captured. This imprisonment of hostages is in accordance with a law which authorizes the seizure and detention of persons or families belonging to criminals who have fled or are in concealment. Such are imprisoned till the guilty relative is brought to justice, for months, years, or even for a lifetime. Two of these women told us that they had been there for twenty years.

There are likewise some single cells—hovels clustering under a wall, in which criminals who can afford to pay the jailer for them may enjoy the luxury of solitude. In each ward there is a single unfettered man—always a felon—who by reason either of bribery or good conduct, is appointed to the place of watchman or spy among his fellows in crime. There is a turnkey for each ward, and these men, with the unchained felons who act as watchmen, torture new arrivals in order to force money from them, and under this process some die.

In the outer wall of the prison there is a port-hole, just large enough to allow of a body being pushed through it, for no malefactor's corpse must be carried through the prison entrance, lest it should defile the

"Gate of Righteousness." There is also a hovel called a deadhouse, into which these bodies are conveyed till a grave has been dug in some "accursed place," by members of an "accursed" class.

In addition to the large mortality arising from poor living and its concomitant diseases, and the exhaustion produced by repeated torture, epidemics frequently break out in the hot weather in those dark and fetid dens, and oftentimes nearly clear out the prison. On such occasions as many as four hundred have succumbed in a month. The number of criminals who are executed from this prison, either as sentenced to death, or as unable to bribe the officials any further, is supposed to be about five hundred annually, and it is further supposed that half this number die annually from starvation and torture. Sometimes one hundred criminals are beheaded in an hour, as it is feared may be the case on the Governor going out of office, when it is not unusual to make a jail delivery in this fashion.

In numerous cases, when there is a press of business before the judgment-seat and a dead-lock occurs, accusers and witnesses are huddled indiscriminately into the Naam-Hoi prison, sometimes for months; and as the Governor or magistrate takes no measures to provide for them during the interval, some of the poorer ones who have no friends to bribe the jailer on their behalf, perish speedily.

At night, in the dens which I have described, the hands of the prisoners are chained to their necks, and even in the daytime only one hand is liberated. I thought that many of the faces looked quite imbecile. The jailer, as we went out, kept holding out his long-clawed, lean, brown hand, muttering about his promised kum-sha, very fearful lest the other turnkeys, who were still lying on their beds smoking opium, should come in for any share of it.

Mr. Henry,* my host and very able cicerone, is an American missionary, and as such carries with him the gospel of peace on earth and good will to men. Surely if the knowledge of Him who came "to preach liberty to the captive, and the opening of the prison to them that are bound," were diffused and received here, and were spread with no niggard hand, the prison of the Naam-Hoi magistrate, with its unspeakable horrors, would go the way of all our dungeons and bedlams.

> [*I cannot forbear adding a note on the extent of Mr. Henry's work in 1881. He preached 190 times in Chinese, and five times in English; held fifty-two Bible-class meetings, and thirteen communion services; baptized forty-five adults and eight children; traveled on mission work by boat 2,540 miles, by chair, eighty miles, and on foot 670 miles; visited 280 different towns and villages, and distributed 14,000 books, receiving assistance in the latter work only on one short journey. His life is a happy combination of American energy and Christian zeal.]

But this is not all. From the prison it is only a short distance to the judgment-seat, and passing once more through the "Gate of Righteousness," we crossed a large court infested by gamblers and fortune-tellers, and presented ourselves at a porch with great figures painted on both its doors, and gay with the red insignia of mandarinism, which is the entrance to the stately residence of the Naam-Hoi magistrate, one of the subordinate dignitaries of Canton. In the porch, as might have been in that of Pilate or Herod, were a number of official palanquins, and many officials and servants of the mandarin with red-crowned hats turned up from their faces, and privates of the city guard, mean and shabby persons. One of these, for a kum-sha of course, took us, not through the closed and curtained doors, but along some passages, from which we passed through a circular brickwork tunnel to the front of the judgment seat at which all the inmates of the Naam-Hoi prison may expect sooner or later to be tried. My nerves were rather shaken with what I had seen, and I trembled as a criminal might on entering this chamber of horror.

In brief, the judgment-seat is a square hall, open at one end, with a roof supported on three columns. In the plan which I send, No. 1 is the three pillars; No. 2, the instruments of torture ranged against the wall;

No. 3, four accused men wearing heavy chains, and kneeling with their foreheads one inch from the ground, but not allowed to touch it. These men are undergoing the mildest form of torture—protracted kneeling without support in one position, with coarse sand under the bare knees. No. 4 is a very old and feeble man, also kneeling, a claimant in an ancient civil suit. No. 6 indicates a motley group of notaries, servants, attendants, lictors, alas! The table (No. 5) is of dark wood, covered with a shabby red cloth. On it are keys, petitions, note-books, pens and ink, an official seal, and some small cups containing tallies, which are thrown down to indicate the number of blows which a culprit is to receive. This was all.

In a high-backed ebony arm-chair, such as might be seen in any English hall, sat the man who has the awful power of life and death in his hands. It is almost needless to say that the judge, who was on the left of the table, and who never once turned to the accused, or indeed to anyone, was the only seated person. He was a young man, with fine features, a good complexion, and a high intellectual brow, and had I seen him under other circumstances, I should have thought him decidedly prepossessing looking. He wore a black satin hat, a rich, blue brocade robe, almost concealing his blue brocade trousers, and over this a sleeved cloak of dark blue satin, lined with ermine fur. A look of singular coldness and hauteur sat permanently on his face, over which a flush of indescribable impatience sometimes passed. He is not of the people, this lordly magistrate. He is one of the privileged literati. His literary degrees are high and numerous. He has both place and power. Little risk does he run of a review of his decisions or of an appeal to the Emperor at Pekin. He spoke loud and with much rapidity and emphasis, and often beat impatiently on the floor with his foot. He used the mandarin tongue, and whether cognizant of the dialect of the prisoners or not, he put all his questions through an interpreter, who stood at his left, a handsomely dressed old man, who wore a gold chain with a dependent ivory comb, with which while he spoke he frequently combed a small and scanty gray mustache.

Notaries, attendants with scarlet-crowned hats, and a rabble of men and boys, in front of whom we placed ourselves, stood down each side. The open hall, though lofty, is shabby and extremely dirty, with an unswept broken pavement, littered at one side with potsherds, and disfigured by a number of more or less broken black pots as well as other rubbish, making it look rather like a shed in an untidy nursery garden than an imperial judgment-hall. On the pillars there are certain classical inscriptions, one of which is said to be an exhortation to mercy. Pieces of bamboo of different sizes are ranged against the south wall. These are used for the bastinado, and there were various instruments ranged against the same wall, at which I could only look fitfully and with a shudder, for they are used in "The Question by Torture," which rapid method of gaining a desired end appears to be practised on witnesses as well as criminals.

The yard, or uncovered part of this place, has a pavement in the middle, and on one side of this the most loathsome trench I ever beheld, such a one as I think could not be found in the foulest slum of the dirtiest city in Europe, not only loathsome to the eye, but emitting a stench which even on that cool day might produce vertigo, and this under the very eye of the magistrate, and not more than thirty feet from the judgment-seat.

On the other side by which we entered, and which also has an entrance direct from the prison, is a slimy, green ditch, at the back of which some guards were lounging, with a heap of felons in chains attached to heavy stones at their feet. Above, the sky was very blue, and the sun of our Father which is in heaven shone upon "the just and the unjust."

The civil case took a long time, and was adjourned, and the aged claimant was so exhausted with kneeling before the judge, that he was obliged to be assisted away by two men. Then another man knelt and presented a petition, which was taken to "avizandum." Then a guard led in by a chain a prisoner, heavily manacled, and with a heavy stone attached to his neck, who knelt with his forehead touching the ground. After some speaking, a boy who was standing dangling a number of keys came forward, and, after much ado, unlocked the rusty padlock which fastened the chain round the man's neck, and he was led away, dragging the stone after him with his hands. He had presented a formal petition for this favor, and I welcomed the granting of it as a solitary gleam of mercy, but I was informed that the mitigation of the sentence came about through bribery on the part of the man's relatives, who had to buy the good-will of four officials before the petition could reach the magistrate's hands.

More than an hour and a half had passed since we entered, and for two hours before that the four chained prisoners had been undergoing the torture of kneeling on a coarsely sanded stone in an immovable and unsupported position. I was standing so close to them that the dress of one touched my feet. I could hear their breathing, which had been heavy at first, become a series of gasps, and cool as the afternoon was, the sweat of pain fell from their brows upon the dusty floor, and they were so emaciated that, even through their clothing, I could see the outlines of their bones. There were no counsel, and no witnesses, and the judge asked but one question as he beat his foot impatiently on the floor, "Are you guilty?" They were accused of an aggravated robbery, and were told to confess, but they said that only two of them were guilty. They were then sent back to the tender mercies of the opium-smoking jailer, probably to come back again and again to undergo the severer forms of torture, till no more money can be squeezed out of their friends, when they will probably be beheaded, death being the legal penalty for robbery with aggravations.

There is no regular legal process, no jury, no one admitted to plead for the accused, and owing to the way in which accusations are made and the intimate association of trial with bribery, it is as certain that many innocent persons suffer as it is that many guilty escape. From such a system one is compelled to fall back upon the righteousness of the Judge of all the earth; and as I stood in that hideous judgment-hall beside the tortured wretches, I could not shut out of my heart a trembling hope that for these and the legion of these, a worthier than an earthly intercessor pleads before a mightier than an earthly judge.

It is not clear whether torture is actually recognized by Chinese law, but it is practised in almost every known form by all Chinese magistrates, possibly as the most expeditious mode of legal procedure which is known. It is also undoubtedly the most potent agent in securing bribes. The legal instruments of summary punishment which hang on the wall of the Naam-Hoi judgment-hall consist of three boards with proper grooves for squeezing the fingers, and the bastinado, which is inflicted with bamboos of different weights. The illegal modes of "putting the question," i.e., of extorting a confession of guilt, as commonly practised are, prolonged kneeling on coarse sand, with the brow within an inch of the ground; twisting the ears with "roughened fingers," and keeping them twisted while the prisoner kneels on chains; beating the lips to a jelly with a thick stick, the result of which was to be seen in several cases in the prison; suspending the body by the thumbs; tying the hands to a bar under the knees, so as to bend the body double during many hours; the thumb-screw; dislocating the arm or shoulder; kneeling upon pounded glass, salt and sand mixed together, till the knees are excoriated, and several others, the product of fiendish ingenuity. Severe flogging with the bamboo, rattan, cudgel, and knotted whip successively is one of the most usual means of extorting confession; and when death results from the process, the magistrate reports that the criminal has died of sickness, and in the few cases in which there may be reason to dread investigation, the administration of a bribe to the deceased man's friends insures silence.

The cangue, if its wearers were properly fed and screened from the sun, is rather a disgrace than a cruel mode of punishment. Death is said to be inflicted for aggravated robbery, robbery with murder, highway robbery, arson, and piracy, even without the form of a trial when the culprits are caught in flagrante delicto; but though it is a frequent punishment, it is by no means absolutely certain for what crimes it is the legal penalty.

We left the judgment-seat as a fresh relay of criminals entered, two of them with faces atrocious enough for any crime, and passed out of the courtyard of the Yamun through the "Gate of Righteousness," where the prisoners, attached to heavy stones, were dragging and clanking their chains, or lying in the shade full of sores, and though the red sunset light was transfiguring all things, the glory had faded from Canton and the air seemed heavy with a curse.

Letter IV

Concluded

The "Covent Garden" of Canton—Preliminaries of Execution—A Death Procession—The "Field of Blood"—"The Death of the Cross"—A Fair Comparison

Although I went to the execution ground two days before my visit to the prison, the account of it belongs to this place. Passing through the fruit-market, the "Covent Garden" of Canton, where now and in their stated seasons are exposed for sale, singly and in fragrant heaps, among countless other varieties of fruits, the orange, pommeloe, apple, citron, banana, rose-apple, pine-apple, custard-apple, pear, quince, guava, carambola, persimmon, loquat, pomegranate, grape, water-melon, musk-melon, peach, apricot, plum, mango, mulberry, date, cocoa-nut, olive, walnut, chestnut, lichi, and papaya, through the unsavory precincts of the "salt-fish market," and along a street the specialty of which is the manufacture from palm leaves of very serviceable rain cloaks, we arrived at the Ma T'au, a cul de sac resembling in shape, as its name imports, a horse's head, with the broad end opening on the street. This "field of blood," which counts its slain by tens of thousands, is also a "potter's field," and is occupied throughout its whole length by the large earthen pots which the Chinese use instead of tubs, either in process of manufacture or drying in the sun. This Ma T'au, the place of execution, on which more than one hundred heads at times fall in a morning, is simply a pottery yard, and at the hours when space is required for the executioner's purposes more or fewer pots are cleared out of the way, according to the number of the condemned. The spectacle is open to the street and to all passers-by. Against the south wall are five crosses, which are used for the crucifixion of malefactors. At the base of the east wall are four large earthenware vessels full of quicklime, into which heads which are afterward to be exposed on poles are cast, until the flesh has been destroyed. From this bald sketch it may be surmised that few accessories of solemnity or even propriety consecrate the last tragedy of justice.

In some cases criminals are brought directly from the judgment-seat to the execution ground on receiving sentence, but as a rule the condemned persons remain in prison ignorant of the date of their doom, till an official, carrying a square board with the names of those who are to die that day pasted upon it, enters and reads the names of the doomed. Each man on answering is made to sit in something like a dust-basket, in which he is borne through the gate of the inner prison, at which he is interrogated and his identity ascertained by an official, who represents the Viceroy or Governor, into the courtyard of the Yamun, where he is pinioned. At this stage it is usual for the friends of the criminal, or the turnkeys in their absence, to give him "auspicious" food, chiefly fat pork and Saam-su, an intoxicating wine. Pieces of betel-nut, the stimulating qualities of which are well known, are invariably given. These delays being over, the criminal is carried into the presence of the judge, who sits not in the judgment-hall but in the porch of the inner gateway of his Yamun. On the prisoner giving his name, a superscription bearing it, and proclaiming his crime and the manner of his death, is tied to a slip of bamboo and bound to his head. A small wooden ticket, also bearing his name and that of the prison from which he is taken to execution, is tied to the back of his neck.

Then the procession starts, the criminals, of whom there are usually several, being carried in open baskets in the following order:—Some spearmen, the malefactors, a few soldiers, a chair of state, bearing the ruler of the Naam-Hoi county, attended by equerries; and another chair of state, in which is seated the official who, after all is over, pays worship to the five protecting genii of Canton, a small temple to whom stands close to the potter's field, and who have power to restrain those feelings of revenge and violence which the spirits of the decapitated persons may be supposed hereafter to cherish against all who were instrumental in their decapitation. Last of all follows a herald on horseback, carrying a yellow banner inscribed "By Imperial Decree," an indispensable adjunct on such occasions, as without it the county ruler would not be justified in commanding the executioner to give the death stroke. This ruler or his deputy sits at a table covered with a red cloth, and on being told that all the preliminaries have been complied with, gives the word for execution. The criminals, who have been unceremoniously pitched out of the dust baskets into the mud or gore or dust of the execution ground, kneel down in a row or rows, and the executioner with a scimitar strikes off head after head, each with a single stroke, an assistant attending to hand him a fresh sword as soon as the first becomes blunt. It is said that Chinese criminals usually meet their doom with extreme apathy, but occasionally they yield to extreme terror, and howl at the top of their voices, "Save life! Save life!" As soon as the heads have fallen, some coolies of a pariah class take up the trunks and put them into wooden shells, in which they are eventually buried in a cemetery outside one of the city gates, called "The trench for the bones of ten thousand men." It is not an uncommon thing, under ordinary circumstances, for fifteen, twenty, or thirty-five wretches to suffer the penalty of death in this spot; and this number swells to very large dimensions at a jail delivery, or during a rebellion, or when the crews of pirates are captured in the act of piracy. My friend Mr. Bulkeley Johnson, of Shanghai, saw one hundred heads fall in one morning.

Mr. Henry says that the reason that most of the criminals meet death with such stoicism or indifference is, that they have been worn down previously by starvation and torture. Some are stupefied with Saam-su. It is possible in some cases for a criminal who is fortunate enough to have rich relations to procure a substitute; a coolie sells himself to death in such a man's stead for a hundred dollars, and for a week before his surrender indulges in every kind of expensive debauchery, and when the day of doom arrives is so completely stupefied by wine and opium, as to know nothing of the terror of death.

We had not gone far into this aceldema when we came to a space cleared from pots, and to a great pool of blood and dust mingled, blackening in the sun, then another and another, till there were five of them almost close together, with splashes of blood upon the adjacent pots, and blood trodden into the thirsty ground. Against the wall opposite, a rudely constructed cross was resting, dark here and there with patches of blood. Among the rubbish at the base of the wall there were some human fragments partly covered with matting; a little farther some jawbones with the teeth in them, then four more crosses, and some human heads lying at the foot of the wall, from which it was evident that dogs had partially gnawed off the matting in which they had been tied up. The dead stare of one human eye amidst the heap haunts me still. A blood-splashed wooden ticket, with a human name on one side and that of the Naam-Hoi prison on the other, was lying near one of the pools of blood, and I picked it up as a memento, as the stroke which had severed its string had also severed at the same time the culprit's neck. The place was ghastly and smelt of blood.

The strangest and most thrilling sight of all was the cross in this unholy spot, not a symbol of victory and hope, but of the lowest infamy and degradation, of the vilest death which the vilest men can die. Nor was it the solid, lofty structure, fifteen or twenty feet high, which art has been glorifying for a thousand years, but a rude gibbet of unplaned wood, roughly nailed together, barely eight feet high, and not too heavy for a strong man to carry on his shoulders. Most likely it was such a cross, elevated but little above the heads of the howling mob of Jerusalem, which Paul had in view when he wrote of Him who hung upon it, "But made Himself obedient unto death, *even the death of the cross.*" To these gibbets infamous criminals, whose crimes are regarded as deserving of a lingering death, are tightly bound with cords, and are then slowly hacked to pieces with sharp knives, unless the friends of the culprit are rich enough to bribe the executioner to terminate the death agony early by stabbing a vital part.

    These facts do not require to be dressed out with words. They are most effective when most baldly stated. I left the execution ground as I left the prison—with the prayer, which has gained a new significance, "For all prisoners and captives we beseech Thee to hear us, good Lord;" but though our hands are nationally clean now as regards the administration of justice and the treatment of criminals, we need not hold them up in holy horror as if the Chinese were guilty above all other men, for the framers of the Litany were familiar with dungeons perhaps worse than the prison of the Naam-Hoi magistrate, and with forms of torture which spared not even women, and the judges' and jailers' palms were intimate with the gold of accused persons. It is simply that heathenism in Canton is practising at this day what Christianity in Europe looked upon with indifference for centuries.

I. L. B.

Letter V

Portuguese Missionaries—A Chinese Hospital—Chinese Anaesthetics—Surgery and Medicine—Ventilation and Cleanliness—A Chinese "Afternoon Tea"—A New Inspiration

HONG KONG, January 10.

The year seems already getting old and frowzy. Under these blue skies, and with all the doors and windows open, I should think it midsummer if I did not look at the calendar. Oh, how I like blue, sunny skies, instead of gray and grim ones, and blazing colors instead of the dismal grays and browns of our nondescript winters!

I left Canton by the Kin-Kiang on Monday, with two thousand Chinese passengers and two Portuguese missionary priests, the latter wearing Chinese costume, and so completely got up as Chinamen that had they not spoken Portuguese their features would not have been sufficient to undeceive me. They were noble-looking men, and bore upon their faces the stamp of consecration to a noble work. On the other steamer, the Tchang, instead of a man with revolvers and a cutlass keeping guard over the steerage grating, a large hose pipe is laid on to each hatch-way, through which, in case of need, boiling water can be sent under strong pressure. Just as we landed here, about five hundred large fishes were passed through a circular net from a well in the steamer into a well in a fishing boat, to which all the fishmongers in Hong Kong immediately resorted.

(I pass over the hospitalities and festivities of Hong Kong, and an afternoon with the Governor in the Victoria Prison, to an interesting visit paid with Mr., now Sir J. Pope Hennessey to the Chinese Hospital.)

We started from Government House, with the Governor, in a chair with six scarlet bearers, attended by some Sikh orderlies in scarlet turbans, for a "State Visit" to the Tung-Wah Hospital, a purely Chinese institution, built some years ago by Chinese merchants, and supported by them at an annual cost of $16,000. In it nothing European, either in the way of drugs or treatment, is tried. There is a dispensary connected with it, where advice is daily given to about a hundred and twenty people; and, though lunacy is rare in China, they are building a lunatic asylum at the back of the hospital.

The Tung-Wah hospital consists of several two-storied buildings of granite, with large windows on each side, and a lofty central building which contains the directors' hall, the accommodation for six resident physicians, and the business offices. The whole is surrounded by a well-kept garden, bounded by a very high wall. We entered by the grand entrance, which has a flagged pavement, each flag consisting of a slab of granite twelve feet long by three broad, and were received at the foot of the grand staircase by the directors and their chairman, the six resident doctors, and Mr. Ng Choy, a rising, Chinese barrister, educated at Lincoln's Inn, who interpreted for us in admirable English. He is the man who goes between the Governor and the Chinese community, and is believed to have more influence with the Governor on all questions which concern Chinamen than anybody else. These gentlemen all wore rich and beautiful dresses of thick ribbed silk and figured brocade, and, unless they were much padded and wadded, they had all attained to a remarkable embonpoint.

The hall in which the directors meet is lofty and very handsome, the roof being supported on massive pillars. One side is open to the garden. It has a superb ebony table in the middle, with a chair massive enough for a throne for the chairman, and six grand, carved ebony chairs on either side.

Our procession consisted of the chairman and the twelve directors, the six stout middle-aged doctors, Mr. Ng Choy, the Governor, the Bishop of Victoria, and myself; but the patients regarded the unwonted spectacle with extreme apathy.

The wards hold twenty each, and are divided into wooden stalls, each stall containing two beds. Partitions seven feet high run down the centre. The beds are matted wooden platforms, and the bedding white futons or wadded quilts, which are washed once a week. The pillows are of wood or bamboo. Each bed has a shelf above it, with a teapot upon it in a thickly wadded basket, which keeps the contents hot all day, the infusion being, of course, poured off the leaves. A ticket, with the patient's name upon it, and the hours at which he is to take his medicine, hangs above each person.

No amputations are performed, but there are a good many other operations, such as the removal of cancers, tumors, etc. The doctors were quite willing to answer questions, within certain limits; but when I asked them about the composition and properties of their drugs they became reticent at once and said that they were secrets. They do not use chloroform in operations, but they all asserted, and their assertions were corroborated by Mr. Ng Choy, that they possess drugs which throw their patients into a profound sleep, during which the most severe operations can be painlessly performed. They asserted further that such patients awake an hour or two afterward quite cheerful, and with neither headache nor vomiting! One of them showed me a bottle containing a dark brown powder which, he said, produced this result, but he would not divulge the name of one of its constituents, saying that it is a secret taught him by his tutor, and that there are several formulas. It has a pungent and slightly aromatic taste.

The surgery and medicine are totally uninfluenced by European science, and are of the most antiquated and barbaric description. There was a woman who had had a cancer removed, and the awful wound, which was uncovered for my inspection, was dressed with musk, lard, and ambergris, with a piece of oiled paper over all. There was also exhibited to us a foot which had been pierced by a bamboo splinter. Violent inflammation had extended up to the knee, and the wound, and the swollen, blackened limb were being treated with musk and tiger's fat. A man with gangrened feet, nearly dropping off, had them rolled up in dark-colored paste, of which musk and oil were two ingredients. All the wounds were deplorably dirty, and no process of cleaning them exists in this system of surgery.

The Governor and Bishop were not allowed to go into the women's ward. It looked very clean and comfortable, but a woman in the last death-agony was unattended. They never bleed, or leech, or blister, or apply any counter-irritants in cases of inflammation. They give powdered rhinoceros' horns, sun-dried tiger's blood, powdered tiger's liver, spiders' eyes, and many other queer things, and for a tonic and febrifuge, where we should use quinine, they rely mainly on the ginseng (Panax quinquefolia?) of which I saw so much in Japan. They judge much by the pulse and tongue. The mortality in this hospital is very large, not only from the nature of the treatment, but because Chinamen who have no friends in Victoria go there when they are dying, in order to secure that their bodies shall be sent to their relations at a distance. There were fifteen sick and shipwrecked junkmen there, covered with sores, who looked very far down in the scale of humanity.

After going through the wards I went into the laboratory, where six men were engaged in preparing drugs, then to the "chemical kitchen," where a hundred and fifty earthen pipkins on a hundred and fifty earthen furnaces were being used in cooking medicines under the superintendence of eight cooks in spotless white clothing; then to the kitchen, which is large and clean; then alone into the dead-house, which no Chinese will enter except an unclean class of pariahs, who perform the last offices for the departed and dress the corpses for burial. This gloomy receptacle is also clean.

Great attention is paid to cleanliness and ventilation. Dry earth is used as a deodorizer, but if there be a bad odor they burn sandalwood. They don't adopt any disinfectants; indeed, they don't appear to know their use. The patients all lie with their backs to the light, and there is a space five feet wide between the beds and the windows. All the windows were open both at the top and bottom, so as to create a complete current of air, and the airiness and freedom from smells and closeness were quite remarkable, considering the state in which the wounds are, which is worse than I dare attempt to describe. The hospital is conducted on strictly "temperance principles," i.e., no alcoholic stimulants are given, which is not remarkable, considering how little comparatively they are used in China, and with what moderation on the whole by those who use them. There were seventy-five patients in the wards yesterday, and the cases were mostly either serious originally, or have been made so by the treatment. There are one hundred and twenty beds. There is much to admire in this hospital, the humane arrangements, the obvious comfort of the patients, and the admirable ventilation and perfect cleanliness of the beds and wards, but the system adopted is one of the most antiquated quackery, and when I think of the unspeakably horrible state of the wounds, the mortifying limbs, and the gangrened feet ready to drop off, I almost question Governor Hennessey's wisdom in stamping the hospital with his approval on his "State Visit."

The Governor and I were received in the boardroom after our two hours' inspection, where we were joined by Mrs. Hennessey, and entertained by the directors at what might be called "afternoon tea." But when is the Chinaman not drinking tea? A monstrous plateau of the preserved and candied fruits, in the making of which the Chinese ladies excel, had been placed upon the ebony table, and when we were seated in the stately ebony chairs on the chairman's right, with the yellow, shining-faced, wadded or corpulent directors opposite to us, excellent tea with an unusual flavor was brought in, and served in cups of antique green dragon china. The Governor made kindly remarks on the hospital, which fluent Mr. Ng Choy doubtless rendered into the most fulsome flattery; the chairman complimented the Governor, and unlimited "soft sawder," in Oriental fashion, passed all round.

It is proper in China on such an occasion to raise the tea-cup with both the hands to a good height and bow to each person, naming at the same time the character so continually seen on tea-cups and sake bottles—Happiness,—which is understood to be a wish for happiness in this formula, "May your happiness be as the Eastern Sea;" but the wish may also mean "May you have many sons." It is strange that these Chinamen, who showed all fitting courtesy to Mrs. Hennessey and me, would only have spoken of their wives apologetically as "the mean ones within the gates!" It was a charming Oriental sight, the grand, open-fronted room with its stone floor and many pillars, the superbly dressed directors and their blue-robed attendants, and the immense costumed crowd outside the gate in the sunshine, kept back by crimson-turbaned Sikh orderlies.

If civilization were to my taste, I should linger in Victoria for the sake of its beauty, its stirring life, its costume and color, its perfect winter climate, its hospitalities, its many charming residents, and for various other reasons, and know nothing of its feuds in state, church, and society. But I am a savage at heart, and weary for the wilds first, and then for the beloved little home on the wooded edge of the moorland above the Northern Sea, which gleams like a guiding star, even through the maze of sunshine and color of this fascinating Eastern world. to-day I lunched at (acting) Chief Justice Snowden's, and he urges me to go to Malacca on my way home. I had never dreamed of the "Golden Chersonese;" but I am much inspired by his descriptions of the neighborhood of the Equator, and as he has lent me Newbold's Malacca for the voyage, and has given me letters to the Governor and Colonial Secretary of the Straits Settlements, you will next hear from me from Singapore!

I. L. B.

Letter VI

A Cochin China River—The Ambition of Saigon—A French Colonial Metropolis—European Life in Saigon-A Cochin-Chinese Village—"Afternoon Tea" in Choquan—Anamese Children—Anamite Costume—Anamite River-Dwellings—An Amphibious Population—An Unsuccessful Colony—"With the Big Toe"—Three Persecuting Kings—Saigon

S.S. "SINDH," CHINA SEA, January.

This steamer, one of the finest of the Messageries Maritimes line, is perfect in all respects, and has a deck like that of an old-fashioned frigate. The weather has been perfect also, and the sea smooth enough for a skiff. The heat increases hourly though, or rather has increased hourly, for hotter it cannot be! Punkahs are going continually at meal times, and if one sits down to write in the saloon, the "punkah-wallah" spies one out and begins his refreshing labors at once. But we took on board a host of mosquitoes at Saigon, and the nights are consequently so intolerable that I weary for the day.

The twenty-four hours spent at Saigon broke the monotonous pleasantness of our voyage very agreeably to me, but most of the passengers complain of the wearisome detention in the heat. In truth, the mercury stood at 92 degrees!

At daybreak yesterday we were steaming up a branch of the great Me-kong river in Cochin China, a muddy stream, densely fringed by the nipah palm, whose dark green fronds, ten and twelve feet long, look as if they grew out of the ground, so dumpy is its stem. The country, as overlooked from our lofty deck, appeared a dead level of rice and scrubby jungle intermixed, a vast alluvial plain, from which the heavy, fever-breeding mists were rising in rosy folds. Every now and then we passed a Cochin Chinese village—a collection of very draughty-looking wooden huts, roofed with palm leaves, built over the river on gridiron platforms supported on piles. Each dwelling of the cluster had its boat tethered below it. It looked a queer amphibious life. Men were lying on the gridirons smoking, women were preparing what might be the breakfast, and babies were crawling over the open floors, born with the instinct not to tumble over the edge into the river below. These natives were small and dark, although of the Mongolian type, with wide mouths and high cheek bones—an ugly race; and their attitudes, their tumble-to-pieces houses, and their general forlornness, gave me the impression that they are an indolent race as well, to be ousted in time possibly by the vigorous and industrious Chinaman.

After proceeding for about forty miles up this mighty Me-kong or Cambodia river, wearying somewhat of its nipah-fringed alluvial flats, and of the monotonous domestic economy of which we had so good a view, we reached Saigon, which has the wild ambition to propose to itself to be a second Singapore! All my attempts to learn anything about Saigon on board have utterly failed. People think that they told me something altogether new and sufficient when they said that it is a port of call for the French mail steamers, and one of the hottest places in the world! This much I knew before I asked them! If they know anything more now, no dexterity of mine can elicit it. There was a general stampede ashore as soon as we moored, and gharries—covered spring carts—drawn by active little Sumatra ponies, and driven by natives of Southern India, known as Klings, were immediately requisitioned, but nothing came of it apparently, and when I came back at sunset I found that, after an hour or two of apparently purposeless wanderings, all my fellow-passengers had returned to the ship, pale and depressed. True, the mercury was above 90 degrees!

Arriving in this condition of most unblissful ignorance, I was astonished when a turn in the river brought us close upon a considerable town, straggling over a great extent of ground, interspersed with abundant tropical greenery, its river front consisting of a long, low line of much-shaded cafes, mercantile offices, some of them flying consular flags and Government offices, behind which lies the city with its streets, shops, and great covered markets or bazaars, and its barracks, churches, and convents.

The Me-kong, though tortuous and ofttimes narrow, is navigable as the Donnai or Saigon branch up to and above Saigon for vessels of the largest tonnage, and the great Sindh steamed up to a wharf and moored alongside it, almost under the shade of great trees. A French three-decker of the old type, moored higher up, serves as an hospital. There were two French ironclads, a few steamers, and some big sailing ships at anchor, but nothing looked busy, and the people on the wharf were all loafers.

After all my fellow-passengers had driven off I stepped ashore and tried to realize that I was in Cochin China or Cambodia, but it would not do. The irrepressible Chinaman in his loose cotton trousers was as much at home as in Canton, and was doing all the work that was done; the shady lounges in front of the cafes were full of Frenchmen, Spaniards, and Germans, smoking and dozing with their feet upon tables or on aught else which raised them to the level of their heads; while men in linen suits and pith helmets dashed about in buggies and gharries, and French officers and soldiers lounged wearily along all the roads. There was not a native to be seen! A little later there was not a European to be seen! There was a universal siesta behind closed jalousies, and Saigon was abandoned to Chinamen and leggy dogs. Then came the cool of the afternoon, i.e., the mercury, with evident reluctance, dawdled down to 84 degrees; military bands performed, the Europeans emerged, smoking as in the morning, to play billiards or ecarte, or sip absinthe at their cafes; then came the mosquitoes and dinner, after which I was told that card-parties were made up, and that the residents played till near midnight. Thus from observation and hearsay, I gathered that the life of a European Saigonese was made up of business in baju and pyjamas with cheroot in mouth from 6 to 9:30 A.M., then the bath, the toilette, and the breakfast of claret and curry; next the sleeping, smoking, and lounging till tiffin; after tiffin a little more work, then the band, billiards, ecarte, absinthe, smoking, dinner, and card-parties, varied by official entertainments.

Rejecting a guide, I walked about Saigon, saw its streets, cafes, fruit markets, bazaars, barracks, a botanic or acclimatization garden, of which tigers were the chief feature, got out upon the wide, level roads, bordered with large trees, which run out into the country for miles in perfectly straight lines, saw the handsome bungalows of the residents, who surround themselves with many of the luxuries of Paris, went over a beautiful convent, where the sisters who educate native girl children received me with kindly courtesy; and eventually driving in a gharrie far beyond the town, and then dismissing it, I got into a labyrinth of lanes, each with a high hedge of cactus, and without knowing it found that I was in a native village, Choquan, a village in which every house seems to be surrounded and hidden by high walls of a most malevolent and obnoxious cactus, so as to insure absolute privacy to its proprietor. Each dwelling is under the shade of pommeloe, orange, and bamboo. By dint of much peeping, and many pricks which have since inflamed, I saw that the poorer houses were built of unplaned planks or split bamboo, thatched with palm leaves, with deep verandas, furnished with broad matted benches with curious, round bamboo pillows. On these men, scarcely to be called clothed, were lying, smoking or chewing the betel-nut, and all had teapots in covered baskets within convenient reach. The better houses are built of an ornamental framework of carved wood, the floor of which is raised about three feet from the ground on brick pillars. The roofs of these are rather steep, and are mostly tiled, and have deep eaves, but do not as elsewhere form the cover of the veranda. While I was looking through the cactus screen of one of these houses, a man came out with a number of low caste, leggy, flop-eared, mangy dogs, who attacked me in a cowardly bullying fashion, yelping, barking, and making surreptitious snaps at my feet. Their owner called them off, however, and pelted them so successfully that some ran away whimpering, and two pretended (as dogs will) to have broken legs. This man carried a cocoa-nut, and on my indicating that I was thirsty, he hesitated, and then turning back, signed to me to follow him into his house. This was rare luck!

Within the cactus screen, which is fully ten feet high, there is a graveled area, on which the neat-looking house stands, and growing out of the very thirsty ground are cocoa palms, bananas, bread fruit, and papayas. There are verandas on each side of the doorway with stone benches; the doorway and window frames are hung with "portieres" of split reeds, and a ladder does duty for door steps. The interior is very dark, and divided into several apartments. As soon as I entered there was a rush as if of bats into the darkness, but on being reassured, about twenty women and boy and girl children appeared, and contemplated me with an apathetic stare of extreme solemnity. Remember the mercury was 92 degrees, so the women may be excused for having nothing more than petticoats or loose trousers on in the privacy of their home, the children for being in a state of nudity, and the man for being clothed in a loin cloth! As I grew used to the darkness I saw a toothless old woman smoking in a corner, fanned by two girls, who, I believe, are domestic slaves. Near one of the window openings a young woman was lounging, and two others were attentively removing vermin from her luxuriant but ill-kept hair. Mats and bamboo pillows covered the floors, and most of the inmates had been rudely disturbed in a siesta.

I was evidently in the principal apartment, for the walls were decorated with Chinese marine pictures, among which were two glaring daubs of a Madonna and an Ecce Homo. There was also a rude crucifix, from which I gather that this is a Roman Catholic family. There were two teapots of tea on a chair, a big tub of pommeloes on the floor, and a glazed red earthenware bowl full of ripe bananas on another chair. A sort of sickle, a gun, and some bullock gear hung against the wall. In the middle of the room there was a sort of trap in the floor, and there was the same in two other apartments. Through this all rubbish is conveniently dropped. A woman brought in a cocoa-nut, and poured the milk into a gourd calabash, and the man handed me the dish of bananas, so I had an epicurean repast, and realized that I was in Cochin China! They were courteous people, and not only refused the quarter dollar which I pressed upon them, but gave me a handkerchief full of bananas when I left them, being pleased, however, to accept a puggree.

The neat gravel area, the covered walls, and neatly tiled roof, the lattice work, the boards suspended from the door-posts, with (as I have since learned) texts from the Chinese Classics in gold upon them, and the large establishment, show that the family belongs to the upper class of Anamites, and leave one quite unprepared for the reeking, festering heap of garbage below the house, the foul, fetid air, and swarming vermin of the interior, and the unwashedness of the inmates. I bowed myself out, the gate was barred behind me, and in two minutes I had lost what I supposed to be my way, and having left the maze of cactus-walled paths behind, was entangled in a maze of narrow village paths through palms and bananas, flowering trees covered with creepers and orchids, and a wonderful profusion of small and great ferns. Getting back into the cactus hidden village I found groups of pretty, dark-skinned children, quite naked, playing in the deep dust, while some no bigger were lounging in the shade smoking cigars, lazily watching the clouds of smoke which they puffed out from their chubby cheeks.

Finding my own footsteps in the deep dust, I got back to a pathway with a monstrous bamboo hedge on one side, and a rice-field on the other, in which was a slimy looking pond with a margin of pink water-lilies, in which a number of pink buffaloes of large size were wallowing with much noise and rough play, plastering their sensitive hides with mud as a protection against mosquitoes.

With some difficulty, by some very queer paths and with much zig-zagging, I at last reached Cholen,* a native town, said to be three or eight miles from Saigon, and was so exhausted by the fatigue of the long walk in such a ferocious temperature that I sat by the roadside on a stump under a huge tropical tree, considering the ways of ants and Anamites.

Children with brown chubby faces which had never been washed since birth, and, according to all accounts, will never be washed till death, stood in a row, staring the stare of apathy, with a quiet confidence. They had no clothes on, and I admired their well-made forms and freedom from skin disease. The Mongolian face is pleasant in childhood. A horde of pariah dogs in the mad excitement of a free fight, passed, covering me with dust. (By the way, I am told that hydrophobia is unknown in Cochin China.) Then some French artillerymen, who politely raised their caps; then a quantity of market girls, dressed like the same class in China, but instead of being bare-headed, they wore basket hats, made of dried leaves, fully twenty-four inches in diameter, by six in depth. These girls walked well, and looked happy. Then a train of Anamese carts passed, empty, the solid wooden wheels creaking frightfully round the ungreased axles, each cart being drawn by two buffaloes, each pair being attached to the cart in front by a rope through the nostrils, so that one driver sufficed for eleven carts. The native men could not be said to be clothed, but, as I remarked before, the mercury was above 90 degrees. They were, however, protected both against sun and rain by hats over three feet in diameter, very conical, peaked at the top, coming down umbrella fashion over the shoulders, and well tilted back.

> [*Cholen, i.e., the big market, has a population which is variously estimated at from 30,000 to 80,000. I am inclined to think that the lowest estimate is nearest the mark.—I. L. B.]

After laboriously reaching Cholen, I found far the greater part of the town to be Chinese, rather than Anamese, with Chinese streets, temples, gaming houses, club houses, and that general air of business and industry which seems characteristic of the Chinese everywhere; but still groping my way about, I came upon what I most wished to see—the real Anamese town. There is a river, the Me-kong, or one of its branches, and the town—the real native Cholen—consists of a very large collection of river-dwellings, little, if at all, superior to those which we passed in coming up. I spent an hour among them, and I never saw any house whose area could be more than twelve feet square, while many were certainly not more than seven feet by six. Such primitive, ramshackle, shaky-looking dwellings I never before have seen. As compared with them, an Aino hut, even of the poorest kind, is a model of solidity and architectural beauty. They looked as if a single gust would topple them and their human contents into the water. Yet, if it were better carried out, it is not a bad idea to avoid paying any Anamese form of rent, to secure perfect drainage, a never-failing water supply, good fishing, immunity from reptiles, and the easiest of all highways at the very door.

These small rooms with thatched roofs and gridiron floors, raised on posts six or eight feet above the stream, are reached from the shore by a path a foot wide, consisting of planks tied on to posts. The river-dwellings, I must add, are tied together with palm fibre rope. One of average size can be put together for eleven shillings. In front of each house a log canoe is moored, into which it is easy to drop from above when the owner desires any change of attitude or scene.

I ventured into two of these strange abodes, but it was dizzy work to walk the plank, and as difficult to walk the gridiron floor in shoes. Both were wretched habitations, but doubtless they suit their inmates, who need nothing more than a shelter from the sun and rain. The men wore only loin cloths. The women were clothed to the throat in loose cotton garments; the children wore nothing. In both the men were fishing for their supper over the edge of their platforms. In one a woman was cooking rice; and in both there was a good store of rice, bananas, and sweet potatoes. There was no furniture in either, except matted platforms for sleeping upon, a few coarse pipkins, a red earthen-ware pitcher or two, and some calabashes. On the wall of one was a crucifix, and on a rafter in the other a wooden carving of a jolly-looking man, mallet in hand, seated on rice bags, intended for Daikoku, the Japanese God of Wealth. The people were quite unwashed, but the draught of the river carried off the bad smells which ought to have been there, and, fortunately, a gridiron floor is unfavorable to accumulations of dirt and refuse. These natives look apathetic, and are, according to our notions, lazy; but I am weary of seeing the fevered pursuit of wealth, and am inclined to be lenient to these narcotized existences, provided, as is the case, that they keep clear of debt, theft, and charity.

Below this amphibious town there is a larger and apparently permanent floating village, consisting of hundreds of boats moored to the shore and to each other, poor and forlorn as compared with the Canton house boats, but yet more crowded, a single thatched roof sheltering one or more families, without any attempt at furniture or arrangement. The children swarmed, and looked healthy, and remarkably free from eye and skin diseases. There were Romish pictures in some of these boats, and two or three of them exhibited the cross in a not inconspicuous place. In my solitary explorations I was not mobbed or rudely treated in any way. The people were as gentle and inoffensive in their manners as the Japanese, without their elaborate courtesy and civilized curiosity.

Having seen all I could see, I turned shipwards, weary, footsore, and exhausted; my feet so sore and blistered, indeed, that long before I reached a gharrie I was obliged to take off my boots and wrap them in handkerchiefs. The dust was deep and made heavy walking, and the level straightness of a great part of the road is wearisome. Overtaking even at my slow rate of progress a string of creaking buffalo carts, I got upon the hindmost, but after a little rest found the noise, dust, and slow progress intolerable, and plodded on as before, taking two and a half hours to walk three miles. About a mile from Cholen there is an extraordinary burial-ground, said to cover an area of twenty square miles. (?) It is thickly peopled with the dead, and profuse vegetation and funereal lichens give it a profoundly melancholy look. It was chosen by the Cambodian kings several centuries ago for a cemetery, on the advice of the astrologers of the court. The telegraph wire runs near it, and so the old and the new age meet.

On my weary way I was overtaken by a young French artillery officer, who walked with me until we came upon an empty gharrie, and was eloquent upon the miseries of Saigon. It is a very important military station, and a sort of depot for the convicts who are sent to the (comparatively) adjacent settlement of New Caledonia. A large force of infantry and artillery is always in barracks here, but it is a most sickly station. At times 40 per cent. of this force is in hospital from climatic diseases, and the number of men invalided home by every mail steamer, and the frequent changes necessary, make Saigon a very costly post. The French don't appear to be successful colonists. This Cochin Chinese colony of theirs, which consists of the six ancient southern provinces of the empire of Anam, was ceded to France in 1874, but its European population is still under twelve thousand, exclusive of the garrison and the Government officials. The Government consists of a governor, aided by a privy council. The population of the colony is under a million and a half, including eighty-two thousand Cambodians and forty thousand Chinese. According to my various informants—this young French officer, a French nun, and a trader of dubious nationality, in whose shop I rested—France is doing its best to promote the prosperity and secure the good-will of the natives. The land-tax, which was very oppressive under the native princes, has been lowered, municipal government has been secured to the native towns, and corporate and personal rights have been respected. These persons believe that the colony, far from being a source of profit to France, is kept up at a heavy annual loss, and they regard the Chinese as the only element in the population worth having. They think the Anamese very superior to the Cambodians, from whom indeed they conquered these six provinces, but the Cambodians are a bigger and finer race physically.

I do not think I have said how hideous I think the adult Anamese. Somewhere I have read that two thousand years before our era the Chinese called them Giao-chi, which signifies "with the big toe." This led me to look particularly at their bare feet, and I noticed even in children such a wide separation of the big toe from the rest as to convey the perhaps erroneous impression that it is of unusual size. The men are singularly wide at the hips, and walk with a laughably swaggering gait, which is certainly not affectation, but is produced by a sufficient anatomical cause. I never saw such ugly, thick-set, rigid bodies, such uniformly short necks, such sloping shoulders, such flat faces and flatter noses, such wide, heavy, thick-lipped mouths, such projecting cheek bones, such low foreheads, such flat-topped heads, and such tight, thick skin, which suggests the word hide-bound. The dark, tawny complexion has no richness of tint. Both men and women are short, and the teeth of both sexes are blackened by the constant chewing of the betel-nut, which reddens the saliva, which is constantly flowing like blood from the corners of their mouths. Though not a vigorous, they appear to be a healthy people, and have very large families. They suffer chiefly from "forest fever" in the forest lands, but the rice swamps, deadly to Europeans, do not harm them.

I rested for some time at a very beautiful convent, and was most kindly entertained by some very calm, sweet-looking sisters, who labor piously among the female Anamese, and have schools for girls. The troops are stationed at Saigon for only two years, owing to the unhealthiness of the climate, but these pious women have no sanitarium, and live and die at their posts. Various things in the convent chapel remind one of the faithfulness unto death both of missionaries and converts. In this century alone three successive kings rivaled each other in persecuting the Christians, both Europeans and native, over and over again murdering all the missionaries. In 1841 the king ordered that all missionaries should be drowned, and in 1851 his successor ordered that whoever concealed a missionary should be cut in two. The terrible and sanguinary persecution which followed this edict never ceased, till years afterward the French frightened the king into toleration, and put an end, one hopes forever, to the persecution of Christians. The sisters compute the native Christians at seven thousand, and have sanguine hopes for the future of Christianity in French Cochin China, as well as in Cambodia, which appears to be under a French protectorate.

I do not envy the French their colony. According to my three informants, Europeans cannot be acclimatized, and most of the children born of white parents die shortly after birth. The shores of the sea and of the rivers are scourged by severe intermittent fevers, and the whole of the colony by dysentery, which among Europeans is particularly fatal. The mean temperature is 83 degrees F., the dampness is unusual, and the nights are too hot to refresh people after the heat of the day.*

> [*The chief production of the country is rice, which forms half the sum total of the exports. The other exports are chiefly salt-fish, salt, undyed cotton, skins of beasts, and pepper. About seven hundred vessels enter and leave Saigon in a year.]

After leaving the convent I resumed my gharrie, and the driver took me, what I suppose is the usual "course" for tourists, through a quaint Asiatic town inhabited by a mixed, foreign population of Hindus, Malays, Tagals, and Chinese merchants, scattered among a large indigenous population of Anamese fishermen, servants, and husbandmen, through the colonial district, which looked asleep or dead, to the markets, where the Chinamen and natives of India were in the full swing and din of buying and selling all sorts of tropical fruits and rubbishy French goods, and through what may be called the Government town or official quarter. It was getting dark when I reached the wharf, and the darkness enabled me to hobble unperceived on board on my bandaged feet. The heat of the murky, lurid evening was awful, and as thousands of mosquitoes took possession of the ship, all comfort was banished, and I was glad when we steamed down the palm-fringed Saigon or Donnai waters, and through the mangrove swamps at the mouths of the Mekong river, and past the lofty Cape St. Jacques, with its fort, into the open China Sea.

I. L. B.

Letter VII

Beauties of the Tropics—Singapore Hospitality—An Equatorial Metropolis—An Aimless Existence—The Growth of Singapore—"Farms" and "Farmers"—The Staple of Conversation—The Glitter of "Barbaric Gold"—A Polyglot Population—A Mediocre People—Female Grace and Beauty—The "Asian Mystery"—Oriental Picturesqueness—The Metamorphosis of Singapore

SINGAPORE, January 19, 1879.

It is hot—so hot!—but not stifling, and all the rich-flavored, colored fruits of the tropics are here—fruits whose generous juices are drawn from the moist and heated earth, and whose flavors are the imprisoned rays of the fierce sun of the tropics. Such cartloads and piles of bananas and pineapples, such heaps of custard-apples and "bullocks' hearts," such a wealth of gold and green giving off fragrance! Here, too, are treasures of the heated, crystal seas—things that one has dreamed of after reading Jules Verne's romances. Big canoes, manned by dark-skinned men in white turbans and loin-cloths, floated round our ship, or lay poised on the clear depths of aquamarine water, with fairy freights— forests of coral white as snow, or red, pink, violet, in massive branches or fern-like sprays, fresh from their warm homes beneath the clear warm waves, where fish as bright-tinted as themselves flash through them like "living light." There were displays of wonderful shells, too, of pale rose-pink, and others with rainbow tints which, like rainbows, came and went—nothing scanty, feeble, or pale!

It is a drive of two miles from the pier to Singapore, and to eyes which have only seen the yellow skins and non-vividness of the Far East, a world of wonders opens at every step. It is intensely tropical; there are mangrove swamps, and fringes of cocoa-palms, and banana-groves, date, sago, and travelers' palms, tree-ferns, India-rubber, mango, custard-apple, jackfruit, durion, lime, pomegranate, pineapples, and orchids, and all kinds of strangling and parrot-blossomed trailers. Vegetation rich, profuse, endless, rapid, smothering, in all shades of vivid green, from the pea-green of spring and the dark velvety green of endless summer to the yellow-green of the plumage of the palm, riots in a heavy shower every night and the heat of a perennial sun-blaze every day, while monkeys of various kinds and bright-winged birds skip and flit through the jungle shades. There is a perpetual battle between man and the jungle, and the latter, in fact, is only brought to bay within a short distance of Singapore.

I had scarcely finished breakfast at the hotel, a shady, straggling building, much infested by ants, when Mr. Cecil Smith, the Colonial Secretary, and his wife called, full of kind thoughts and plans of furtherance; and a little later a resident, to whom I had not even a letter of introduction, took me and my luggage to his bungalow. All the European houses seem to have very deep verandas, large, lofty rooms, punkahs everywhere, windows without glass, brick floors, and jalousies and "tatties" (blinds made of grass or finely split bamboo) to keep out the light and the flies. This equatorial heat is neither as exhausting or depressing as the damp summer heat of Japan, though one does long "to take off one's flesh and sit in one's bones."

I wonder how this unexpected and hastily planned expedition into the Malay States will turn out? It is so unlikely that the different arrangements will fit in. It seemed an event in the dim future; but yesterday my host sent up a "chit" from his office to say that a Chinese steamer is to sail for Malacca in a day or two, and would I like to go? I was only allowed five minutes for decision, but I have no difficulty in making up my mind when an escape from civilization is possible. So

I wrote back that if I could get my money and letters of introduction in time I would go, and returned to dine at Mr. Cecil Smith's, where a delightfully cultured and intellectual atmosphere made civilization more than tolerable. The needed letters were written, various hints for my guidance were thrown out, and I drove back at half-past ten under heavens which were one blaze of stars amidst a dust of nebulae, like the inlaid gold spots amidst a dust of gold on old Japanese lacquer, and through a moist, warm atmosphere laden with the heavy fragrance of innumerable night-blossoming flowers.

Singapore, as the capital of the Straits Settlements and the residence of the Governor, has a garrison, defensive works, ships of war hanging about, and a great deal of military as well as commercial importance, and "the roll of the British drum" is a reassuring sound in the midst of the unquiet Chinese population. The Governor is assisted by lieutenant-governors at Malacca and Pinang, and his actual rule extends to the three "protected" States of the Malay Peninsula—Sungei Ujong, Selangor, and Perak—the affairs of which are administered by British Residents, who are more or less responsible to him.

If I fail in making you realize Singapore it is partly because I do not care to go into much detail about so well-known a city, and partly because my own notions of it are mainly of overpowering greenery, a kaleidoscopic arrangement of colors, Chinese predominance, and abounding hospitality. I almost fail to realize that it is an island; one of many; all, like itself, covered with vegetation down to the water's edge; about twenty-seven miles long by fourteen broad, with the city at its southern end. It is only seventy miles from the equator, but it is neither unhealthy nor overpoweringly hot! It is low and undulating, its highest point, Bukit Timor, or the Hill of Tin, being only five hundred and twenty feet high. The greatest curse here used to be tigers, which carried off about three hundred people yearly. They were supposed to have been extirpated, but they have reappeared, swimming across from the mainland State of Johore it is conjectured; and as various lonely Chinese laborers have been victimized, there is something of a "scare," in the papers at least. Turtles are so abundant that turtle-soup is anything but a luxury, and turtle flesh is ordinarily sold in the meat shops.

Rain is officially said to fall on two hundred days of the year, but popularly every day! The rainfall is only eighty-seven inches, however, and the glorious vegetation owes its redundancy to the dampness of the climate. Of course, Singapore has no seasons. The variety is only in the intensity of the heat, the mercury being tolerably steady between 80 degrees and 84 degrees, the extreme range of temperature being from 71 degrees to 92 degrees. People sleep on Malay mats spread over their mattresses for coolness, some dispense with upper sheets, and others are fanned all night by punkahs. The soft and tepid land and sea breezes mitigate the heat to a slight extent, but I should soon long for a blustering north-easter to break in upon the oppressive and vapor-bath stillness.

As Singapore is a military station, and ships of war hang about constantly, there is a great deal of fluctuating society, and the officials of the Straits Settlements Government are numerous enough to form a large society of their own. Then there is the merchant class, English, German, French, and American; and there is the usual round of gayety, and of the amusements which make life intolerable. I think that in most of these tropical colonies the ladies exist only on the hope of going "home!" It is a dreary, aimless life for them—scarcely life, only existence. The greatest sign of vitality in Singapore Europeans that I can see is the furious hurry in writing for the mail. To all sorts of claims and invitations, the reply is, "But it's mail day, you know," or, "I'm writing for the mail," or, "I'm awfully behind hand with my letters," or, "I can't stir till the mail's gone!" The hurry is desperate, and even the feeble Englishwomen exert themselves for "friends at home." To judge from the flurry and excitement, and the driving down to the post-office at the last moment, and the commotion in the parboiled community, one would suppose the mail to be an uncertain event occurring once in a year or two, rather than the most regular of weekly fixtures! The incoming mail is also a great event, though its public and commercial news is anticipated by four weeks by the telegraph.

The Americans boast of the rapid progress of San Francisco, with which the Victorians boast that Melbourne is running a neck and neck race; but, if boasting is allowable, Singapore may boast, for in 1818 the island was covered with dense primeval forest, and only a few miserable fishermen and pirates inhabited its creeks and rivers. The prescience of Sir Stamford Raffles marked it out in 1819 as the site of the first free port in the Malayan Seas, but it was not till 1824 that it was formally ceded to the East India Company by the Sultan of Johore, and it only became a Crown colony in 1867, when it was erected into the capital of the Straits Settlements, which include Malacca and Pinang.

Like Victoria, Singapore is a free port, and the vexatiousness of a custom-house is unknown. The only tax which shipping pays is 1-1/2 per cent. for the support of sundry lighthouses. The list of its exports suggests heat. They are chiefly sugar, pepper, tin, nutmegs, mace, sago, tapioca, rice, buffalo hides and horns, rattans, gutta, india rubber, gambier, gums, coffee, dye-stuffs, and tobacco, but the island itself, though its soil looks rich from its redness, only produces pepper and gambier. It is a great entrepot, a gigantic distributing point.*

[*The exports and imports of Singapore amounted in 1823 to 2,120,000 pounds, in 1859-60 to 10,371,000 pounds, and in 1880, to 23,050,000 pounds! In the latter year, tonnage to the amount of three millions of tons arrived in its harbor. It must be observed that the imports, to a very large extent, are exported to other places.]

The problem of raising a revenue without customs duties is solved by a stamp-tax, land-revenue, and (by far the most important), the sale of the monopolies of the preparation and retailing of opium for smoking, and of spirits and other excisable commodities, these monopolies being "farmed" to private individuals, mostly Chinamen. It is rather puzzling to hear "farmers" spoken of so near the equator. A revenue of nearly half a million annually and a public debt of one hundred thousand pounds is not bad for so young a colony. The prosperity of the Straits Settlements ports is a great triumph for free traders, and a traveler, even if, like myself, he has nothing but a canvas roll and a "Gladstone bag," congratulates himself on being saved from the bother of unstrapping and restrapping stiffened and refractory straps, and from the tiresome delays of even the most courteous custom-house officers.

The official circle is large, as I before remarked. A Crown colony where the Government has it all its own way must be the paradise of officials, and the high sense of honor and the righteous esprit de corps which characterize our civil servants in the Far East, and a conscientious sense of responsibilities for the good government and well-being of the heterogeneous populations over which they rule, seem as good a check as the general run of colonial parliaments.

The Governor, Sir William Robinson (now Sir F. A. Weld), is assisted by an Executive Council of eight members, and a Legislative Council consisting of nine official and six non-official members, including Mr. Whampoa, C.M.G., a Chinaman of great wealth and enlightened public spirit, who is one of the foremost men in the colony. Then on the Civil Establishment there are a legion of departments, the Colonial Secretary's office with a branch office and Chinese Protectorate, a Land Office, Printing Office, Treasury, Audit Office, Post Office, Public Works and Survey Department, Marine Department, Judicial Department, Attorney-General's Department, Sheriff's Department, Police Court and Police Department, and Ecclesiastical, Educational, Medical, and Prison Staffs.

It is natural that when the mail has been worn threadbare and no stirring incidents present themselves, such as the arrival of a new ship of war or a touring foreign prince, and the receptions of Mr. Whampoa and the Maharajah of Johore have grown insipid, that much of local conversation should consist of speculations as to when or whether Mr. —— will get promotion, when Mr. —— will go home, or how much he has saved out of his salary; what influence has procured the appointment of Mr. —— to Selangor or Perak, instead of Mr. ——, whose qualifications are higher; whether Mr. ——'s acting appointment will be confirmed; whether Mr. —— will get one or two years' leave; whether some vacant appointment is to be filled up or abolished, and so on ad infinitum. Such talk girdles the colonial world as completely as the telegraph, which has revolutionized European business here as elsewhere.

The island is far less interesting than the city. Its dense, dark jungle is broken up mainly by pepper and gambier plantations, the latter specially in new clearings. The laborers on these are Chinese, and so are the wood-cutters and sawyers, who frequent the round-topped wooded undulations. The climate is hotter and damper, to one's sensations at least, than the hottest and dampest of the tropical houses at Kew, and heat-loving insects riot. The ants are a pest of the second magnitude, mosquitoes being of the first, the palm-trees and the piles of decaying leaves and bark being excellent nurseries for larvae. The vegetation is luxuriant, and in the dim, green twilight which is created by enormous forest trees there are endless varieties of ferns, calladiums, and parasitic plants; but except where a road has been cut and is kept open by continual labor, the climbing rattan palms make it impossible to explore.

My short visit has been mainly occupied with the day at the Colonial Secretary's Lodge, and in walking and driving through the streets. The city is ablaze with color and motley with costume. The ruling race does not show to advantage. A pale-skinned man or woman, costumed in our ugly, graceless clothes, reminds one not pleasingly, artistically at least, of our dim, pale islands. Every Oriental costume from the Levant to China floats through the streets—robes of silk, satin, brocade, and white muslin, emphasized by the glitter of "barbaric gold;" and Parsees in spotless white, Jews and Arabs in dark rich silks; Klings in Turkey red and white; Bombay merchants in great white turbans, full trousers, and draperies, all white, with crimson silk girdles; Malays in red sarongs, Sikhs in pure white Madras muslin, their great height rendered nearly colossal by the classic arrangement of their draperies; and Chinamen of all classes, from the coolie in his blue or brown cotton, to the wealthy merchant in his frothy silk crepe and rich brocade, make up an irresistibly fascinating medley.

The English, though powerful as the ruling race, are numerically nowhere, and certainly make no impression on the eye. The Chinese, who number eighty-six thousand out of a population of one hundred and thirty-nine thousand, are not only numerous enough, but rich and important enough to give Singapore the air of a Chinese town with a foreign settlement. Then there are the native Malays, who have crowded into the island since we acquired it, till they number twenty-two thousand, and who, besides being tolerably industrious as boatmen and fishermen, form the main body of the police. The Parsee merchants, who like our rule, form a respectable class of merchants here, as in all the great trading cities of the East. The Javanese are numerous, and make good servants and sailors. Some of the small merchants and many of the clerks are Portuguese immigrants from Malacca; and traders from Borneo, Sumatra, Celebes, Bali, and other islands of the Malay Archipelago are scattered among the throng. The washermen and grooms are nearly all Bengalees. Jews and Arabs make money and keep it, and are, as everywhere, shrewd and keen, and only meet their equals among the Chinese. Among the twelve thousand natives of India who have been attracted to Singapore, and among all the mingled foreign nationalities, the Klings from the Coromandel coast, besides being the most numerous of all next to the Chinese, are the most attractive in appearance, and as there is no check on the immigration of their women, one sees the unveiled Kling beauties in great numbers.*

[*The Singapore census returns for 1881 are by no means "dry reading," and they give a very imposing idea of the importance of the island. It is interesting to note that of the 434 enumerators employed only seven were Europeans!

THE GOLDEN CHERSONESE AND THE WAY THITHER (TRAVELS IN MALAYSIA)

The number of houses on the island is 20,462; the total population is 139,208 souls, viz., 105,423 males and 33,785 females. The total increase in ten years is divided as follows:—

Europeans and Americans	*823*
Eurasians	*930*
Chinese	*32,194*
Malays and other natives of the Archipelago	*6,954*
Tamils and other natives of India	*637*
Other nationalities	*559*

Among these "other nationalities" the great increase has been among the Arabs, who have nearly doubled their numbers. Among the "Malays and other natives of the Archipelago" are included, Achinese, Boyanese, Bugis, Dyaks, Jawi-Pekans, and Manilamen.

The European resident population, exclusive of the soldiers, is only 1,283. The Chinese population is 86,766; the Malay, 22,114; the Tamil, 10,475; the Javanese, 5,881; and the Eurasian, 3,091. In the very small European population 19 nationalities are included, the Germans numerically following the British. Of 15,368 domestic servants, only 844 are women.]

These Klings are active and industrious, but they lack fibre apparently, and that quick-sightedness for opportunities which makes the Chinese the most successful of all emigrants. Not a Malay or a Kling has raised himself either as a merchant or in any other capacity to wealth or distinction in the colony. The Klings make splendid boatmen, they drive gharries, run as syces, lend small sums of money at usurious interest, sell fruit, keep small shops, carry "chit books," and make themselves as generally useful as their mediocre abilities allow. They are said to be a harmless people so far as deeds go. They neither fight, organize, nor get into police rows, but they quarrel loudly and vociferously, and their vocabulary of abuse is said to be inexhaustible. The Kling men are very fine-looking, lithe and active, and, as they clothe but little, their forms are seen to great advantage. The women are, I think, beautiful—not so much in face as in form and carriage. I am never weary of watching and admiring their inimitable grace of movement. Their faces are oval, their foreheads low, their eyes dark and liquid, their noses shapely, but disfigured by the universal adoption of jewelled nose-rings; their lips full, but not thick or coarse; their heads small, and exquisitely set on long, slender throats; their ears small, but much dragged out of shape by the wearing of two or three hoop-earrings in each; and their glossy, wavy, black hair, which grows classically low on the forehead, is gathered into a Grecian knot at the back. Their clothing, or rather drapery, is a mystery, for it covers and drapes perfectly, yet has no *make*, far less fit, and leaves every graceful movement unimpeded. It seems to consist of ten wide yards of soft white muslin or soft red material, so ingeniously disposed as to drape the bust and lower limbs, and form a girdle at the same time. One shoulder and arm are usually left bare. The part which may be called a petticoat—though the word is a slur upon the graceful drapery—is short, and shows the finely turned ankles, high insteps, and small feet. These women are tall, and straight as arrows; their limbs are long and rounded; their appearance is timid, one might almost say modest, and their walk is the poetry of movement. A tall, graceful Kling woman, draped as I have described, gliding along the pavement, her statuesque figure the perfection of graceful ease, a dark pitcher on her head, just touched by the beautiful hand, showing the finely moulded arm, is a beautiful object, classical in form, exquisite in movement, and artistic in coloring, a creation of the tropic sun. What thinks she, I wonder, if she thinks at all, of the pale European, paler for want of exercise and engrossing occupation, who steps out of her carriage in front of her, an ungraceful heap of poufs and frills, tottering painfully on high heels, in tight boots, her figure distorted into the shape of a Japanese sake bottle, every movement a struggle or a jerk, the clothing utterly unsuited to this or any climate, impeding motion, and affecting health, comfort, and beauty alike?

THE GOLDEN CHERSONESE AND THE WAY THITHER (TRAVELS IN MALAYSIA)

It is all fascinating. Here is none of the indolence and apathy which one associates with Oriental life, and which I have seen in Polynesia. These yellow, brown, tawny, swarthy, olive-tinted men are all intent on gain; busy, industrious, frugal, striving, and, no matter what their creed is, all paying homage to Daikoku. In spite of the activity, rapidity, and earnestness, the movements of all but the Chinese are graceful, gliding, stealthy, the swarthy faces have no expression that I can read, and the dark, liquid eyes are no more intelligible to me than the eyes of oxen. It is the "Asian mystery" all over.

It is only the European part of Singapore which is dull and sleepy looking. No life and movement congregate round the shops. The merchants, hidden away behind jalousies in their offices, or dashing down the streets in covered buggies, make but a poor show. Their houses are mostly pale, roomy, detached bungalows, almost altogether hidden by the bountiful vegetation of the climate. In these their wives, growing paler every week, lead half-expiring lives, kept alive by the efforts of ubiquitous "punkah-wallahs;" writing for the mail, the one active occupation. At a given hour they emerge, and drive in given directions, specially round the esplanade, where for two hours at a time a double row of handsome and showy equipages moves continuously in opposite directions. The number of carriages and the style of dress of their occupants are surprising, and yet people say that large fortunes are not made now-a-days in Singapore! Besides the daily drive, the ladies, the officers, and any men who may be described as of "no occupation," divert themselves with kettle-drums, dances, lawn tennis, and various other devices for killing time, and this with the mercury at 80 degrees! Just now the Maharajah of Johore, sovereign of a small state on the nearest part of the mainland, a man much petted and decorated by the British Government for unswerving fidelity to British interests, has a house here, and his receptions and dinner parties vary the monotonous round of gayeties.

The native streets monopolize the picturesqueness of Singapore with their bizarre crowds, but more interesting still are the bazaars or continuous rows of open shops which create for themselves a perpetual twilight by hanging tatties or other screens outside the sidewalks, forming long shady alleys, in which crowds of buyers and sellers chaffer over their goods, the Chinese shopkeepers asking a little more than they mean to take, and the Klings always asking double. The bustle and noise of this quarter are considerable, and the vociferation mingles with the ringing of bells and the rapid beating of drums and tom-toms—an intensely heathenish sound. And heathenish this great city is. Chinese joss-houses, Hindu temples, and Mohammedan mosques almost jostle each other, and the indescribable clamor of the temples and the din of the joss-houses are faintly pierced by the shrill cry from the minarets calling the faithful to prayer, and proclaiming the divine unity and the mission of Mahomet in one breath.

How I wish I could convey an idea, however faint, of this huge, mingled, colored, busy, Oriental population; of the old Kling and Chinese bazaars; of the itinerant sellers of seaweed jelly, water, vegetables, soup, fruit, and cooked fish, whose unintelligible street cries are heard above the din of the crowds of coolies, boatmen, and gharriemen waiting for hire; of the far-stretching suburbs of Malay and Chinese cottages; of the sheet of water, by no means clean, round which hundreds of Bengalis are to be seen at all hours of daylight unmercifully beating on great stones the delicate laces, gauzy silks, and elaborate flouncings of the European ladies; of the ceaseless rush and hum of industry, and of the resistless, overpowering, astonishing Chinese element, which is gradually turning Singapore into a Chinese city! I must conclude abruptly, or lose the mail.

I. L. B.

Letter VIII

St. Andrew's Cathedral—Singapore Harbor Scenes—Chinese Preponderance—First Impressions of Malacca—A Town "Out of the Running"

S.S. "RAINBOW," MALACCA ROADS, January 20.

Yesterday I attended morning service in St. Andrew's, a fine colonial cathedral, prettily situated on a broad grass lawn among clumps of trees near the sea. There is some stained glass in the apse, but in the other windows, including those in the clerestory, Venetian shutters take the place of glass, as in all the European houses. There are thirty-two punkahs, and the Indians who worked them, anyone of whom might have been the model of the Mercury of the Naples Museum, sat or squatted outside the church. The service was simple and the music very good, but in the Te Deum, just as the verse "Thou art the King of Glory, O Christ," I caught sight of the bronze faces of these "punkah-wallahs," mostly bigoted Mussulmen, and was overwhelmed by the realization of the small progress which Christianity has made upon the earth in nineteen centuries. A Singhalese D.D. preached an able sermon. Just before the communion we were called out, as the Rainbow was about to sail, and a harbor boat, manned by six splendid Klings, put us on board.

The Rainbow is a very small vessel, her captain half Portuguese and half Malay, her crew Chinese, and her cabin passengers were all Chinese merchants. Her engineer is a Welshman, a kindly soul, who assured Mr. ——, when he commended me to his care, that "he was a family man, and that nothing gave him greater pleasure than seeing that ladies were comfortable," and I owe to his good offices the very small modicum of comfort that I had. Waiting on the little bridge was far from being wearisome, there was such a fascination in watching the costumed and manifold life of the harbor, the black-hulled, sullen-looking steamers from Europe discharging cargo into lighters, Malay prahus of all sizes but one form, sharp at both ends, and with eyes on their bows, like the Cantonese and Cochin China boats, reeling as though they would upset under large mat sails, and rowing-boats rowed by handsome, statuesque Klings. A steamer from Jeddah was discharging six hundred pilgrims in most picturesque costumes; and there were boats with men in crimson turbans and graceful robes of pure white muslin, and others a mass of blue umbrellas, while some contained Brahmins with the mark of caste set conspicuously on their foreheads, all moving in a veil of gold in the setting of a heavy fringe of cocoa-palms.

We sailed at four, with a strong favorable breeze, and the sea was really delightful as we passed among green islets clothed down to the water's edge with dense tropical vegetation, right out into the open water of the Straits of Malacca, a burning, waveless sea, into which the sun was descending in mingled flame and blood. Then, dinner for three, consisting of an excellent curry, was spread on the top of the cabin, and eaten by the captain, engineer, and myself, after which the engineer took me below to arrange for my comfort, and as it was obviously impossible for me to sleep in a very dirty and very small hole, tenanted by cockroaches disproportionately large, and with a temperature of eighty-eight degrees, he took a mattress and pillows upon the bridge, told me his history, and that of his colored wife and sixteen children under seventeen, of his pay of 35 pounds a month, lent me a box of matches, and vanished into the lower regions with the consoling words, "If you want anything in the night, just call 'Engineer' down the engine skylight." It does one's heart good to meet with such a countryman.

The Rainbow is one of the many tokens of preponderating Chinese influence in the Straits of Malacca. The tickets are Chinese, as well as the ownership and crew. The supercargo who took my ticket is a sleek young Chinaman in a pigtail, girdle, and white cotton trousers. The

THE GOLDEN CHERSONESE AND THE WAY THITHER (TRAVELS IN MALAYSIA)

cabin passengers are all Chinamen. The deck was packed with Chinese coolies on their way to seek wealth in the diggings at Perak. They were lean, yellow, and ugly, smoked a pipe of opium each at sundown, wore their pigtails coiled round their heads, and loose blue cotton trousers. We had slipped our cable at Singapore, because these coolies were clambering up over every part of the vessel, and defying all attempts to keep them out, so that "to cut and run" was our only chance. The owners do not allow any intoxicant to be brought on board, lest it should be given to the captain and crew, and they should take too much and lose the vessel. I am the only European passenger and the only woman on board. I had a very comfortable night lying on deck in the brisk breeze on the waveless sea, and though I watched the stars, hoping to see the Southern Cross set, I fell asleep, till I was awoke at the very earliest dawn by a most formidable Oriental shouting to me very fiercely I thought, with a fierce face; but it occurred to me that he was trying to make me understand that they wanted to wash decks, so I lifted my mattress on a bench and fell asleep again, waking to find the anchor being let go in the Malacca roads six hours before we should have arrived.

I am greatly interested with the first view of Malacca, one of the oldest European towns in the East, originally Portuguese, then Dutch, and now, though under English rule, mainly Chinese. There is a long bay with dense forests of cocoa-palms, backed by forests of I know not what, then rolling hills, and to the right beyond these a mountain known as Mount Ophir, rich in gold. Is this possibly, as many think, the Ophir of the Bible, and this land of gems and gold truly the "Golden Chersonese?" There are islets of emerald green lying to the south, and in front of us a town of antiquated appearance, low houses, much colored, with flattish, red-tiled roofs, many of them built on piles, straggling for a long distance, and fringed by massive-looking bungalows, half buried in trees. A hill rises near the middle, crowned by a ruined cathedral, probably the oldest Christian church in the Far East, with slopes of bright green grass below, timbered near their base with palms and trees of a nearly lemon-colored vividness of spring-green, and there are glimpses of low, red roofs behind the hill. On either side of the old-world-looking town and its fringe of bungalows are glimpses of steep, reed roofs among the cocoa-palms. A long, deserted-looking jetty runs far out into the shallow sea, a few Chinese junks lie at anchor, in the distance a few Malay fishermen are watching their nets, but not a breath stirs, the sea is without a ripple, the gray clouds move not, the yellow plumes of the palms are motionless; the sea, the sky, the town, look all alike asleep in a still, moist, balmy heat.

Stadthaus, Malacca, 4 P.M.—Presently we were surrounded by a crowd of Malay boats with rude sails made of mats, but their crews might have been phantoms for any noise they made. By one of these I sent my card and note of introduction to the Lieutenant-Governor. An hour afterward the captain told me that the Governor usually went into the country early on Monday morning for two days, which seemed unfortunate. Soon after, the captain and engineer went ashore, and I was left among a crowd of Chinamen and Malays without any possibility of being understood by any of them, to endure stifling heat and provoking uncertainty, much aggravated by the want of food, for another three hours. At last, when very nearly famished, and when my doubts as to the wisdom of this novel and impromptu expedition had become very serious indeed, a European boat appeared, moving with the long steady stroke of a man-of-war's boat, rowed by six native policemen, with a frank-looking bearded countryman steering, and two peons in white, with scarlet-and-gold hats and sashes, in the bow, and as it swept up to the Rainbow's side the man in white stepped on board, and introduced himself to me as Mr. Biggs, the colonial chaplain, deputed to receive me on behalf of the Governor, who was just leaving when my card arrived. He relieved all anxiety as to my destination by saying that quarters were ready for me in the Stadthaus.

We were soon on a lovely shore under the cathedral-crowned hill, where the velvety turf slopes down to the sea under palms and trees whose trunks are one mass of ferns, brightened by that wonderful flowering tree variously known as the "flamboyant" and the "flame of the forest" (Poinciana regia). Very still, hot, tropical, sleepy, and dreamy, Malacca looks, a town "out of the running," utterly antiquated, mainly un-English, a veritable Sleepy Hollow.

I. L. B.

Letter IX

The Lieutenant-Governor of Malacca—A Charming Household—The Old Stadthaus—A Stately Habitation—An Endless Siesta—A Tropic Dream—Chinese Houses—Chinese Wealth and Ascendency—"Opium Farming"—The Malacca Jungle—Mohammedan Burial-Places—Malay Villages—Malay Characteristics—Costume and Ornament—Bigotry and Pilgrimage—The Malay Buffalo

STADTHAUS, MALACCA, January 21-23.

This must surely fade like a dream, this grand old Stadthaus, this old-world quiet, this quaint life; but when it fades I think I shall have a memory of having been "once in Elysium." Still, Elysium should have no mosquitoes, and they are nearly insupportable here; big spotted fellows, with a greed for blood, and a specially poisonous bite, taking the place at daylight of the retiring nocturnal host. The Chinese attendant is not careful, and lets mosquitoes into my net, and even one means a sleepless night. They are maddening.

I was introduced to my rooms, with their floors of red Dutch tiles, their blue walls, their white-washed rafters, their doors and windows consisting of German shutters only, their ancient beds of portentous height, and their generally silent and haunted look, and then went to tiffin with Mr. and Mrs. Biggs. Mr. Biggs is a student of hymnology, and we were soon in full swing on this mutually congenial subject. Mrs. Biggs devotes her time and strength to the training and education of young Portuguese girls. I pass their open bungalow as I go to and from the Governor's cottage, and it usually proves a trap.

THE GOLDEN CHERSONESE AND THE WAY THITHER (TRAVELS IN MALAYSIA)

Captain Shaw, who has been for many years Lieutenant-Governor of Malacca, is a fine, hearty, frank, merry, manly, Irish naval officer, well read and well informed, devoted to Malacca and its interests, and withal a man of an especially unselfish, loving, and tender nature, considerate to an unusual degree of the happiness and comfort of those about him. Before I had been here many hours I saw that he was the light of a loving home.* He can be firm and prompt when occasion requires firmness, but his ordinary rule is of the gentlest and most paternal description, so that from the Chinese he has won the name of "Father," and among the Malays, the native population, English rule, as administered by him, has come to be known as "the rule of the just." The family, consisting of the Governor, his, wife, and two daughters just grown up, is a very charming one, and their quiet, peaceful life gives me the opportunity which so rarely falls to the lot of a traveler of becoming really intimate with them.

[*I should not have reproduced this paragraph of my letter were Captain Shaw still alive, but in five weeks after my happy visit he died almost suddenly, to the indescribable grief of his family and of the people of Malacca, by whom he was greatly beloved.]

The Government bungalow, in which I spend most of my time, is a comfortable little cottage, with verandas larger than itself. In the front veranda, festooned with trailers and orchids, two Malay military policemen are always on guard, and two scornful-looking Bengalis in white trousers, white short robes, with sashes of crimson silk striped with gold, and crimson-and-gold flat hats above their handsome but repellent faces, make up the visible part of the establishment. One of these Bengalis has been twice to Mecca, at an expense of 40 pounds on each visit, and on Friday appears in a rich Hadji suit, in which he goes through the town, and those Mussulmen who are not Hadji bow down to him. I saw from the very first that my project of visiting the native States was not smiled upon at Government House.

The Government bungalow being scarcely large enough for the Governor's family, I am lodged in the old Dutch Stadthaus, formerly the residence of the Dutch Governor, and which has enough of solitude and faded stateliness to be fearsome, or at the least eerie, to a solitary guest like myself, to whose imagination, in the long, dark nights, creeping Malays or pilfering Chinamen are far more likely to present themselves than the stiff beauties and formal splendors of the heyday of Dutch ascendancy. The Stadthaus, which stands on the slope of the hill, and is the most prominent building in Malacca, is now used as the Treasury, Post Office, and Government offices generally. There are large state reception-rooms, including a ballroom, and suites of apartments for the use of the Governor of the Straits Settlements, the Chief-Justice, and other high officials, on their visits to Malacca. The Stadthaus, at its upper end on the hill, is only one story high, but where it abuts on the town it is three and even four. The upper part is built round three sides of a Dutch garden, and a gallery under the tiled veranda runs all round. A set of handsome staircases on the seaside leads to the lawn-like hill with the old cathedral, and the bungalows of the Governor and colonial chaplain. Stephanotis, passiflora, tuberose, alamanda, Bougainvillea, and other trailers of gorgeous colors, climb over everything, and make the night heavy with their odors. There must be more than forty rooms in this old place, besides great arched corridors, and all manner of queer staircases and corners. Dutch tiling and angularities and conceits of all kinds abound.

My room opens on one side upon a handsome set of staircases under the veranda, and on the other upon a passage and staircase with several rooms with doors of communication, and has various windows opening on the external galleries. Like most European houses in the Peninsula, it has a staircase which leads from the bedroom to a somewhat grim, brick-floored room below, containing a large high tub, or bath, of Shanghai pottery, in which you must by no means bathe, as it is found by experience that to take the capacious dipper and pour water upon yourself from a height, gives a far more refreshing shock than immersion when the water is at 80 degrees and the air at 83 degrees.

The worst of my stately habitation is, that after four in the afternoon there is no one in it but myself, unless a Chinese coolie, who has a lair somewhere, and appears in my room at all sorts of unusual hours after I think I have bolted and barred every means of ingress. However, two Malay military policemen patrol the verandas outside at intervals all night, and I have the comfort of imagining that I hear far below the clank of the British sentries who guard the Treasury. In the early morning my eyes always open on the Governor's handsome Mohammedan servant in spotless white muslin and red head-dress and girdle, bringing a tray with tea and bananas. The Chinese coolie who appears mysteriously attends on me, and acts as housemaid, our communications being entirely by signs. The mosquitoes are awful. The view of the green lawns, the sleeping sea, the motionless forest of cocoa-palms along the shore, the narrow stream and bridge, and the quaint red-tiled roofs of the town, is very charming and harmonious; yet I often think, if these dreamy days went on into months, that I should welcome an earthquake shock, or tornado, or jarring discord of some rousing kind, to break the dream produced by the heated, steamy, fragrant air, and the monotonous silence.

I have very little time for writing here, and even that is abridged by the night mosquitoes, which muster their forces for a desperate attack as soon as I retire to the Stadthaus for two hours of quiet before dinner, so I must give the features of Malacca mainly in outline. Having written this sentence, I am compelled to say that the feature of Malacca is that it is featureless! It is a land where it is "always afternoon"—hot, still, dreamy. Existence stagnates. Trade pursues its operations invisibly. Commerce hovers far off on the shallow sea. The British and French mail steamers give the port a wide offing. It has no politics, little crime, rarely gets even two lines in an English newspaper, and does nothing toward making contemporary history. The Lieutenant-Governor has occupied the same post for eleven years. A company of soldiers vegetates in quarters in a yet sleepier region than the town itself. Two Chinese steamers make it a port of call, but, except that they bring mails, their comings and goings are of no interest to the very small English part of the population. Lying basking in the sun, or crawling at the heads of crawling oxen very like hairless buffaloes, or leaning over the bridge looking at nothing, the Malays spend their time when they come into the town, their very movements making the lack of movement more perceptible.

The half-breed descendants of the Portuguese, who kept up a splendid pomp of rule in the days of Francis Xavier, seem to take an endless siesta behind their closely covered windows. I have never seen an Englishman out of doors except Mr. Hayward, the active superintendent of military police, or Mr. Biggs, who preserves his health and energies by systematic constitutionals. Portuguese and Dutch rule have passed away, leaving, as their chief monuments—the first, a ruined cathedral, and a race of half-breeds; and the last, the Stadthaus and a flat-faced meetinghouse. A heavy shower, like a "thunder-plump," takes up a part of the afternoon, after which the Governor's carriage, with servants in scarlet liveries, rolls slowly out of Malacca, and through the sago-palms and back again. If aught else which is European breaks the monotony of the day I am not aware of it. The streets have no particular features, though one cannot but be aware that a narrow stream full of boats, and spanned by a handsome bridge, divides the town into two portions, and that a handsome clock-tower (both tower and bridge erected by some wealthy Chinese merchants) is a salient object below the Stadthaus. Trees, trailers, fruits, smother the houses, and blossom and fruit all the year round; old leaves, young leaves, buds, blossom, and fruit, all appearing at once. The mercury rarely falls below 79 degrees or rises above 84 degrees. The softest and least perceptible of land and sea breezes blow alternately at stated hours. The nights are very still. The days are a tepid dream. Since I arrived not a leaf has stirred, not a bird has sung, the tides ebb and flow in listless and soundless ripples. Far off, on the shallow sea, phantom ships hover and are gone, and on an indefinite horizon a blurred ocean blends with a blurred sky. On Mount Ophir heavy cloud-masses lie always motionless. The still, heavy, fragrant nights pass with no other sounds than the aggressive hum of mosquitoes and the challenge of the sentries. But through the stormy days and the heavy nights Nature is always busy in producing a rapidity and profusion of growth which would turn Malacca into a jungle were it not for axe and billhook, but her work does not jar upon the general silence. Yet with all this indefiniteness, dreaminess, featurelessness, indolence, and silence, of which I have attempted to convey an idea, Malacca is very fascinating, and no city in the world, except Canton, will leave so vivid an impression upon me, though it may be but of a fragrant tropic dream and nothing more.

Yesterday Mrs. Biggs took me a drive through Malacca and its forest environs. It was delightful; every hour adds to the fascination which this place has for me. I thought my tropic dreams were over, when seven years ago I saw the summit peaks of Oahu sink sunset flushed into a golden sea, but I am dreaming it again. The road crosses the bridge over the narrow stream, which is, in fact, the roadway of a colored and highly picturesque street, and at once enters the main street of Malacca, which is parallel to the sea. On the sea side each house consists of three or four divisions, one behind the other, each roof being covered with red tiles. The rearmost division is usually built over the sea, on piles. In the middle of each of the three front divisions there is a courtyard. The room through which you enter from the street always has an open door, through which you see houses showing a high degree of material civilization, lofty rooms, handsome altars opposite the doors, massive, carved ebony tables, and carved ebony chairs with marble seats and backs standing against the walls, hanging pictures of the kind called in Japan kakemono, and rich bronzes and fine pieces of porcelain on ebony brackets. At night, when these rooms are lighted up with eight or ten massive lamps, the appearance is splendid. These are the houses of Chinese merchants of the middle class.

And now I must divulge the singular fact that Malacca is to most intents and purposes a Chinese city. The Dutch, as I wrote, have scarcely left a trace. The Portuguese, indolent, for the most part poor, and lowered by native marriages, are without influence, a most truly stagnant population, hardly to be taken into account. Their poor-looking houses resemble those of Lisbon. The English, except in so far as relates to the administration of government, are nowhere, though it is under our equitable rule that the queerly mixed population of Chinese, Portuguese, half-breeds, Malays, Confucianists, Buddhists, Tauists, Romanists, and Mohammedans "enjoy great quietness."*

[*By the census of 1881 the resident European population of the Settlement of Malacca consists of 23 males and 9 females, a "grand" total of 32! The Eurasian population, mainly of Portuguese mixed blood, is 2,213. The Chinese numbers 19,741, 4,020 being females. The Malay population is 67,488, the females being 2,000 in excess of the males, the Tamils or Klings are 1,781, the Arabs 227, the Aborigines of the Peninsula 308, the Javanese 399, the Boyanese 212, and the Jawi-Pekans 867. Besides these there are stray Achinese, Africans, Anamese, Bengalis, Bugis, Dyaks, Manilamen, Siamese, and Singhalese, numbering 174. The total population of the territory is 93,579, viz., 52,059 males and 41,520 females, an increase in ten years of 15,823. The decrease in the number of resident Europeans is 31.9 per cent. In "natives of India" 42 per cent., and in "other nationalities" 48.9 per cent. On the other hand the Chinese population has increased by 6,259 or 46.4 per cent., and the Malays by 11,264, or 19.3 per cent. The town of Malacca contains 5,538 houses, and the country districts 11,177. The area of the settlement is 640 square miles, and the density of the population 146 to the square mile; only twelve of the population are lunatics.]

Of the population of the town the majority are said to be Chinese, and still their crowded junks are rolling down on the north-east monsoon. As I remarked before, the coasting trade of the Straits of Malacca is in their hands, and to such an extent have they absorbed the trade of this colony, that I am told there is not a resident British merchant in Malacca. And it is not, as elsewhere, that they come, make money, and then return to settle in China, but they come here with their wives and families, buy or build these handsome houses, as well as large bungalows in the neighboring cocoa-groves, own most of the plantations up the country, and have obtained the finest site on the hill behind the town for their stately tombs. Every afternoon their carriages roll out into the country, conveying them to their substantial bungalows to smoke and gamble. They have fabulous riches in diamonds, pearls, sapphires, rubies, and emeralds. They love Malacca, and take a pride in beautifying it. They have fashioned their dwellings upon the model of those in Canton, but whereas cogent reasons compel the rich Chinaman at home to conceal the evidences of his wealth, he glories in displaying it under the security of British rule. The upper class of the Chinese merchants live in immense houses within walled gardens. The wives of all are secluded, and inhabit the back regions and have no share in the remarkably "good time" which the men seem to have. Along with their industrious habits and their character for fair trading, the Chinese have brought to Malacca gambling and opium-smoking. One-seventh of the whole quantity of opium exported from India to China is intercepted and consumed in the Straits Settlements, and the Malacca Government makes a large revenue from it. The Chinaman who "farms the opium"—i.e., who purchases from the Government the exclusive right to sell it—pays for his monopoly about 50 pounds per day. It must be remembered, however, that every man who smokes opium is not what we understand by an "opium-smoker," and that between the man who takes his daily pipe of opium after his supper, and the unhappy opium-slave who reduces himself to imbecility in such dens as I saw in Canton, there is just as much difference as there is in England between the "moderate drinker" and the "habitual drunkard." Slavery is prohibited in Malacca, and slaves from the neighboring State fly for freedom to the shelter of the British flag; but there is reason to suppose that the numerous women in the households of the Chinese merchants, though called servants, are persons who have been purchased in China, and are actually held in bondage. Apart from these exceptions, the Chinese population is a valuable one, and is, in its upper classes, singularly public-spirited, law-abiding, and strongly attached to British rule.

I saw no shops except those for the sale of fish, fruit, and coarse native pottery, but doubtless most things which are suited to the wants of the mixed population can be had in the bazaars. As we drove out of the town the houses became fewer and the trees denser, with mosques here and there among them, and in a few minutes we were in the great dark forest of cocoa, betel, and sago palms, awfully solemn and oppressive in the hot stillness of the evening. Every sight was new, for though I have seen the cocoa-palm before, the palm-fringes of the coral islands, with their feathery plumes have little kinship with the dark, crowded cocoa-forests of Malacca, with their endless vistas and mysterious gloom. These forests are intersected by narrow, muddy streams, suggestive of alligators, up which you can go in canoes if you lie down, and are content with the yet darker shade produced by the nipah, a species of stemless palm, of which the poorer natives make their houses, and whose magnificent fronds are often from twenty to twenty-two feet in length. The soft carriage road passes through an avenue of trees of great girth and a huge spread of foliage, bearing glorious yellow blossoms of delicious fragrance. Jungles of sugar-cane often form the foreground of dense masses of palms, then a jungle of pine-apples surprises one, then a mass of lianas, knotted and tangled, with stems like great cables, and red blossoms as large as breakfast cups. The huge trees which border the road have their stems and branches nearly hidden by orchids and epiphytes—chiefly that lovely and delicate one whose likeness to a hovering dove won for it the name of the "Flower of the Holy Ghost," an orchid (Peristeria elata) which lives but for a day, but in its brief life fills the air with fragrance. Then the trees change, the long tresses of an autumn-flowering orchid fall from their branches over the road;

dead trees appear transformed into living beauty by multitudes of ferns, among which the dark-green shining fronds of the Asplenium nidus, measuring four feet in length, specially delight the eye; huge tamarinds and mimosa add the grace of their feathery foliage; the banana unfolds its gigantic fronds above its golden fruitage; clumps of the betel or areca palms, with their slender and absolutely straight shafts, make the cocoa-palms look like clumsy giants; the gutta-percha, india rubber, and other varieties of ficus, increase the forest gloom by the brown velvety undersides of their shining dark-green leafage; then comes the cashew-nut tree, with its immense spread of branches, and its fruit an apple with a nut below; and the beautiful bread-fruit, with its green "cantalupe melons," nearly ripe, and the gigantic jak and durion, and fifty others, children of tropic heat and moisture, in all the promise of perpetual spring, and the fulfillment of endless summer, the beauty of blossom and the bounteousness of an unfailing fruitage crowning them through all the year. At their feet is a tangle of fungi, mosses, ferns, trailers, lilies, nibongs, reeds, canes, rattans, a dense and lavish undergrowth, in which reptiles, large and small, riot most congenially, and in which broods of mosquitoes are hourly hatched, to the misery of man and beast. Occasionally a small and comparatively cleared spot appears, with a crowded cluster of graves, with a pawn-shaped stone at the head of each, and the beautiful Frangipani,* the "Temple Flower" of Singhalese Buddhism, but the "Grave Flower" of Malay Mohammedanism, sheds its ethereal fragrance among the tombs. The dead lie lonely in the forest shade, under the feathery palm-fronds, but the living are not far to seek. [*Plumieria sp.]

It is strange that I should have written thus far and have said nothing at all about the people from whom this Peninsula derives its name, who have cost us not a little blood and some treasure, with whom our relations are by no means well defined or satisfactory, and who, though not the actual aborigines of the country, have at least that claim to be considered its rightful owners which comes from long centuries of possession. In truth, between English rule, the solid tokens of Dutch possession, the quiet and indolent Portuguese, the splendid memories of Francis Xavier, and the numerical preponderance, success, and wealth of the Chinese, I had absolutely forgotten the Malays, even though a dark-skinned military policeman, with a gliding, snake-like step, whom I know to be a Malay, brings my afternoon tea to the Stadthaus! Of them I may write more hereafter. They are symbolized to people's minds in general by the dagger called a kris, and by the peculiar form of frenzy which has given rise to the phrase "running amuck."

The great cocoa groves are by no means solitary, for they contain the kampongs, or small raised villages of the Malays. Though the Malay builds his dismal little mosques on the outskirts of Malacca, he shuns the town, and prefers a life of freedom in his native jungles, or on the mysterious rivers which lose themselves among the mangrove swamps. So in the neighborhood of Malacca these kampongs are scattered through the perpetual twilight of the forest. They do not build the houses very close together, and whether of rich or poor, the architecture is the same. Each dwelling is of planed wood or plaited palm leaves, the roof is high and steep, the eaves are deep, and the whole rests on a gridiron platform, supported on posts from five to ten feet high, and approached by a ladder in the poorer houses, and a flight of steps in the richer. In the ordinary houses mats are laid here and there over the gridiron, besides the sleeping mats; and this plan of an open floor, though trying to unaccustomed Europeans, has various advantages. As, for instance, it insures ventilation, and all debris can be thrown through it, to be consumed by the fire which is lighted every evening beneath the house to smoke away the mosquitoes. A baboon, trained to climb the cocoa palms and throw down the nuts, is an inmate of most of the houses.

The people lead strange and uneventful lives. The men are not inclined to much effort except in fishing or hunting, and, where they possess rice land, in ploughing for rice. They are said to be quiet, temperate, jealous, suspicious, some say treacherous, and most bigoted Mussulmen. The women are very small, keep their dwellings very tidy, and weave mats and baskets from reeds and palm leaves. They are clothed in cotton or silk from the ankles to the throat, and the men, even in the undress of their own homes, usually wear the sarong, a picturesque tightish petticoat, consisting of a wide piece of stuff kept on by a very ingenious knot. They are not savages in the ordinary sense, for they have a complete civilization of their own, and their legal system is derived from the Koran.

They are dark brown, with rather low foreheads, dark and somewhat expressionless eyes, high cheek bones, flattish noses with broad nostrils, and wide mouths with thick lips. Their hair is black, straight and shining, and the women dress it in a plain knot at the back of the head. To my thinking, both sexes are decidedly ugly, and there is a coldness and aloofness of manner about them which chills one even where they are on friendly terms with Europeans, as the people whom we visited were with Mrs. Biggs.

The women were lounging about the houses, some cleaning fish, others pounding rice; but they do not care for work, and the little money which they need for buying clothes they can make by selling mats, or jungle fruits. Their lower garment, or sarong, reaching from the waist to the ankles, is usually of red cotton of a small check, with stripes in the front, above which is worn a loose sleeved garment, called a kabaya, reaching to the knees, and clasped in front with silver or gold, and frequently with diamond ornaments. They also wear gold or silver pins in their hair, and the sarong is girt or held up by a clasp of enormous size, and often of exquisite workmanship, in the poorer class of silver, and in the richer of gold jeweled with diamonds and rubies. The sarong of the men does not reach much below the knee and displays loose trousers. They wear above it a short-sleeved jacket, the baju, beautifully made, and often very tastefully decorated in fine needlework, and with small buttons on each side, not for use, however. I have seen one Malay who wore about twenty buttons, each one a diamond solitaire! The costume is completed by turbans or red handkerchiefs tied round their heads.

In these forest kampongs the children, who are very pretty, are not encumbered by much clothing, specially the boys. All the dwellings are picturesque, and those of the richer Malays are beautiful. They rigidly exclude all ornaments which have "the likeness of anything in heaven or earth," but their arabesques are delicately carved, and the verses from the Koran, which occasionally run under the eaves, being in the Arabic character, are decidedly decorative. Their kampongs are small, and they have little of the gregarious instinct; they are said to live happily, and to have a considerable amount of domestic affection. Captain Shaw likes the Malays, and the verdict on them here is that they are chaste, gentle, honest and hospitable, but that they tell lies, and that their "honor" is so sensitive that blood alone can wipe out some insults to it. They seclude their women to a great extent, and under ordinary circumstances the slightest courtesy shown by a European man to a Malay woman would be a deadly insult; and at the sight of a man in the distance the women hastily cover their faces.

There is a large mosque with a minaret just on the outskirts of Malacca, and we passed several smaller ones in the space of three miles. Scarcely any kampong is so small as not to have a mosque. The Malays are bigoted, and for the most part ignorant and fanatical Mohammedans, and I firmly believe that the Englishman whom they respect most is only a little removed from being "a dog of an infidel." They are really ruled by the law of the Koran, and except when the Imaum, who interprets the law, decides (which is very rarely the case) contrary to equity, the British magistrate confirms his decision. In fact, Mohammedan law and custom rule in civil cases, and the Imaum of the mosque assists the judge with his advice. The Malays highly appreciate the manner in which law is administered under English rule, and the security they enjoy in their persons and property, so that they can acquire property without risk, and accumulate and wear the costliest jewels even in the streets of Malacca without fear of robbery or spoliation. This is by no means to write that the Malays love us, for I doubt whether the entente cordiale between any of the dark-skinned Oriental races and ourselves is more than skin deep. It is possible that they prefer being equitably taxed by us, with the security which our rule brings, to being plundered by native princes, but we do not understand them, or they us, and where they happen to be Mohammedans, there is a gulf of contempt and dislike on their part which is rarely bridged by amenities on ours. The pilgrimage to Mecca is the great object of ambition. Many Malays, in spite of its expense and difficulties, make it twice, and even three times. We passed three women clothed in white from head to foot, their drapery veiling them closely, leaving holes for their eyes. These had just returned from Mecca. The picturesqueness of the drive home was much heightened by the darkness, and the brilliancy of the fires underneath the Malay houses. The great gray buffalo which they use for various purposes—and which, though I have written gray, is as often pink—has a very thin and sensitive skin, and is almost maddened by mosquitoes; and we frequently passed fires lighted in the jungle, with these singular beasts standing or lying close to them in the smoke on the leeward side, while Malays in red sarongs and handkerchiefs, and pretty brown children scarcely clothed at all, lounged in the firelight. Then Chinese lamps and lanterns, and the sound of what passes for music; then the refinement and brightness of the Government bungalow, and at ten o'clock my chair with three bearers, and the solitude of the lonely Stadthaus.

I. L. B.

Letter X

Malacca Mediaevalism—Tiger Stories—The Chinese Carnival—Gold and Gems—A Weight of Splendor—New-Year Rejoicings—Syed Abdulrahman—A Mohammedan Princess—A Haunted City—Francis Xavier—The Reward of "Pluck"—Projects of Travel

STADTHAUS, MALACCA, January 23.

Malacca fascinates me more and more daily. There is, among other things, a mediaevalism about it. The noise of the modern world reaches it only in the faintest echoes; its sleep is almost dreamless, its sensations seem to come out of books read in childhood. Thus, the splendid corpse of a royal tiger has been brought in in a bullock-cart, the driver claiming the reward of fifteen dollars, and its claws were given to me. It was trapped only six miles off, and its beautiful feline body had not had time to stiffen. Even when dead, with its fierce head and cruel paws hanging over the end of the cart, it was not an object to be disrespected. The same reward is offered for a rhinoceros, five dollars for a crocodile (alligator?) and five dollars for a boa-constrictor or python. Lately, at five in the morning, a black tiger (panther?) came down the principal street of Malacca, tore a Chinamen in pieces, and then, scared by a posse of police in pursuit, jumped through a window into a house. Every door in the city was barred, as the rumor spread like wildfire. The policemen very boldly entered the house, but the animal pinned the Malay corporal to the wall. The second policeman, a white man, alas! ran away. The third, a Malay, at the risk of his life, went close up to the tiger, shot him, and beat him over the head with the butt of his rifle, which made the beast let go the corporal and turn on him, but fortunately he had scarcely got hold of him when he fell dead. The corporal is just coming out of hospital, almost completely paralyzed, to be taken care of for the rest of his life, and the man who rescued him has got promotion and a pension. A short time ago a fine young tiger was brought alive to Captain Shaw, and he ordered a proper cage to be made, in which to send him to England, telling Babu, the "double Hadji," to put it into the "godown" in its bamboo cage; but the man put it into the kitchen, and in the morning the cage was found broken into pieces, the kitchen shutters torn down, and the tiger gone! There was a complete panic in Malacca; people kept their houses shut, and did not dare to go out even on business, and not only was the whole police force turned out in pursuit, but the English garrison. It was some days before the scare subsided and the people believed that the beast had escaped to its natural home in the jungle.

A tropical thunderstorm of the most violent kind occurred yesterday, when I was quite alone in the Stadthaus. The rain fell in sheets, deluges, streams, and the lightning flashed perfectly blue through a "darkness which could be felt." There is a sort of grandeur about this old Dutch Stadthaus, with its tale of two centuries. Its smooth lawns, sloping steeply to the sea, are now brilliant with the gaudy parrot-like blossoms of the "flame of the forest," the gorgeous Poinciana regia, with which they are studded. Malacca is such a rest after the crowds of Japan and the noisy hurry of China! Its endless afternoon remains unbroken except by the dreamy, colored, slow-moving Malay life which passes below the hill. There is never any hurry or noise.

So had I written without prescience! The night of the awful silence which succeeded the thunderstorm was also the eve of the Chinese New Year, and Captain Shaw gave permission for "fireworks" from 7 P.M. till midnight. The term "fireworks" received a most liberal construction. The noise was something awful, and as it came into the lonely Stadthaus, and red, blue, crimson, and greenish-yellow glares at short intervals lighted up the picturesque Malacca steam and its blue and yellow houses, with their steep red-tiled roofs and balconies and quaint projections, and the streets were traced in fire and smoke, while crackers, squibs, and rockets went off in hundreds, and cannon, petards, and gingalls were fired incessantly, and gongs, drums, and tom-toms were beaten, the sights, and the ceaseless, tremendous, universal din made a rehearsal of the final assault on a city in old days. At 1 A.M., every house being decorated and illuminated, the Chinese men began to make their New Year's calls, and at six the din began again. After breakfast the Governor drove out in state to visit the leading Chinese merchants, with whom he is on terms of the most cordial amity, and at each house was offered two dishes of cakes, twelve dishes of candied and preserved fruits, mandarin tea (the price of this luxury is from 25s. to 45s. a pound), and champagne from the finest Rhenish vineyards! At eleven all the Chinese children came forth in carriages shaped like boats, turned up at both ends, painted red and yellow, and with white-fringed canopies over them. These were drawn by servants, and in the case of the wealthy, a train of servants accompanied each carriage. It was a sight worthy of a fabled age. The wealth of the East in all its gorgeousness was poured out upon these dignified and solemn infants, who wore coronals of gold and diamonds, stuffs of cloth of gold brocade, and satin sewn with pearls, and whose cloth-of-gold shoes flashed with diamonds!

During the morning four children of a rich Chinese merchant, attended by a train of Chinese and Malay servants, came to see Mrs. Shaw. There were a boy and girl of five and six years old, and two younger children. A literal description of their appearance reads like fiction. The girl wore a yellow petticoat of treble satin (mandarin yellow) with broad box plaits in front and behind, exquisitely embroidered with flowers in shades of blue silk, with narrow box plaits between, with a trail of blue silk flowers on each. Over this there was a short robe of crimson brocaded silk, with a broad border of cream-white satin, with the same exquisite floral embroidery in shades of blue silk. Above this was a tippet of three rows of embroidered lozenge-shaped "tabs" of satin. The child wore a crown on her head, the basis of which was black velvet. At the top was an aigrette of diamonds of the purest water, the centre one as large as a sixpenny-piece. Solitaires flashing blue flames blazed all over the cap, and the front was ornamented with a dragon in fine filigree work in red Malay gold set with diamonds. I fear to be thought guilty of exaggeration when I write that this child wore seven necklaces, all of gorgeous beauty. The stones were all cut in facets at the back; and highly polished, and their beauty was enhanced by the good taste and skilful workmanship of the setting. The first necklace was of diamonds set as roses and crescents, some of them very large, and all of great brilliancy; the second of emeralds, a few of which were as large as acorns, but spoilt by being pierced; the third of pearls set whole; the fourth of hollow filigree beads in red, burned gold; the fifth of sapphires and diamonds; the sixth a number of finely worked chains of gold with a pendant of a gold filigree fish set with diamonds; the seventh, what they all wear, a massive gold chain, which looked heavy enough even by itself to weigh down the fragile little wearer, from which depended a gold shield, on which the Chinese characters forming the child's name were raised in rubies, with fishes and flowers in diamonds round it, and at the back a god in rubies similarly surrounded. Magnificent diamond earrings and heavy gold bracelets completed the display.

And all this weight of splendor, valued at the very least at $40,000, was carried by a frail human mite barely four feet high, with a powdered face, gentle, pensive expression, and quiet grace of manner, who came forward and most winsomely shook hands with us, as did all the other grave gentle mites. They were also loaded with gold and diamonds. Some sugar-plums fell on the floor, and as the eldest girl stooped to pick them up, diamond solitaires fell out of her hair, which were gathered up by her attendants as if they were used to such occurrences. Whenever she moved her diamonds flashed, scintillated, and gave forth their blue light. Then came the children of the richest Chinaman in Malacca, but the little gentle creatures were motherless, and mourning for a mother lasts three years, so they were dressed in plain blue and white, and as ornaments wore only very beautiful sapphires and diamonds set in silver.

Do not suppose that the Chinese New Year is a fixed, annual holiday lasting a day, as in Scotland, and to a minor extent in England. In Canton a month ago active preparations were being made for it, and in Japan nine weeks ago. It is a "movable feast," and is regulated by the date on which the new moon falls nearest to the day "when the sun reaches the 15 degrees of Aquarius," and occurs this year on January 21st. Everything becomes cheap before it, for shopkeepers are anxious to realize ready money at any loss, for it is imperative that all accounts be closed by the last day of the old year, on pain of a man being disgraced, losing all hope of getting credit, and of having his name written up on his door as a defaulter. It appears also that debts which are not settled by the New Year's Eve cannot thereafter be recovered, though it is lawful for a creditor who has vainly hunted a debtor throughout that last night to pursue him for the first hours after daybreak, provided he still carries a lantern!

The festival lasts a fortnight, and is a succession of feasts and theatrical entertainments, everybody's object being to cast care and work to the winds. Even the official seals of the mandarins are formally and with much rejoicing sealed up and laid aside for one month. On the 20th day of the 12th month houses and temples are thoroughly washed and cleaned, rich and poor decorate with cloth-of-gold, silk embroideries, artificial and real flowers, banners, scrolls, lucky characters, illuminated strips of paper, and bunches of gilt-paper flowers, and even the poorest coolie contrives to greet the festival with some natural blossom. There is no rest either by night or day, joss-sticks burn incessantly, and lamps before the ancestral tablets, gongs are beaten, gingalls fire incessantly, and great crackers like cartridges fastened together in rows are let off at intervals before every door to frighten away evil spirits; there are family banquets of wearisome length, feasts to the household gods, offerings in the temples, processions in the street by torch and lantern light, presents are given to the living, and offerings to the dead, the poor are feasted, and the general din is heightened by messengers perambulating the streets with gongs, calling them to the different banquets. When the fortnight of rejoicing is over its signs are removed, and after the outbreak of extravagant expenditure the Chinese return to their quiet, industrious habits and frugal ways.

Just as this brilliant display left the room, a figure in richer coloring of skin appeared—Babu, the head servant, in his beautiful Hadji dress. He wore white full trousers, drawn in tightly at the ankles over black shoes, but very little of these trousers showed below a long, fine, linen tunic of spotless white, with a girdle of orange silk. Over this was a short jacket of rich green silk, embroidered in front with green of the same color, and over all a pure white robe falling from the shoulders. The turban was a Mecca turban made of many yards of soft white silk, embroidered in white silk. It was difficult to believe that this gorgeous Mussulman, in the odor of double sanctity, with his scornful face and superb air, could so far demean himself as to wait on "dogs of infidels" at dinner, or appear in my room at the Stadthaus, with matutinal tea and bananas!

This magnificence heralded the Datu Klana, Syed Abdulrahman, the reigning prince of the native State of Sungei Ujong, his principal wife, and his favorite daughter, a girl of twelve. It has been decided that I am to go to Sungei Ujong, and that I am to be escorted by Mr. Hayward, the superintendent of police, but, unfortunately, I am to go up in the Datu Klana's absence, and one object of his visit was to express his regret. This prince has been faithful to British interests, and is on most friendly terms with the resident, Captain Murray, and the Governor of Malacca. During his visit Babu interpreted, but Miss Shaw, who understands Malay, said that, instead of interpreting faithfully, he was making enormous demands on my behalf! At all events, Syed Abdulrahman, with truly exaggerated Oriental politeness, presented me with the key of his house in the interior.

This prince is regarded by British officials as an enlightened ruler, though he is a rigid Mussulman. His dress looked remarkably plain beside that of the splendid Babu. He wore a Malay bandana handkerchief round his head, knotted into a peak, a rich brocade baju or short jacket, a dark Manilla sarong, trousers of Mandarin satin striped with red, a girdle clasp set with large diamonds, and sandals with jeweled cloth-of-gold straps. His wife, though elderly and decidedly plain looking, has a very pleasing expression. She wore a black veil over her head, and her kabaya, or upper garment, was fastened with three diamond clasps. The bright little daughter wore a green veil with gold stars upon it over her head, and ornaments of rich, red gold elaborately worked. The Datu Klana apologized for the extreme plainness of their dress by saying that they had only just arrived, and that they had called before changing their traveling clothes. When they departed the two ladies threw soft silk shawls over their heads, and held them so as to cover their faces except their eyes.

There are now sixty-seven thousand Malays in the British territory of Malacca, and the number is continually increased by fugitives from the system of debt-slavery which prevails in some of the adjacent States, and by immigration from the same States of Malays who prefer the security which British rule affords.

> *[The police force is Malay, and it seems as if the Malays had a special aptitude for this semi-military service, for they not only form the well-drilled protective forces of Malacca, Sungei Ujong, and Selangor, but that fine body of police in Ceylon of which Mr. George Campbell has so much reason to be proud. Otherwise very few of them enter British employment, greatly preferring the easy, independent life of their forest kampongs.]*

The commercial decay of Malacca is a very interesting fact.* Formerly fifty merchantmen were frequently lying in its roads at one time. Here the Portuguese fleet lay which escorted Xavier from Goa, and who can say how many galleons freighted with the red gold of Ophir floated on these quiet waters! Now, Chinese junks, Malay prahus, a few Chinese steamers, steam-launches from the native States, and two steamers which call in passing, make up its trade. There is neither newspaper, banker, hotel, nor resident English merchant, The half-caste descendants of the Portuguese are, generally speaking, indolent, degraded with the degradation that is born of indolence, and proud. The Malays dream away their lives in the jungle, and the Chinese, who number twenty thousand, are really the ruling population.

> [*Linscholt, two hundred and seventy years ago, writes:—"This place is the market of all India, of China, and the Moluccas, and of other islands round about, from all which places, as well as from Banda, Java, Sumatra, Siam, Pegu, Bengal, Coromandil, and India, arrive ships which come and go incessantly charged with an infinity of merchandises."]

The former greatness of Malacca haunts one at all times. The romantic exploits of Albuquerque, who conquered it in 1511, apostrophized in the Lusiad—

> "Not eastward far though fair Malacca lie,
> Her groves embosomed in the morning sky,
> Though with her amorous sons the valiant line
> Of Java's isle in battle rank combine,
> Though poisoned shafts their ponderous quivers store,
> Malacca's spicy groves and golden ore,
> Great Albuquerque, thy dauntless toils shall crown,"

live again, though my sober judgment is that Albuquerque and most of his Portuguese successors were little better than buccaneers.

I like better to think of Francis Xavier passing through the thoroughfares of what was then the greatest commercial city of the East, ringing his bell, with the solemn cry, "Pray for those who are in a state of mortal sin." For among the "Jews, Turks, infidels, and heretics" who then thronged its busy streets, there were no worse livers than the roistering soldiers who had followed Albuquerque. Tradition among the present Portuguese residents says that coarse words and deeds disappeared from the thoroughfares under his holy influence, and that little altars were set up in public places, round which the children sang hymns to Jesus Christ, while the passers-by crossed themselves and bowed their heads reverently. Now, the cathedral which crowns the hill, roofless and ruinous, is only imposing from a distance, and a part of it is used for the storage of marine or lighthouse stores under our prosaic and irreverent rule. Xavier preached frequently in it and loved it well, yet the walls are overgrown with parasites, and the floor, under which many prelates and priests lie, is hideous with matted weeds, which are the haunt of snakes and lizards. Thus, in the city which was so dear to Xavier that he desired to return to it to die (and actually did die on his way thither), the only memento of him is the dishonored ruin of the splendid church in which his body was buried, with all the population of Malacca following it from the yellow strand up the grass-crowned hill, bearing tapers. This wretched ruin is a contrast to the splendid mausoleum at Goa, where his bones now lie, worthily guarded, in coffins of silver and gold.

If the Portuguese were little better than buccaneers, the Dutch, who drove them out, were little better than hucksters—mean, mercenary traders, without redeeming qualities; content to suck the blood of their provinces and give nothing in return. I should think that the colony is glad to be finally rid of them. The English took possession of it in 1795, but restored it to the Dutch in 1818, regaining it again by treaty in 1824, giving Bencoolen, in Sumatra, in exchange for it, stipulating at the same time that the Dutch were not to meddle with Malayan affairs, or have any settlement on the Malay Peninsula. The ruined cathedral of Notre Dame del Monte is a far more interesting object than the dull, bald, commonplace, flat-faced, prosaic, Dutch meeting-house, albeit the latter is in excellent repair. Even this Stadthaus, with its stately solitudes, smells of trade, and suggests corpulent burgomasters and prim burgomasters' wives in wooden hoops and stiff brocades. The influence of Holland has altogether vanished, as is fitting, for she cared only for nutmegs, sago, tapioca, tin and pepper.

The variety of races here produces a ludicrous effect sometimes. In the Stadthaus one never knows who is to appear—whether Malay, Portuguese, Chinaman, or Madrassee. Yesterday morning, at six, the Chinaman who usually "does" my room, glided in, murmuring something unintelligible, and on my not understanding him, brought in a Portuguese interpreter. At seven, came in the Madrassee, Babu, with a cluster of bananas, and after him, two Malays, in red sarongs, who brushed and dusted all my clothes as slowly as they could—men of four races in attendance before I was up in the morning! This Chinese attendant, besides being a common coolie in a brown cotton shirt over a brown cotton pair of trousers, is not a good specimen of his class, and is a great nuisance to me. My doors do not bolt properly, and he appears in the morning while I am in my holoku, writing, and slowly makes the bed and kills mosquitoes; then takes one gown after another from the rail, and stares at me till I point to the one I am going to wear, which he holds out in his hands; and though I point to the door, and say "Go!" with much emphasis, I never get rid of him, and have to glide from my holoku into my gown with a most unwilling dexterity.

Two days ago Captain Shaw declared that "pluck should have its reward," and that I should have facilities for going to Sungei Ujong. Yesterday, he asked me to take charge of his two treasured daughters. Then Babu said, "If young ladies go, me go," and we are to travel under the efficient protection of Mr. Hayward, the superintendent of police. This expedition excites great interest in the little Malacca world. This native State is regarded as "parts unknown;" the Governor has never visited it, and there are not wanting those who shake their heads and wonder that he should trust his girls in a region of tigers, crocodiles, rogue elephants and savages! The little steam-launch Moosmee (in reality by far the greatest risk of all) has been brought into the stream below the Stadthaus, ready for an early start to-morrow, and a runner has been sent to the Resident to prepare him for such an unusual incursion into his solitudes.

I. L. B.

A CHAPTER ON SUNGEI UJONG

The Puzzles of the Peninsula—Sungei Ujong—A Malay Confederation —Syed Abdulrahman—The Revenue of Sungei Ujong—Scenery and Productions—The New Datu Klana—A "Dual Control"

I had never heard of this little State until I reached Singapore, and probably many people are as ignorant as I was. The whole peninsula, from Johore in the south to Kedah in the north, is a puzzle, what with British colonies, Singapore, Malacca, and Province Wellesley, and "Protected States," Sungei Ujong, Selangor, and Perak, north, south, and east of which lie a region of unprotected Malay States, with their independent rulers, such as Kedah, Patani, Tringganu, Kelantan, Pahang, Johore, etc.* In several of these States, more or less anarchy prevails, owing to the ambitions and jealousies of the Rajahs and their followers, and a similar state of things in the three protected States formerly gave great annoyance to the Straits-Settlements Government, and was regarded as a hindrance to the dominant interests of British trade in the Straits.

[*A number of small States are united into a sort of confederation known as the Negri Sembilan, or Nine States. Their relative positions and internal management, as well as their boundaries, remain unknown, as from dread of British annexation they have refused to allow Europeans to pass through their territory.]

In 1874, Sir A. Clark, the then Governor, acting in British interests, placed British residents in Perak, Selangor, and the small State of Sungei

Ujong. These residents were to advise the rulers in matters of revenue and general administration, but, it may be believed, that as time has passed, they have become more or less the actual rulers of the States which they profess to advise merely. They are the accredited agents of England, reporting annually to the Straits Government, which, in its turn, reports to the Colonial Office, and the amount of pressure which they can bring to bear is overwhelming.

It is not easy to give the extent and boundaries of Sungei Ujong, the "boundary question" being scarcely settled, and the territory to the eastward being only partially explored. It is mainly an inland State, access to its very limited seaboard being by the Linggi river. The "protected" State of Selangor bounds it on the north, and joining on to it and to each other on the east, are the small "independent" States of Rumbow, Johol, Moar, Sri Menanti, Jelabu, Jompol, and Jelai. The Linggi river, which in its lower part forms the boundary between Selangor and Malacca, forks in its upper part, the right branch becoming for some distance the boundary between Sungei Ujong and Rumbow. It is doubtful whether the area of the State exceeds seven hundred square miles.

The Malays of Sungei Ujong and several of the adjacent States are supposed to be tolerably directly descended from those of the parent empire Menangkabau in Sumatra, who conquered and have to a great extent displaced the tribes known as Jakuns, Orang Bukit, Rayet Utan, Samangs, Besisik, Rayet Laut, etc., the remnants of which live mainly in the jungles of the interior, are everywhere apart from the Malays, and are of a much lower grade in the scale of civilization. The story current among the best informed Malays of this region is that a Sumatran chief with a large retinue crossed to Malacca in the twelfth century, and went into the interior, which he found inhabited only by the Jakuns, or "tree people." There his followers married Jakun women, and their descendants spread over Sungei Ujong, Rumbow, and other parts, the Rayet Laut, or "sea-people," the supposed Ichthyophagi of the ancients, and the Rayet Utan, or "forest-people," betaking themselves to the woods and the sea-board hills.

This mixed race rapidly increasing, divided into nine petty States, under chiefs who rendered feudal service to the Sultans of Malacca before its conquest by the Portuguese, and afterward to the Sultan of Johore, at whose court they presented themselves once a year. This confederation, called the Negri Sembilan, in the seventeenth and eighteenth centuries made various commercial treaties with the Dutch, but its domestic affairs were in a state of chronic feud, and four of the States, late in the eighteenth century, becoming disgusted with the arbitrary proceedings of a ruler who, aided by Dutch influence, had gained the ascendency over the whole nine, sent to Sumatra, the original source of government, for a prince of the blood-royal of Menangkabau, and after a prolonged conflict this prince became sovereign of the little States of Sungei Ujong, Rumbow, Johol, and Sri Menanti, the chiefs of these States constituting his Council of State. This dynasty came to an end in 1832, and intrigues and discord prevailed for many years, till the Datu Klana of Sungei Ujong, troubled by a hostile neighbor in Rumbow and a hostile subject or rival at home, conceived the bright idea of supporting his somewhat shaky throne by British protection.

After some curious negotiations, he succeeded in obtaining both a Resident and the English flag to protect his little fortunes; but it is obvious that his calling in foreign intervention was not likely to make him popular with his independent neighbors or disaffected subjects, and the troubles culminated in a "little war," in which the attacking force was composed of a few English soldiers, Malay military police, and a body of about eighty so-called Arabs, enlisted in Singapore and taken to the scene of action by Mr. Fontaine. The "enemy" was seldom obvious, but during the war it inflicted a loss upon us of eight killed and twenty-three wounded. We took various stockades, shot from sixty to eighty Malays, burned a good deal of what was combustible, and gave stability to the shaky rule of the Datu Klana, Syed Abdulrahman. Of this prince, who owed his firm seat on the throne to British intervention, the Resident wrote in 1880:—"Loyal to his engagements, he had gained the good will of the British Government. Straightforward, honest, and truly charitable, he had gained the love and respect of almost everyone in Sungei Ujong, Chinese as well as Malay, and if he had a fault he erred on the side of a weak belief in the goodness of human nature, and often suffered in consequence." This was Captain Murray's verdict after nearly five years' experience.

The population of this tiny State, which in 1832 consisted of three thousand two hundred Malays and four hundred Chinese, at the time of my visit had risen to twelve thousand, composed of three Europeans, a few Klings, two thousand Malays, and ten thousand Chinese. It exports tin in large quantities, gutta-percha collected in the interior by the aborigines, coffee, which promises to become an important production, buffalo hides, gum dammar, and gharroo. In 1879 the exports amounted to 81,976 pounds; 81,451 pounds being the value of tin. Its imports are little more than half this amount. Rice heads the list with an import of 18,150 pounds worth, and opium comes next, valued at 14,448 pounds. The third import in value is oil; the next Chinese tobacco, the next sugar, the next salt fish, and the next pigs! The Chinese, of course, consume most of what is imported, being in a majority of five to one, and here as elsewhere they carry with them their rigid conservatism in dress, mode of living, food, and amusements, and have a well-organized and independent system of communication with China. It is the Chinese merchant, not the British, who benefits by the rapidly augmenting Chinese population. Thus in the import list the Chinese tobacco, pigs, lard, onions, beans, vermicelli, salted vegetables, tea, crackers, joss-sticks, matches, Chinese candles, Chinese clothing, Chinese umbrellas, and several other small items, are all imported from China.

Having been debited with a debt of 10,000 pounds for war expenses, to be paid off by installments, the finances were much hampered, and the execution of road-making and other useful work has been delayed. This war debt, heavy as it was, was exclusive of 6,000 pounds previously paid off, and of heavy disbursements made to supply food and forage for the British soldiers who were quartered in Sungei Ujong for a considerable time. Apart from this harassing debt, the expenses are pre-eminently for "establishments," the construction of roads and bridges, and pensions to Rajahs whose former sources of revenue have been interfered with or abolished. The sources of revenue are to some extent remarkable, and it is possible that some of them might be altogether abolished if public attention became focussed upon them. Export duties are levied only on tin, the great product of Sungei Ujong, and gutta-percha. The chief import duty is on opium, and in 1879 this produced 4,182 pounds, or about one-fourth of the whole revenue. Besides this fruitful and growing source of income, 3,074 pounds was raised in 1879 under the head "Farms;" a most innocuous designation of a system which has nothing to do with the "kindly fruits of the earth" at all, but with spirits, gambling, oil, salt, opium, and a lottery! In other words, the "farms" are so many monopolies, sold at intervals to the highest bidder, the "gambling farm" being the most lucrative of the lot to the Government, and of course to the "farmer"!

The prison expenses are happily small, and the hospital expenses also, owing mainly in the former case to the efforts of the "Capitans China," who are responsible for their countrymen, and in the latter to the extreme healthiness of the climate. The military police force now consists of a European superintendent, ninety-four constables, paid 45s. per month, and twelve officers, all Malays; but as it is Malay nature to desire a change, and it is found impossible to retain the men for any lengthened periods, it is proposed to employ Sikhs, as in Perak.

Sungei Ujong, like the other States of the Peninsula, is almost entirely covered with forests, now being cleared to some extent by tapioca, gambier, and coffee-planters. Its jungles are magnificent, its hill scenery very beautiful, and its climate singularly healthy. Pepper, coffee, tapioca, cinchona, and ipecacuanha, are being tried successfully; burnt earth, of which the natives have a great opinion, and leaf mould being used in the absence of other manure.

The rainfall is supposed to average 100 inches a year, and since thermometrical observations have been taken the mercury has varied from

68 degrees to 92 degrees. From the mangrove swamps at the mouths of turbid, sluggish rivers, where numberless alligators dwell in congenial slime, the State gradually rises inland, passing through all the imaginable wealth of tropical vegetation and produce till it becomes hilly, if not mountainous. Sparkling streams dash through limestone fissures, the air is clear, and the nights are fresh and cool. Its mineral wealth lies in its tin mines, which have been worked mainly by Chinamen for a great number of years.

The British Resident, who was called in to act as adviser, is practically the ruler of this little State, and the arrangement seems to give tolerable satisfaction. At all events it has secured to Sungei Ujong since the war an amount of internal tranquillity which is not possessed by the adjacent States which are still under native rule, though probably the dread of British intervention and of being reduced to mere nominal sovereignty, being "pensioned off" in fact, keeps the Rajahs from indulging in the feuds and exactions of former years. Since my visit the Datu Klana died of dysentery near Jeddah in Arabia in returning from a pilgrimage to Mecca, and three out of six of his followers perished of the same disease. The succession was quietly arranged, but the hope that the State to which its late ruler was intensely, even patriotically attached might remain prosperous under the new Rajah, has not been altogether fulfilled. Affairs are certainly not as satisfactory as they were, judging from recent official statements. The import of opium has largely increased. Rice planting had failed owing to the mortality and sickness among the buffaloes used in ploughing, the scanty crop was nearly destroyed by rats, and the Malays had shown a "determined opposition" to taking out titles to their lands.

The new Datu Klana is very unpopular, and so remarkably weak in character as not to be able to bring any influence to bear upon the settlement of any difficult question. The Datu Bandar (alluded to in my letter) is entirely opposed to progress of every kind, and, having a great deal of influence, obstructs the present Resident in every attempt to come to an understanding on the land grant question. A virulent cattle disease had put an end for the time being to cart traffic; and the Linggi, the great high-road to the tin mines, had become so shallow that the means of water transport were very limited. Large numbers of jungle workers had returned to Malacca. The Resident's report shows very significantly the formidable difficulties which attend on the system of a "Dual Control," and on making any interference with "Malay custom" regarding land, etc. It is scarcely likely, however, that Sungei Ujong and the other feeble protected States which have felt the might of British arms, and are paying dearly through long years for their feeble efforts at independence, will ever seek to shake off the present system, which, on the whole, gives them security and justice.

Letter XI

*A Mangrove Swamp—Jungle Dwellers—The Sempang Police Station—
Shooting Alligators—The River Linggi—A Somber-Faced Throng—
Stuck Fast at Permatang Pasir—Fair Impediments*

SEMPANG POLICE STATION

(At the junction of the Loboh-Chena, and Linggi rivers), Territory of the Datu Klana of Sungei Ujong, Malay Peninsula. January 24, 1 P.M. Mercury, 87 degrees.)

We left Malacca at seven this morning in the small, unseaworthy, untrustworthy, unrigged steam-launch Moosmee, and after crawling for some hours at a speed of about five miles an hour along brown and yellow shores with a broad, dark belt of palms above them, we left the waveless, burning sea behind, and after a few miles of tortuous steaming through the mangrove swamps of the Linggi river, landed here to wait for sufficient water for the rest of our journey.

This is a promontory covered with cocoa-palms, bananas, and small jungle growths. On either side are small rivers densely bordered by mangrove swamps. The first sight of a real mangrove swamp is an event. This mangi-mangi of the Malays (the Rhizophera mangil of botanists) has no beauty. All along this coast within access of tidal waters there is a belt of it many miles in breadth, dense, impenetrable, from forty to fifty feet high, as nearly level as may be, and of a dark, dull green. At low water the mangroves are seen standing close packed along the shallow and muddy shores on cradles or erections of their own roots five or six feet high, but when these are covered at high tide they appear to be growing out of the water. They send down roots from their branches, and all too quickly cover a large space. Crabs and other shell-fish attach themselves to them, and aquatic birds haunt their slimy shades. They form huge breeding grounds for alligators and mosquitoes, and usually for malarial fevers, but from the latter the Peninsula is very free. The seeds germinate while still attached to the branch. A long root pierces the covering and grows rapidly downward from the heavy end of the fruit, which arrangement secures that when the fruit falls off the root shall at once become embedded in the mud. Nature has taken abundant trouble to insure the propagation of this tree, nearly worthless as timber. Strange to say, its fruit is sweet and eatable, and from its fermented juice wine can be made. The mangrove swamp is to me an evil mystery.

Behind, the jungle stretches out—who can say how far, for no European has ever penetrated it?—and out of it rise, jungle-covered, the Rumbow hills. The elephant, the rhinoceros, the royal tiger, the black panther, the boar, the leopard, and many other beasts roam in its tangled, twilight depths, but in this fierce heat they must be all asleep in their lairs. The Argus-pheasant too, one of the loveliest birds of a region whose islands are the home of the Bird of Paradise, haunts the shade, and the shade alone. In the jungle too, is the beautiful bantam fowl, the possible progenitor of all that useful race. The cobra, the python (?), the boa-constrictor, the viper, and at least fourteen other ophidians, are winding their loathsome and lissom forms through slimy jungle recesses; and large and small apes and monkeys, flying foxes, iguanas, lizards, peacocks, frogs, turtles, tortoises, alligators, besides tapirs, rarely seen, and the palandok or chevrotin, the hog deer, the spotted deer, and the sambre, may not be far off. I think that this part of the country, intersected by small, shallow, muddy rivers, running up through slimy mangrove swamps into a vast and impenetrable jungle, must be like many parts of Western Africa.

One cannot walk three hundred yards from this station, for there are no tracks. We are beyond the little territory of Malacca, but this bit of land was ceded to England after the "Malay disturbances" in 1875, and on it has been placed the Sempang police station, a four-roomed shelter, roofed with attap, a thatch made of the fronds of the nipah palm, supported on high posts—an idea perhaps borrowed from the mangrove—and reached by a ladder. In this four Malay policemen and a corporal have dwelt for three years to keep down piracy. "Piracy," by which these rivers were said to be infested, is a very ugly word, suggestive of ugly deeds, bloody attacks, black flags, and no quarter; but here it meant, in our use of the word at least, a particular mode of raising revenue, and no boat could go up or down the Linggi without paying black-mail to one or more river rajahs.

Our wretched little launch, moored to a cocoa-palm, flies a blue ensign, and the Malay policemen wear an imperial crown upon their caps, both representing somewhat touchingly in this equatorial jungle the might of the small island lying far off amidst the fogs of the northern seas, and in this instance at least not her might only, but the security and justice of her rule.

Two or three canoes hollowed out of tree trunks have gone up and down the river since we landed, each of the inward bound being paddled by four men, who ply their paddles facing forward, which always has an aboriginal look, those going down being propelled by single, square sails made of very coarse matting. It is very hot and silent. The only sounds are the rustle of the palm fronds and the sharp din of the cicada, abruptly ceasing at intervals. In this primitive police station the notices are in both Tamil and Arabic, but the reports are written in Arabic only. Soon after we sat down to drink fresh cocoa-nut milk, the great beverage of the country, a Malay bounded up the ladder and passed through us, with the most rapid and feline movements I have ever seen in a man. His large prominent eyes were fixed, tiger-like, on a rifle which hung on the wall, at which he darted, clutched it, and, with a feline leap, sprang through us again.

I have heard much of amok running lately, and have even seen the two-pronged fork which was used for pinning a desperate amok runner to the wall, so that for a second I thought that this Malay was "running amuck;" but he ran down toward Mr. Hayward, our escort, and I ran after him, just in time to see a large alligator plunge from the bank into the water. Mr. Hayward took a steady aim at the remaining one, and hit him, when he sprang partly up as if badly wounded, and then plunged into the river after his companion, staining the muddy water with his blood for some distance.

Police Station, Permatang Pasir, Sungei Ujong, 5 P.M.—We are now in a native State, in the Territory of the friendly Datu Klana, Syed Abdulrahman, and the policemen wear on their caps not an imperial crown, but a crescent, with a star between its horns.

This is a far more adventurous expedition than we expected. Things are not going altogether as straight as could be desired, considering that we have the Governor's daughters with us, who, besides being very precious, are utterly unseasoned and inexperienced travelers, quite unfit for "roughing it." For one thing, it turns out to be an absolute necessity for us to be out all night, which I am very sorry for, as one of the girls is suffering from the effects of exposure to the intense heat of the sun.

We left Sempang at two, the Misses Shaw reeling rather than walking to the launch. I cannot imagine what the mercury was in the sun, but the copper sheathing of the gunwale was too hot to be touched. Above Sempang the river narrows and shoals rapidly, and we had to crawl, taking soundings incessantly, and occasionally dragging heavily over mud banks. We saw a large alligator sleeping in the sun on the mud, with a mouth, I should think, a third of the length of his body; and as he did not wake as we panted past him, a rifle was loaded and we backed up close to him; but Babu, who had the weapon, and had looked quite swaggering and belligerent so long as it was unloaded, was too frightened to fire; the saurian awoke, and his hideous form and corrugated hide plunged into the water, so close under the stern as to splash us.

After this, alligators were so common, singly or in groups, or in families, that they ceased to be exciting. It is difficult for anything to produce continuous excitement under this fierce sun; and conversation, which had been flagging before noon, ceased altogether. It was awfully hot in the launch, between fire and boiler-heat and solar fury. I tried to keep cool by thinking of Mull, and powdery snow and frosty stars, but it would not do.

It was a solemn afternoon, as the white, unwinking sun looked down upon our silent party, on the narrow turbid river, silent too, except for the occasional plunge of an alligator or other water monster—on mangrove swamps and nipah palms dense along the river side, on the blue gleam of countless kingfishers, on slimy creeks arched over to within a few feet of their surface by grand trees with festoon of lianas, on an infinite variety of foliage, on an abundance of slender-shafted palms, on great fruits brilliantly colored, on wonderful flowers on the trees, on the hoya carnosa and other waxen-leaved trailers matting the forest together and hanging down in great festoons, the fiery tropic sunblaze stimulating all this over-production into perennial activity, and vivifying the very mud itself.

Occasionally we passed a canoe with a "savage" crouching in it fishing, but saw no other trace of man, till an hour ago we came upon large cocoa groves, a considerable clearing in the jungle, and a very large Malayan-Chinese village with mosques, one on either side of the river, houses built on platforms over the water, large and small native boats covered and thatched with attap, roofed platforms on stilts answering the purpose of piers, bathing-houses on stilts carefully secluded, all forming the (relatively) important village of Permatang Pasir.

Up to this time we had expected to find perfectly smooth sailing, as a runner was sent from Malacca to the Resident yesterday. We supposed that we should be carried in chairs six miles through the jungle to a point where a gharrie could meet us, and that we should reach the Residency by nine tonight at the latest. On arriving at Sempang,

Mr. Hayward had sent a canoe to this place with instructions to send another runner to the Resident; but

"The best laid schemes of men and mice gang aft aglee."

The messenger seemed to have served no other purpose than to assemble the whole male population of Permatang Pasir on the shore—a sombre-faced throng, with an aloofness of manner and expression far from pleasing. The thatched piers were crowded with turbaned Mussulmen in their bajus or short jackets, full white trousers, and red sarongs or plaitless kilts—the boys dressed in silver fig-leaves and silver bangles only. All looked at our unveiled faces silently, and, as I thought, disapprovingly.

After being hauled up the pier with great difficulty, owing to the lowness of the water, we were met by two of the Datu Klana's policemen, who threw cold water on the idea of our getting on at all unless Captain Murray sent for us. These men escorted us to this police station—a long walk through a lane of much decorated shops, exclusively Chinese, succeeded by a lane of detached Malay houses, each standing in its own fenced and neatly sanded compound under the shade of cocoa-palms and bananas.

The village paths are carefully sanded and very clean. We emerged upon the neatly sanded open space on which this barrack stands, glad to obtain shelter, for the sun is still fierce. It is a genuine Malay house on stilts; but where there should be an approach of eight steps there is only a steep ladder of three round rungs, up which it is not easy to climb in boots! There is a deep veranda under an attap roof of steep slope, and at either end a low bed for a constable, with the usual very hard, circular Malay bolsters, with red silk ends, ornamented with gold and silk embroidery.

Besides this veranda there is only a sort of inner room, with just space enough for a table and four chairs. The wall is hung with rifles, krises, and handcuffs, with which a "Sam Slick" clock, an engraving from the Graphic, and some curious Turkish pictures of Stamboul, are oddly mixed up.

Babu, the Hadji, having recovered from a sulk into which he fell in consequence of Mr. Hayward having quizzed him for cowardice about an alligator, has made everything (our very limited everything) quite comfortable, and, with as imposing an air as if we were in Government House, asks us when we will have dinner! One policeman has brought us fresh cocoa-nut milk, another sits outside pulling a small punkah, and two more have mounted guard over us. This stilted house is the barrack of eleven Malay constables. Under it are four guns of light calibre, mounted on carriages, and outside is a gong on which the policemen beat the hours.

At the river we were told that the natives would not go up the shallow, rapid stream by night, and now the corporal says that no man will carry us through the jungle; that trees are lying across the track; that there are dangerous swamp holes; that though the tigers which infest the jungle never attack a party, we might chance to see their glaring eyeballs; that even if men could be bribed to undertake to carry us, they would fall with us, or put us down and run away, for no better reason than that they caught sight of the "spectre bird" (the owl); and he adds, with a gallantry remarkable in a Mohammedan, that he should not care about Mr. Hayward, "but it would not do for the ladies."

So we are apparently stuck fast, the chief cause for anxiety and embarrassment being that the youngest Miss Shaw is lying huddled up and shivering on one of the beds, completely prostrated by a violent sick headache, brought on by the heat of the sun in the launch. She declares that she cannot move; but our experienced escort, who much fears bilious fever for her, is resolved that she shall as soon as any means of transit can be procured. Heretofore, I have always traveled "without encumbrance." Is it treasonable to feel at this moment that these fair girls are one?

I. L. B.

Letter XII

The Tomb of "A Great Prophet"—"Durance Vile"—Fragile Travelers—Our Craft—A Night in the Jungle—Nocturnal Revelations—January in the Perak Jungle—Glories of the Jungle—Activity and Stillness—An Uneasy Night—A Slim Repast—Betel-Chewing—A Severe Disappointment—Police Station at Rassa

BRITISH RESIDENCY, SERAMBANG, SUNGEI UJONG, January 26.

By the date of my letter you will see that our difficulties have been surmounted. I continue my narrative in a temperature which, in my room—shaded though it is—has reached 87 degrees. After hearing many pros and cons, and longing much for the freedom of a solitary traveler, I went out and visited the tomb of a famous Hadji, "a great prophet," the policeman said, who was slain in ascending the Linggi. It is a raised mound, like our churchyard graves, with a post at each end, and a jar of oil upon it, and is surrounded by a lattice of reeds on which curtains are hanging, the whole being covered with a thatched roof supported on posts.

The village looks prosperous, and the Chinaman as much at home as in China,—striving, thriving, and oblivious of everything but his own interests, the sole agent in the development of the resources of the country, well satisfied with our, or any rule, under which his gains are quick and safe.

There are village officers, or headmen, Pangulus, in all villages, and every hamlet of more than forty houses has its mosque and religious officials, though Mohammedanism does not recognize the need of a priesthood. If one see a man, with the upper part of his body unclothed, paddling a log canoe, face forward, one is apt to call him a savage, specially if he be dark-skinned; but the Malays would be much offended if they were called savages, and, indeed, they are not so. They have an elaborate civilization, etiquette, and laws of their own; are the most rigid of monotheists, are decently clothed, build secluded and tolerably comfortable houses, and lead domestic lives after their fashion, especially where they are too poor to be polygamists, though I am of opinion that the peculiar form of domesticity which we still cultivate to some extent in England, and which is largely connected with the fireside, cannot exist in a tropical country. After the obtrusive nudity and promiscuous bathing of the Japanese, there is something specially pleasing in the little secluded bathing sheds by the Malay rivers, used by one person at a time, who throws a sarong on the thatch to show that the shed is occupied.

Babu made some excellent soup, which, together with curry made with fresh cocoa-nut, was a satisfactory meal, and though only in a simple, white, Indian costume, he waited as grandly as at Malacca. Mr. Hayward's knowledge of the peculiarities of the Malay character, at last obtained our release from what was truly "durance vile." He sent for a boatman apart from his fellows, and induced him to make a bargain for taking us up the river at night; but the man soon returned in a state of great excitement, complaining that the villagers had set on him, and were resolved that we should not go up, upon which the police went down and interfered. Even after everything was settled, Miss Shaw was feeling so ill that she wanted to stay in the police station all night, at least; but Mr. Hayward and I, who consulted assiduously about her, were of opinion that we must move her, even if we had to carry her, for if she were going to have fever, I could nurse her at Captain Murray's, but certainly not in the veranda of a police station!

This worthy man, who is very brave, and used to facing danger—who was the first European to come up here, who acted as guide to the troops during the war, and afterward disarmed the population—positively quailed at having charge of these two fragile girls. "Oh," he repeated several times, "if anything were to happen to the Misses Shaw I should never get over it, and they don't know what roughing it is; they never should have been allowed to come." So I thought, too, as I looked at one of them lying limp and helpless on a Malay bed; but my share of the responsibility for them was comparatively limited. Doubtless his thoughts strayed, as mine did, to the days of traveling "without encumbrance." There was another encumbrance of a literal kind. They had a trunk! This indispensable impediment had been left at Malacca in the morning, and arrived in a four-paddled canoe just as we were about to start!

Mr. Hayward prescribed two tablespoonfuls of whisky for Miss Shaw, for it is somewhat of a risk to sleep out in the jungle at the rainy season, for the miasma rises twenty feet, and the day had been exceptionally hot. Our rather dismal procession started at seven, Mr. Hayward leading the way, carrying a torch made of strips of palm branches bound tightly together and dipped in gum dammar, a most inflammable resin; then a policeman; the sick girl, moaning and stumbling, leaning heavily on her sister and me; Babu, who had grown very plucky; a train of policemen carrying our baggage; and lastly, several torch-bearers, the torches dripping fire as we slowly and speechlessly passed along. It looked like a funeral or something uncanny. We crawled dismally for fully three-quarters of a mile to cut off some considerable windings of the river, crossed a stream on a plank bridge, and found our boat lying at a very high pier with a thatched roof.

The mystery of night in a strange place was wildly picturesque; the pale, greenish, undulating light of fireflies, and the broad, red waving glare of torches flashing fitfully on the skeleton pier, the lofty jungle trees, the dark, fast-flowing river, and the dark, lithe forms of our half-naked boatmen.

The prahu was a flattish-bottomed boat about twenty-two and a half feet long by six and a half feet broad, with a bamboo gridiron flooring resting on the gunwale for the greater part of its length. This was covered for seven feet in the middle by a low, circular roof, thatched with attap. It was steered by a broad paddle loosely lashed, and poled by three men who, standing at the bow, planted their poles firmly in the mud and then walked half-way down the boat and back again. All craft must ascend the Linggi by this laborious process, for its current is so strong that the Japanese would call it one long "rapid." Descending loaded with tin, the stream brings boats down with great rapidity, the poles being used only to keep them off the banks and shallows. Our boat was essentially "native."

The "Golden Chersonese" is very hot, and much infested by things which bite and sting. Though the mercury has not been lower than 80 degrees at night since I reached Singapore, I have never felt the heat overpowering in a house; but the night on the river was awful, and after the intolerable blaze of the day the fighting with the heat and mosquitoes was most exhausting, crowded as we were into very close and uneasy quarters, a bamboo gridiron being by no means a bed of down. Bad as it was, I was often amused by the thought of the unusual feast which the jungle mosquitoes were having on the blood of four white people. If it had not been for the fire in the bow, which helped to keep them down by smoking them (and us), I at least should now be laid up with "mosquito fever."

The Misses Shaw and I were on a blanket on the gridiron under the roof, which just allowed of sitting up; Mr. Hayward, who had never been up the river before, and was anxious about the navigation, sat, vigilant and lynx-eyed, at the edge of it; Babu, who had wrapped himself in Oriental impassiveness and a bernouse, and Mr. Hayward's police attendant sat in front, all keeping their positions throughout the night as dutifully as the figures in a tableau vivant, and so we silently left Permatang Pasir for our jungle voyage of eighteen hours, in which time, by unintermitting hard work, we were propelled about as many miles, though some say twenty-nine.

No description could exaggerate the tortuosity of the Linggi or the abruptness of its windings. The boatmen measure the distance by turns. When they were asked when we should reach the end they never said in so many hours, but in so many turns.

Silently we glided away from the torchlight into the apparently impenetrable darkness, but the heavens, of which we saw a patch now and then, were ablaze with stars, and ere long the forms of trees above and around us became tolerably distinct. Ten hours of darkness followed as we poled our slow and tedious way through the forest gloom, with trees to right of us, trees to left of us, trees before us, trees behind us, trees above us, and, I may write, trees under us, so innumerable were the snags and tree trunks in the river. The night was very still,—not a leaf moved, and at times the silence was very solemn. I expected, indeed, an unbroken silence, but there were noises that I shall never forget. Several times there was a long shrill cry, much like the Australian "Coo-ee," answered from a distance in a tone almost human. This was the note of the grand night bird, the Argus pheasant, and is said to resemble the cry of the "orang-outang," the Jakkuns, or the wild men of the interior. A sound like the constant blowing of a steam-whistle in the distance was said to be produced by a large monkey. Yells, hoarse or shrill, and roars more or less guttural, were significant of any of the wild beasts with which the forest abounds, and recalled the verse in Psalm civ., "Thou makest darkness that it may be night, wherein all the beasts of the forest do move." Then there were cries as of fierce gambols, or of pursuit and capture, of hunter and victim; and at times, in the midst of profound stillness, came huge plungings, with accompanying splashings, which I thought were made by alligators, but which Captain Murray thinks were more likely the riot of elephants disturbed while drinking. There were hundreds of mysterious and unfamiliar sounds great and small, significant of the unknown beast, reptile, and insect world which the jungle hides, and then silences.

Sheet lightning, very blue, revealed at intervals the strong stream swirling past under a canopy of trees falling and erect, with straight stems one hundred and fifty feet high probably, surmounted by crowns of drooping branches; palms with their graceful plumage; lianas hanging, looping, twisting—their orange fruitage hanging over our heads; great black snags; the lithe, wiry forms of our boat-men always straining to their utmost; and the motionless white turban of the Hadji,—all for a second relieved against the broad blue flame, to be again lost in darkness.

The Linggi above Permatang Pasir, with its sharp turns and muddy hurry, is, I should say, from thirty to sixty feet wide, a mere pathway through the jungle. Do not think of a jungle, as I used to think of it, as an entanglement or thicket of profuse and matted scrub, for it is in these regions at least a noble forest of majestic trees, many of them supported at their roots by three buttresses, behind which thirty men could find shelter. On many of the top branches of these, other trees have taken root from seeds deposited by birds, and have attained considerable size; and all send down, as it *appears*, extraordinary cylindrical strands from two to six inches in diameter, and often one hundred and fifty feet in length, smooth and straight until they root themselves, looking like the guys of a mast. Under these giants stand the lesser trees grouped in glorious confusion,—cocoa, sago, areca, and gomuti palms, nipah and nibong palms, tree ferns fifteen and twenty feet high, the bread-fruit, the ebony, the damar, the india rubber, the gutta-percha, the cajeput, the banyan, the upas, the bombax or cotton tree, and hosts of others, many of which bear brilliant flowers, but have not yet been botanized; and I can only give such barbarous names as chumpaka, Kamooning, marbow, seum, dadap; and, loveliest of all, the waringhan, a species of ficus, graceful as a birch; and underneath these again great ferns, ground orchids, and flowering shrubs of heavy, delicious odor, are interlocked and interwoven. Oh that you could see it all! It is wonderful; no words could describe it, far less mine. Mr. Darwin says so truly that a visit to the tropics (and such tropics) is like a visit to a new planet. This new wonder-world, so enchanting, tantalizing, intoxicating, makes me despair, for I cannot make you see what I am seeing! Amidst all this wealth of nature and in this perennial summer heat I quite fail to realize that it is January, and that with you the withered plants are shriveling in the frost-bound earth, and that leafless twigs and the needles of half-starved pines are shivering under the stars in the aurora-lighted winter nights.

But to the jungle again, The great bamboo towers up along the river sides in its feathery grace, and behind it the much prized Malacca cane, the rattan, creeping along the ground or climbing trees and knotting them together, with its tough strands, from a hundred to twelve hundred feet in length, matted and matting together while ferns, selaginellas, and lycopodiums struggle for space in which to show their fragile beauty, along with hardier foliaceous plants, brown and crimson, green and crimson, and crimson flecked with gold; and the great and lesser trees alike are loaded with trailers, ferns, and orchids, among which huge masses of the elk-horn fern and the shining five-foot fronds of the Asplenium Nidus are everywhere conspicuous.

Not only do orchids crowd the branches, and the hoya carnosa, the yam, the blue-blossomed Thunbergia, the vanilla (?), and other beautiful creepers, conceal the stems, while nearly every parasitic growth carries another parasite, but one sees here a filament carelessly dangling from a branch sustaining some bright-hued epiphyte of quaint mocking form; then a branch as thick as a clipper's main-mast reaches across the river, supporting a festooned trailer, from whose stalks hang, almost invisibly suspended, oval fruits, almost vermilion colored; then again the beautiful vanilla and the hoya carnosa vie with each other in wreathing the same tree; or an audacious liana, with great clusters of orange or scarlet blossoms, takes possession of several trees at once, lighting up the dark greenery with its flaming splotches; or an aspiring trailer, dexterously linking its feebleness to the strength of other plants, leaps across the river from tree to tree at a height of a hundred feet, and, as though in mockery, sends down a profusion of crimson festoons far out of reach. But it is as useless to attempt to catalogue as to describe. To realize an equatorial jungle one must see it in all its wonderment of activity and stillness—the heated, steamy stillness through which one fancies that no breeze ever whispers, with its colossal flowering trees, its green twilight, its inextricable involvement, its butterflies and moths, its brilliant but harsh voiced birds, its lizards and flying foxes, its infinite variety of monkeys, sitting, hanging by hands or tails, leaping, grimacing, jabbering, pelting each other with fruits; and its loathsome saurians, lying in wait on slimy banks under the mangroves. All this and far more the dawn revealed upon the Linggi river; but strange to say, through all the tropic splendor of the morning, I saw a vision of the Trientalis Europea, as we saw it first on a mossy hillside in Glen Cannich!

But I am forgetting that the night with its blackness and mystery came before the sunrise, that the stars seldom looked through the dense leafage, and that the pale green lamps of a luminous fungus here and there, and the cold blue sheet-lightning only served to intensify the solemnity of the gloom. While the blackest part of the night lasted the "view" was usually made up of the black river under the foliage, with scarcely ten yards of its course free from obstruction—great snags all along it sticking up menacingly, trees lying half or quite across it, with barely room to pass under them, or sometimes under water, when the boat "drave heavily" over them, while great branches brushed and ripped the thatch continually; and as one obstacle was safely passed, the rapidity of the current invariably canted us close on another, but the vigilant skill of the boatmen averted the slightest accident. "Jaga! Jaga!"—caution! caution!—was the constant cry. The most unpleasant sensations were produced by the constant ripping and tearing sounds as we passed under the low tunnel of vegetation, and by the perpetual bumping against timber.

The Misses Shaw passed an uneasy night. The whisky had cured the younger one of her severe sick headache, and she was the prey of many terrors. They thought that the boat would be ripped up; that the roof would be taken off; that a tree would fall and crush us; that the boatmen, when they fell overboard, as they often did, would be eaten by alligators; that they would see glaring eyeballs whenever the cry "Rimou!"—a tiger!—was raised from the bow; and they continually awoke me with news of something that was happening or about to happen, and were drolly indignant because they could not sleep; while I, a blasee old campaigner, slept whenever they would let me. Day broke in a heavy mist, which disappeared magically at sunrise. As the great sun wheeled rapidly above the horizon and blazed upon us with merciless fierceness, all at once the jungle became vociferous. Loudly clattered the busy cicada, its simultaneous din, like a concentration of the noise of all the looms in the world, suddenly breaking off into a simultaneous silence; the noisy insect world chirped, cheeped, buzzed, whistled; birds hallooed, hooted, whooped, screeched; apes in a loud and not inharmonious chorus greeted the sun; and monkeys chattered, yelled, hooted, quarreled, and spluttered. The noise was tremendous. But the forest was absolutely still, except when some heavy fruit, over ripe, fell into the river with a splash. The trees above us were literally alive with monkeys, and the curiosity of some of them about us was so great that they came down on "monkey ropes" and branches for the fun of touching the roof of the boat with their hands while they hung by their tails. They were all full of frolic and mischief.

Then we had a slim repast of soda water and bananas, the Hadji worshiped with his face toward Mecca, and the boatmen prepared an elaborate curry for themselves, with salt fish for its basis, and for its tastiest condiment blachang—a Malay preparation much relished by European lovers of durion and decomposed cheese. It is made by trampling a mass of putrefying prawns and shrimps into a paste with bare feet. This is seasoned with salt. The smell is penetrating and lingering. Our men made the boat fast, rinsed their mouths, washed their hands, and ate, using their fingers instead of chopsticks. Poor fellows! they had done twelve hours of splendid work.

Then one of them prepared the betel-nut for the rest. I think I have not yet alluded to this abominable practice of betel-nut chewing, which is universal among the inhabitants of the Malay Peninsula; the betel-nut being as essential to a Malay as tobacco is to a Japanese, or opium to the confirmed Chinese opium-smoker. It is a revolting habit, and if a person speaks to you while he is chewing his "quid" of betel, his mouth looks as if it were full of blood. People say that the craving for stimulants is created by our raw, damp climate; but it is as strong here, at the equator, in this sunny, balmy air. I have not yet come across a region in which men, weary in body or spirit, are not seeking to stimulate or stupefy themselves. The Malay men and women being prohibited by the Koran from using alcohol, find the needed fillip in this nut, but it needs preparation before it suits their palates.

The betel-nut is the fruit of the lovely, graceful, slender-shafted areca palm. This tree at six years old begins to bear about one hundred nuts a year, which grow in clusters, each nut being about the size of a nutmeg, and covered with a yellow, fibrous husk. The requisites for chewing are: a small piece of areca nut, a leaf of the Sirih or betel pepper, a little moistened lime, and, if you wish to be very luxurious, a paste made of spices. The Sirih leaf was smeared with a little fine lime taken from a brass box; on this was laid a little, brownish paste; on this, a bit of the nut; the leaf was then folded neatly round its contents, and the men began to chew, and to spit—the inevitable consequence. The practice stains the teeth black. I tasted the nut, and found it pungent and astringent, not tempting. The Malays think you look like a beast if you have white teeth.

The heat was exhausting; the mercury 87 degrees in the shade as early as 8:30, and we all suffered, more or less, from it in our cramped position and enforced inactivity. At nine, having been fourteen hours on the river, we came on a small cleared space, from which a bronzed, frank-faced man, dressed in white linen, hallooed to us jovially, and we were soon warmly greeted by Captain Murray, the British Resident in the State of Sungei Ujong. On seeing him, we hoped to find a gharrie and to get some breakfast; and he helped us on shore, as if our hopes were to be realized, and dragged us under the broiling sun to a long shed, the quarters of a hundred Chinese coolies, who are making a road through the jungle. We sat down on one of the long matted platforms, which serve them for beds, and talked; but there was no hint of breakfast; and we soon learned that the Malacca runner had not reached the Residency at all, and that the note sent from Permatang Pasir, which should have been delivered at 1 A.M., had not been received till 8 A.M., so that Captain Murray had not been able to arrange for our transport, and had had barely time to ride down to meet us at such "full speed," as a swampy and partially made road would allow. So our dreams of breakfast ended in cups of stewed tea, given to us by a half-naked Chinaman, and, to our chagrin, we had to go back to the boat and be poled up the shallowing and narrowing river for four hours more, getting on with difficulty, the boat-men constantly jumping into the water to heave the boat off mud banks.

When we eventually landed at Nioto, a small village, Captain Murray again met us, and we found a road; and two antiquated buggies, sent by a Chinaman, with their component parts much lashed together with rope. I charioteered one of these, with reins so short that I could only reach them by sitting on the edge of the seat, and a whip so short that I could not reach the pony with it. At a Chinese village some policemen brought us cocoa-nut milk. After that, the pony could not, or would not, go; and the Malay syce with difficulty got it along by dragging it, and we had to walk up every hill in the fierce heat of a tropic noon. At the large Chinese village of Rassa, a clever little Sumatra pony met us; and after passing through some roughish clearings, on which tapioca is being planted, we arrived here at 4 P.M., having traveled sixty miles in thirty-three hours.

The Residency is on a steepish hill in the middle of an open valley, partially cleared and much defaced by tin diggings. The Chinese town of Serambang lies at the foot of the hill. The valley is nearly surrounded by richly wooded hills, some of them fully three thousand feet high. These, which stretch away to the northern State of Selangor, are bathed in indigo and cobalt, slashed with white here and there, where cool streams dash over forest-shaded ledges. The house consists of two attap roofed bungalows, united by their upper verandas. Below there are a garden of acclimatization and a lawn, on which the Resident instructs the bright little daughter of the Datu Klana in lawn tennis. It was very hot, but the afternoon airs were strong enough to lift the British ensign out of its heavy folds and to rustle the graceful fronds of the areca palms.

Food was the first necessity, then baths, then sleep, then dinner at 7:30, and then ten hours more sleep.

I. L. B.

Letter XIII

The Appurtenances of Civilization—Babu—Characteristics of Captain Murray—An Embodied Government—Chinese Mining Enterprise—A Chinese Gaming-House—The "Capitans China"—New-Year Visits—Sittings "In Equity"—A Court of Justice—The Serambang Prison—"Plantation Hill"—A Monster Bonfire—An Ant World—An Ant Funeral—Night on "Plantation Hill"—The Murder of Mr. Lloyd—A Chinese Dragon Play—A Visit to a Malay Prince—The Datu Bandar's House—A Great Temptation—The Return Journey—An Obituary Quotation

RESIDENCY, SUNGEI UJONG, January 30.

We have been here for four days. The heat is so great that it is wonderful that one can walk about in the sunshine; but the nights, though the mercury does not fall below 80 degrees, are cool and refreshing, and the air and soil are both dry, though a hundred inches of rain fall in the year. These wooden bungalows are hot, for the attap roofs have no lining, but they are also airy. There is no-one but myself at night in the one in which my room is, but this is nothing after the solitude of the great, rambling Stadthaus. Since we came a sentry has been on duty always, and a bull-dog is chained at the foot of the ladder which leads to both bungalows. But there is really nothing to fear from these "treacherous Malays." It is most curious to see the appurtenances of civilization in the heart of a Malay jungle, and all the more so because our long night journey up the Linggi makes it seem more remote than it is. We are really only sixty miles from Malacca.

The drawing-room has a good piano, and many tasteful ornaments, books, and china—gifts from loving friends and relations in the far off home—and is as livable as a bachelor would be likely to make it. There is a billiard table in the corridor. The dining-room, which is reached by going out of doors, with its red-tiled floor and walls of dark, unpolished wood, is very pretty. In the middle of the dinner table there is a reflecting lake for "hot-house flowers;" and exquisite crystal, menu cards with holders of Dresden china, four classical statuettes in Parian, with pineapples, granadillas, bananas, pomegranates, and a durion blanda, are the "table decorations." The cuisine is almost too elaborate for a traveler's palate, but plain meat is rarely to be got, and even when procurable is unpalatable unless disguised. Curry is at each meal, but it is not made with curry powder. Its basis is grated cocoa-nut made into a paste with cocoa-nut milk, and the spices are added fresh. Turtles when caught are kept in a pond until they are needed, and we have turtle soup, stewed turtle, curried turtle and turtle cutlets ad nauseam. Fowls are at every meal, but never plain roasted or plain boiled. The first day there was broiled and stewed elephant trunk, which tastes much like beef.

Babu, who is always en grand tenue, has taken command of everything and saves our host all trouble. He carves at the sideboard, scolds the servants in a stage whisper, and pushes them indignantly aside when they attempt to offer anything to "his young ladies," reduces Captain Murray's butler to a nonentity, and as far as he can turns the Residency into Government House, waiting on us assiduously in our rooms, and taking care of our clothes. The dinner bell is a bugle.

In houses in these regions there is always a brick-floored bath-room, usually of large size, under your bedroom, to which you descend by a ladder. This is often covered by a trap-door, which is sometimes concealed by a couch, and in order to descend the sofa cushion is lifted. Here it is an open trap in the middle of the room. A bath is a necessity —not a luxury—so near the equator, and it is usual to take one three, four, or even five times a day, with much refreshment. One part of

Babu's self-imposed duty is to look under our pillows for snakes and centipedes, and the latter have been found in all our rooms.

I must now make you acquainted with our host, Captain Murray. He was appointed when the Datu Klana asked for a Resident four years ago. He devotes himself to Sungei Ujong as if it were his own property, though he has never been able to acquire the language. He is a man about thirty-eight, a naval officer, and an enterprising African traveler; under the middle height, bronzed, sun-browned, disconnected in his conversation from the habit of living without anyone in or out of the house to speak to; professing a misanthropy which he is very far from feeling, for he is quite unsuspicious, and disposed to think the best of every one; hasty when vexed, but thoroughly kind-hearted; very blunt, very undignified, never happy (he says) out of the wilds; thoroughly well disposed to the Chinese and Malays, but very impatient of their courtesies, thoroughly well meaning, thoroughly a gentleman, but about the last person that I should have expected to see in a position which is said to require much tact if not finesse. His success leads me to think, as I have often thought before, that if we attempt to deal with Orientals by their own methods, we are apt to find them more than a match for us, and that thorough honesty is the best policy.

He lives alone, unguarded; trusts himself by night and day without any escort among the people; keeps up no ceremony at all, and is approachable at all hours. Like most travelers, he has some practical knowledge of medicine, and he gives advice and medicines most generously, allowing himself to be interrupted by patients at all hours. There is no doctor nearer than Malacca. He has been so successful that people come from the neighboring States for his advice. There is very little serious disease, but children are subject to a loathsome malady called puru. Two were brought with it to-day. The body and head are covered with pustules containing matter, looking very much like small-pox, and the natives believe that it must run its course for a year. Captain Murray cures it in a few days with iodide of potassium and iodine, and he says that it is fast disappearing.

Captain Murray is judge, "sitting in Equity," Superintendent of Police, Chancellor of the Exchequer, and Surveyor of Taxes, besides being Board of Trade, Board of Works, and I know not what besides. In fact, *he is the Government*, although the Datu Klana's signature or seal is required to confirm a sentence of capital punishment, and possibly in one or two other cases; and his Residential authority is subject only to the limitations of his own honor and good sense, sharpened somewhat, were he other than what he is, by possible snubs from the Governor of the Straits Settlements or the Colonial Secretary. He is a thoroughly honorable man, means well by all the interests of his little kingdom, and seems both beloved and trusted.

On Sunday morning we had English service and a sermon, the congregation being augmented by the only other English people—a man from Australia who is here road-making, and his wife; and in the afternoon, disregarding a temperature of 85 degrees, we went through the Chinese village of Serambang.

Tin is the staple product of Sungei Ujong, and until lately the Malay peninsula and the adjacent regions were supposed to be the richest tin producing countries in the world. There is not a single tin mine, however, properly so-called. The whole of the tin exported from Sungei Ujong, which last year (1879), even at its present reduced price, was valued at 81,400 pounds, and contributed as export duty to the Government 5,800 pounds, is found in the detritus of ancient mountains, and is got, in mining parlance, in "stream works"—that is, by washing the soil, just as gold is washed out of the soil in Australia and California. It is supposed that there is a sufficient supply to last for ages, even though the demand for tin for new purposes is always on the increase. It is tin mining which has brought the Chinese in such numbers to these States, and as miners and smelters they are equally efficient and persevering. In 1828, the number of Chinese working the mines here was one thousand; and in the same year they were massacred by the Malays. They now number ten thousand, and under British protection have nothing to fear.

It is still the New Year holidays, and hundreds of Chinamen were lounging about, and every house was gayly decorated. The Malays never join house to house, the Chinese always do so, and this village has its streets and plaza. The houses are all to a certain extent fire-proof—that is, when a fire occurs, and the attap-thatched roofs are burned, the houses below, which are mostly shops, are safe. These shops, some of which are very large, are nearly dark. They deal mainly in Chinese goods and favorite Chinese articles of food, fireworks, mining tools, and kerosene oil. In one shop twenty "assistants," with only their loose cotton trousers on, were sitting at round tables having a meal—not their ordinary diet, I should think, for they had seventeen different sorts of soups and stews, some of them abominations to our thinking.

We visited the little joss-house, very gaudily decorated, the main feature of the decorations being two enormous red silk umbrellas, exquisitely embroidered in gold and silks. The crowds in this village remind me of Canton, but the Chinese look anything but picturesque here, for none of them—or at all events, only their "Capitans"—wear the black satin skull cap; and their shaven heads, with the small patch of hair which goes into the composition of the pigtail, look very ugly. The pig-tail certainly begins with this lock of hair, but the greater part of it is made up of silk or cotton thread plaited in with the hair, and blue or red strands of silk in a pigtail indicate mourning or rejoicing. None of the Chinese here wear the beautiful long robes used by their compatriots in China and Japan. The rich wear a white, shirt-like garment of embroidered silk crepe over their trousers and petticoat, and the poorer only loose blue or brown cotton trousers, so that one is always being reminded of the excessive leanness of their forms. Some of the rich merchants invited us to go in and drink champagne, but we declined everything but tea, which is ready all day long in tea-pots kept hot in covered baskets very thickly padded, such as are known with us as "Norwegian Kitchens."

In the middle of the village there is a large, covered, but open-sided building like a market, which is crowded all day—and all night too—

by hundreds of these poor, half-naked creatures standing round the gaming tables, silent, eager, excited, staking every cent they earn on the turn of the dice, living on the excitement of their gains—a truly sad spectacle. Probably we were the first European ladies who had ever walked through the gambling-house, but the gamblers were too intent even to turn their heads. There also they are always drinking tea. Some idea of the profits made by the men who "farm" the gambling licenses may be gained from the fact that the revenue derived by the Government from the gambling "farms" is over 900 pounds a year.

Spirits are sold in three or four places; and the license to sell them brings in nearly 700 pounds a year, but a drunken Chinaman is never seen. There are a few opium inebriates, lean like skeletons, and very vacant in expression; and every coolie smokes his three whiffs of opium every night. Only a few of the richer Chinamen have wives, and there are very few women, as is usual in a mining population. A good many roads have been made in the State, and the Chinese are building buggies, gharries, and wagons, and many of the richer ones own them and import Sumatra ponies to draw them. To say that the Chinese make as good emigrants as the British is barely to give them their due. They have equal stamina and are more industrious and thrifty, and besides that they are always sober, can bear with impunity the fiercest tropical heat, and can thrive and save where Englishmen would starve. The immense immigration of Chinese, all affiliated to clubs or secret societies, might be a great risk to the peace of the State were it not that they recognize certain leaders known as "Capitans China," who contrive to preserve order, so far as is known by a wholesome influence merely; and who in all cases, in return for the security which property enjoys under our flag, work cordially with the Resident in all that concerns the good of the State. How these "Capitans" are elected, and how they exercise their authority, is as inscrutable as most else belonging to the Chinese. The Chinese seem not so much broadly patriotic as provincial or clannish, and the "Hoeys," or secret societies, belong to the different southern provinces. The fights between the factions, and the way in which the secret societies screen criminals by false swearing and other means, are among the woes of the Governor and Lieutenant-Governors of these Settlements. Though they get on very well up here, thanks to the "Capitan China," the clans live in separate parts of the village, have separate markets and gaming houses, and a wooden arch across the street divides the two "Nations."

We went to pay complimentary visits for the New Year to these "Capitans" with the Malay interpreter, and were received with a curious mixture of good-will and solemnity. Wine, tea and sweet-meats were produced at each house. Their houses are very rude, considering their ample means, and have earthen floors. They have comfortable carriages, and their gentle, sweet-mannered children were loaded with gold and diamonds. In one house, a sweet little girl handed round the tea and cake, and all, even to babies who can scarcely toddle across the floor, came up and shook hands. A Chinese family impresses one by its extreme orderliness, filial reverence being regarded as the basis of all the virtues. The manners of these children are equally removed from shyness and forwardness. They all wore crowns of dark red gold of very beautiful workmanship, set with diamonds. When these girl-children are twelve years old, they will, according to custom, be strictly secluded, and will not be seen by any man but their father till the bridegroom lifts the veil at the marriage ceremony.

After these visits, in which the "Capitans China," through the interpreter, assured us of their perpetual and renewed satisfaction with British rule, Mr. Hayward, the interpreter, and I, paid another visit of a more leisurely kind to one of the Chinese gambling houses, which, as usual, was crowded. At one end several barbers were at work. A Chinaman is always being shaved, for he keeps his head and face quite smooth, and never shaves himself. The shaving the head was originally a sign of subjection imposed by the Tartar conquerors, but it is now so completely the national custom that prisoners feel it a deep disgrace when their hair is allowed to grow. Coolies twist their five feet of pigtail round their heads while they are at work, but a servant or other inferior, only insults his superior if he enter his presence with his pigtail otherwise than pendent. The gaming house, whose open sides allow it to present a perpetual temptation, is full of tables, and at each sits a croupier, well clothed, and as many half-naked Chinamen as can see over each others' shoulders crowd round him. Their silent, concentrated eagerness is a piteous sight, as the cover is slowly lifted from the heavy brass box in which the dice are kept, on the cast of which many of them have staked all they possess. They accept their losses as they do their gains, with apparent composure. They work very hard, and live on very little; but they are poor just now, for the price of tin has fallen nearly one-half in consequence of the great tin discoveries in Australia.

Along with Mr. Hayward I paid a visit to the Court House, a large whitewashed room, with a clean floor of red tiles, a tiled dais, with a desk for the judge, a table with a charge sheet and some books upon it, and three long benches at the end for witnesses and their friends. A punkah is kept constantly going. There are a clerk, a Chinese interpreter, who speaks six Chinese dialects, and a Malay interpreter, who puts the Chinese interpreter's words into English. As the judge does not understand Malay, it will be observed that justice depends on the fidelity of this latter official. Though I cannot say that the dignity of justice is sustained in this court, there is not a doubt that the intentions of the judge are excellent, and if some of the guilty escape, it is not likely that any of the innocent suffer. The Datu Bandar sometimes sits on the bench with the Resident.

The benches were crowded almost entirely with Chinamen, and a number of policemen stood about. I noticed that these were as anxious as our own are to sustain a case. The case which I heard, and which occupied more than an hour, was an accusation against a wretched Chinaman for stealing a pig. I sat on the bench and heard every word that was said, and arrived at no judicial conclusion, nor did the Resident, so the accused was dismissed. He did steal that pig though! I don't see how truth can be arrived at in an Oriental court, especially where the witnesses are members of Chinese secret societies. Another case of alleged nocturnal assault, was tried, in which the judge took immense pains to get at the truth, and the prisoner had every advantage; and when he was found guilty, was put into a good jail, from which he will be taken out daily to work on the roads.

Malays being Mussulmen, are mostly tried by the "Divine Law" of the Koran, and Chinamen are dealt with "in equity." The question to be arrived at simply is, "Did the prisoner commit this crime or did he not?" If he did he is punished, and if he did not he is acquitted. There are no legal technicalities by which trial can be delayed or the ends of justice frustrated. Theft is the most common crime. One hundred and fourteen persons were convicted last year, which does not seem a large proportion (being less than one per cent.) out of an unsettled mining population of twelve thousand. Mr. Hayward, through whose hands the crime of Singapore and Malacca has filtered for twenty years, was very critical on the rough and ready method of proceeding here, and constantly interjected suggestions, such as "You don't ask them questions before you swear them," etc. Informal as its administration is, I have no doubt that justice is substantially done, for the Resident is conscientious and truly honorable. He is very lovable, and is evidently much beloved, and is able to go about in unguarded security.

It is not far from the Court House to the prison, a wholesomely situated building on a hill, made of concrete, with an attap roof. The whole building is one hundred feet long by thirty feet broad. There are six cells for solitary confinement. A jailer, turnkey, and eight warders constitute the prison staff. The able-bodied prisoners are employed on the roads and other public works, and attend upon the scavengers' cart, which outcome of civilization goes round every morning! The diet, which costs fourpence a day for each prisoner, consists of rice and salt fish, but those who work get two-pence halfpenny a day in addition, with which they can either buy luxuries or accumulate a small sum against the time when their sentences expire. Old and weakly people do light work about the prison. One man was executed for murder last year under a sentence signed by the Datu Klana. I have not been in a prison since I was in that den of horrors, the prison of the Naam-Hoi magistrate at Canton, and I felt a little satisfaction in the contrast.

The same afternoon we all made a very pleasant expedition to the Sanitarium, a cabin which the Resident has built on a hill three miles from here. A chair with four Chinese bearers carried Miss Shaw up, her sister and the two gentlemen walked, and I rode a Sumatra pony, on an Australian stock-man's saddle, not only up the steep jungle path, but up a staircase of two hundred steps in which it terminates, the sagacious animal going up quite cunningly. One charm of a tropical jungle is that every few yards you come upon something new, and every hundred feet of ascent makes a decided difference in the vegetation. This is a very grand forest, with its straight, smooth stems running up over one hundred feet before branching, and the branches are loaded with orchids and trailers. One cannot see what the foliage is like which is borne far aloft into the summer sunshine, but on the ground I found great red trumpet flowers and crimson corollas, like those of a Brobdingnagian honeysuckle, and flowers like red dragon-flies enormously magnified, and others like large, single roses in yellow wax, falling slowly down now and then, messengers from the floral glories above, "wasting (?) their sweetness on the desert air." A traveler through a tropical jungle may see very few flowers and be inclined to disparage it. It is necessary to go on adjacent rising ground and look down where trees and trailers are exhibiting their gorgeousness. Unlike the coarse weeds which form so much of the undergrowth in Japan, everything which grows in these forests rejoices the eye by its form or color; but things which hurt and sting and may kill, lurk amidst all the beauties. A creeping plant with very beautiful waxy leaves, said by Captain Murray to be vanilla, grows up many of the trees.

When we got up to the top of this, which the Resident calls "Plantation Hill," I was well pleased to find that only the undergrowth had been cleared away, and that "The Sanitarium" consists only of a cabin with a single room divided into two, and elevated on posts like a Malay house. The deep veranda which surrounds it is reached by a stepladder.

A smaller house could hardly be, or a more picturesque one, from the steepness and irregularity of its roof. The cook-house is a small attap shed, in a place cut into the hill, and an inclosure of attap screens with a barrel in it under the house is the bath-room. The edge of the hill, from which a few trees have been cleared, is so steep that but for a bamboo rail one might slip over upon the tree-tops below. Some Liberian coffee shrubs, some tea, cinchona, and ipecacuanha, and some heartless English cabbages, are being grown on the hillside, and the Resident hopes that the State will have a great future of coffee.

The view in all directions was beautiful—to the north a sea of densely wooded mountains with indigo shadows in their hollows; to the south the country we had threaded on the Linggi river, forests, and small tapioca clearings, little valleys where rice is growing, and scars where tin- mining is going on; the capital, the little town of Serambang with its larger clearings, and to the west the gleam of the shining sea. In the absence of mosquitoes we were able to sit out till after dark, a rare luxury. There was a gorgeous sunset of the gory, furnace kind, which one only sees in the tropics—waves of violet light rolling up over the mainland, and the low Sumatran coast looking like a purple cloud amidst the fiery haze.

Dinner was well cooked, and served with coffee after it, just as at home. The primitive bath-room was made usable by our eleven servants and chair-bearers being sent to the hill, where the two gentlemen mounted guard over them. After dark the Chinamen made the largest bonfire I ever saw, or at all events the most brilliant, with trunks of trees and pieces of gum dammar, several pounds in weight, which they obtained by digging, and this was kept up till daylight, throwing its splendid glare over the whole hill-top, lighting up the forest, and bringing the cabin out in all its picturesqueness.

I should have liked to be there some time to study the ways of a tribe of ants. Near the cabin, under a large tree, there was an ant-dwelling, not exactly to be called an ant-hill, but a subterranean ant-town, with two entrances. Into this an army of many thousand largish ants, in an even column three and a half inches wide, marched continually, in well "dressed" ranks, about twenty-seven in each, with the regularity of a crack regiment on the "march past," over all sorts of inequalities, rough ground, and imbedded trunks of small trees, larger ants looking like officers marching on both sides of the column, and sometimes turning back as if to give orders. Would that Sir John Lubbock had been there to interpret their speech!

Each ant of the column bore a yellowish burden, not too large to interfere with his activity. A column marshaled in the same fashion, but only half the width of the other, emerged equally continuously from the lower entrance. From the smaller size of this column I suppose that a number of the carrier ants remain within, stowing away their burdens in store-houses. Attending this latter column for eighteen paces, I came upon a marvelous scene of orderly activity. A stump of a tree, from which the outer bark had been removed, leaving an under layer apparently permeated with a rich, sweet secretion, was completely covered with ants, which were removing the latter in minute portions. Strange to say, however, a quantity of reddish ants of much larger size and with large mandibles seemed to do the whole work of stripping off this layer. They were working from above, and had already bared some inches of the stump, which was four feet six inches in diameter. As the small morsels fell among the myriads of ants which swarmed round the base they were broken up, three or four ants sometimes working at one bit till they had reduced it into manageable portions. It was a splendid sight to see this vast and busy crowd inspired by a common purpose, and with the true instinct of discipline, forever forming into column at the foot of the stump.

Toward dusk the reddish ants, which may be termed quarriers, gave up work, and this was the signal for the workers below to return home. The quarriers came down the stump pushing the laborers, rather rudely as I thought, out of their way; and then forming in what might be called "light skirmishing order," they marched to the lower entrance of the town, meeting as they went the column of workers going up to the stump. They met it of course at once, and a minute of great helter-skelter followed, this column falling back on itself as if assailed, in great confusion. If this be the ordinary day's routine, why does that column fall into confusion, and why, after throwing it into disorder, do the reddish ants close their ranks and march into the town in compact order, parallel with the working column going the other way, and which they seemed to terrorize? Is it possible that the smaller ants are only slaves of the larger? Inscrutable are the ways of ants! However, when the advancing column had recovered from its confusion it formed up, and, wheeling round in most regular order, fell behind the rear-guard of the working column, and before dark not an ant remained outside except a dead body.

Soon after the last of its living comrades had disappeared, six ants, with a red one (dare I say?) "in command," came out and seemed to hold a somewhat fussy consultation round the corpse which had fallen on the line of march to the stump. After a minute or two, three of them got hold of it, and with the other four as spectators or mourners, they dragged it for about six feet and concealed it under a leaf, after which they returned home; all this was most fascinating. A little later Captain Murray destroyed both entrances to the town, but before daylight, by dint of extraordinary labor, they were reconstructed lower down the slope, and the work at the stump was going on as if nothing so unprecedented had happened.

I should have liked also to study the ways of the white ant, the great timber-destroying pest of this country, which abounds on this hill. He is a large ant of a pale buff color. Up the trunk of a tree he builds a tunnel of sand, held together by a viscid secretion, and under this he works, cutting a deep groove in the wood, and always extending the tunnel upward. I broke away two inches of such a tunnel in the afternoon, and by the next morning it was restored. Among many other varieties of ants, there is one found by the natives, which people call the "soldier ant." I saw many of these big fellows, more than an inch long, with great mandibles. Their works must be on a gigantic scale, and their bite or grip very painful; but being with a party, I was not able to make their acquaintance.

When it grew dark, tiny lamps began to move in all directions. Some came from on high, like falling stars, but most moved among the trees a few feet from the ground with a slow undulatory motion, the fire having a pale blue tinge, as one imagines an incandescent sapphire might have. The great tree-crickets kept up for a time the most ludicrous sound I ever heard—one sitting in a tree and calling to another. From the deafening noise, which at times drowned our voices, one would suppose the creature making it to be at least as large as an eagle.

The accommodation of the "Sanitarium" is most limited. The two gentlemen, well armed, slept in the veranda, the Misses Shaw in camp beds in the inner cabin, and I in a swinging cot in the outer, the table being removed to make room for it. The bull-dog mounted guard over all, and showed his vigilance by an occasional growl. The eleven attendants stowed themselves away under the cabin, except a garrulous couple, who kept the fire blazing till daylight. My cot was most comfortable, but I failed to sleep. The forest was full of quaint, busy noises, broken in upon occasionally by the hoot of the "spectre bird," and the long, low, plaintive cry of some animal.

All the white residents in the Malacca Settlements have been greatly excited about a tragedy which has just occurred at the Dindings, off this coast, in which Mr. Lloyd, the British superintendent, was horribly murdered by the Chinese; his wife, and Mrs. Innes, who was on a visit to her, narrowly escaping the same fate. Lying awake I could not help thinking of this, and of the ease with which the Resident could be overpowered and murdered by any of our followers who might have a grudge against him, when, as I thought, the door behind my head from the back ladder was burst open, and my cot and I came down on the floor at the head, the simple fact being, that the head-rope, not having been properly secured, gave way with a run. An hour afterward the foot-ropes gave way, and I was deposited on the floor altogether, and was soon covered with small ants.

Early in the morning the apes began to call to each other with a plaintive "Hoo-houey," and in the gray dawn I saw an iguana fully four feet long glide silently down the trunk of a tree, the branches of which were loaded with epiphytes. Captain Shaw asked the imaum of one of the mosques of Malacca about alligator's eggs a few days ago, and his reply was, that the young that went down to the sea became alligators, and those which came up the rivers became iguanas. At daylight, after coffee and bananas, we left the hill, and after an accident, promptly remedied by Mr. Hayward, reached Serambang when the sun was high in the heavens. I should think that there are very few circumstances which Mr. Hayward is not prepared to meet. He has a reserve of quiet strength which I should like to see fully drawn upon. He has the scar of a spear wound on his brow, which Captain Murray says was received in holding sixty armed men at bay, while he secured the retreat of some helpless persons. Yet he continues to be much burdened by his responsibility for these fair girls, who, however, are enjoying themselves thoroughly, and will be none the worse.

We had scarcely returned when a large company of Chinamen, carrying bannerets and joss-sticks, came to the Residency to give a spectacle or miracle-play, the first part consisting of a representation of a huge dragon, which kicked, and jumped, and crawled, and bellowed in a manner totally unworthy of that ancient and splendid myth; and the second, of a fierce melee, or succession of combats with spears, shields, and battle-axes. The performances were accompanied by much drumming, and by the beating of tom-toms, an essentially infernal noise, which I cannot help associating with the orgies of devil-worship. The "Capitan China," in a beautiful costume, sat with us in the veranda to see the performance.

I have written a great deal about the Chinese and very little about the Malays, the nominal possessors of the country, but the Chinese may be said to be everywhere, and the Malays nowhere. You have to look for them if you want to see them. Besides, the Chinese are as ten to two of the whole population. Still the laws are administered in the name of the Datu Klana, the Malay ruler. The land owned by Malays is being measured, and printed title-deeds are being given, a payment of 2s. an acre per annum being levied instead of any taxes on produce. Export duties are levied on certain articles, but the navigation of the rivers is free. Debt slavery, one curse of the Malay States, has been abolished by the energy of Captain Murray with the cordial co-operation of the Datu Klana, and now the whole population have the status and rights of free men. It is a great pity that this Prince is in Malacca, for he is said to be a very enlightened ruler. The photograph which I inclose (from which the engraving is taken) is of the marriage of his daughter, a very splendid affair. The buffalo in front was a marriage present from the Straits Government, and its covering was of cloth of gold thick with pearls and precious stones.

We visited yesterday a Malay kampong called Mambu, in order to pay an unceremonious visit to the Datu Bandar, the Rajah second in rank to the reigning prince. His house, with three others, a godown on very high stilts, and a mound of graves whitened by the petals of the Frangipani, with a great many cocoa-nut and other trees, was surrounded, as Malay dwellings often are, by a high fence, within which was another inclosing a neat, sanded level, under cocoa-palms, on which his "private residence" and those of his wives stand. His secretary, a nice-looking lad in red turban, baju, and sarong, came out to meet us, followed by the Datu Bandar, a pleasant, able-looking man, with a cordial manner, who shook hands and welcomed us. No notice had been given of our visit, and the Rajah, who is reclaiming and bringing into good cultivation much of his land, and who sets the example of working with his own hands, was in a checked shirt, and a common, checked, red sarong. Vulgarity is surely a disease of the West alone, though, as in Japan, one sees that it can be contagious, and this Oriental, far from apologizing for his dishabille, led us up the steep and difficult ladder by which his house is entered with as much courteous ease as if he had been in his splendors.

I thoroughly liked his house. It is both fitting and tasteful. We stepped from the ladder into a long corridor, well-matted, which led to a doorway with a gold-embroidered silk or valance, and a looped-up portiere of white-flowered silk or crepe. This was the entrance to a small room very well proportioned, with two similar doorways, curtained with flowered silk, one leading to a room which we did not see, and the other to a bamboo gridiron platform, which in the better class of Malay houses always leads to a smaller house at the back, where cooking and other domestic operations are carried on, and which seems given up to the women. There was a rich, dim light in the room, which was cool and wainscoted entirely with dark red wood, and there was only one long, low window, with turned bars of the same wood. There were three handsome cabinets with hangings of gold and crimson embroidery, and an ebony frame containing a verse of the Koran in Arabic characters hung over one doorway. In accordance with Mohammedan prohibitions, there was no decoration which bore the likeness of any created thing, but there were some artistic arabesques under the roof. The furniture, besides the cabinets, consisted of a divan, several ebony chairs, a round table covered with a cool yellow cloth, and a table against the wall draped with crimson silk flowered with gold. The floor was covered with fine matting, over which were Oudh rugs in those mixtures of toned-down rich colors which are so very beautiful. Richness and harmony characterized the room, and it was distinctively Malay; one could not say that it reminded one of anything except of the flecked and colored light which streams through dark, old, stained glass.

The Datu Bandar's brother and uncle came in, the first a very handsome Hadji, with a bright, intelligent countenance. He has lived in Mecca for eight years studying the Koran under a renowned teacher, and in this quest of Mussulman learning has spent several thousand dollars. "We never go to Mecca to trade," he said; "we go for religious purposes only." These men looked superb in their red dresses and turbans, although the Malays are anything but a handsome race. Their hospitality was very graceful. Many of the wealthier Mohammedans, though they don't drink wine, keep it for their Christian guests, and they offered us champagne, which is supposed to be an irresistible temptation to the Christian palate. On our refusing it they brought us cow's milk and most delicious coffee with a very fragrant aroma, and not darker in color than tea of an average strength. This was made from roasted coffee leaves. The berries are exported. A good many pretty, quiet children stood about, but though the Rajah gave us to understand that they were the offspring of three mothers, we were not supposed to see any of "the mean ones within the gates."

Our hosts had a good deal to say, and did not leave us to entertain them, though we are but "infidel dogs." That we are regarded as such, along with all other unbelievers, always makes me feel shy with Mohammedans. Some time ago, when Captain Shaw pressed on the Malays the impropriety of shooting Chinamen, as they were then in the habit of doing, the reply of one of them was, "Why not shoot Chinamen? they've no religion;" and though it would be highly discourteous in members of a ruled race to utter this sentiment regarding their rulers, I have not the least doubt that it is their profound conviction concerning ourselves.

Nothing shows more the honesty and excellence of Captain Murray's purposes than that he should be as much respected and loved as he is in spite of a manner utterly opposed to all Oriental notions of dignity, whether Malay or Chinese. I have mentioned his abruptness, as well as his sailor-like heartiness, but they never came into such strong relief as at the Datu Bandar's, against the solemn and dignified courtesy of our hosts.

We returned after dark, had turtle-soup and turtle-steak, not near so good as veal, which it much resembles, for dinner; sang "Auld Lang Syne," which brought tears into the Resident's kindly eyes, and are now ready for an early start to-morrow.

Stadthaus, Malacca.—We left Serambang before daylight on Thursday in buggies, escorted by Captain Murray, the buggies, as usual, being lent by the Chinese "Capitans." Horses had been sent on before, and after changing them we drove the second stage through most magnificent forest, until they could no longer drag the buggies through the mud, at which point of discomfiture three saddled ponies and two chairs were waiting to take us through the jungle to the river. We rode along an infamous track, much of it knee-deep in mud, through a green and silent twilight, till we emerged upon something like English park and fox-cover scenery, varied by Malay kampongs under groves of palms. In the full blaze of noon we reached the Linggi police station, from which we had started in the sampan, and were received by a company of police with fixed bayonets. We dined in the police station veranda, and as the launch had been obliged to drop down the river because the water was falling, we went to Sempang in a native boat, paddled by four Malays with paddles like oval-ended spades with spade handles, a guard of honor of policemen going down with us. There we took leave of our most kind and worthy host, who, with tears in his kind eyes, immediately turned up the river to dwell alone in his bungalow with his bull-dog, his revolver, and his rifle, a self-exiled man.*

[*In 1881, Captain Murray, feeling ill after prolonged exposure to the sun, went to Malacca, where he died a few days afterward at the house of his friend Mr. Hayward. Sir F. A. Weld writes of him in a dispatch to Lord Kimberley:—"I cannot close this notice of the State of Sungei Ujong without recalling the memory of Captain Murray, so lately its Resident, to whom it owes much, and who was devoted to its people and interests. A man of great honesty of purpose and kindliness of heart, Captain Murray possessed many of those qualities which are required for the successful administration of a Malay State, and though he labored under the disadvantage of want of knowledge of the native tongue, he yet was able to attach to himself, in a singular manner, the affections of all around him. For the last six years, Captain Murray has successfully advised in the administration of the Government of Sungei Ujong, consolidating order and good government, and doing much to open out the country and develop its resources. His name will ever be associated *with its prosperity, and his memory be long fresh in the hearts of its inhabitants."]*

After it grew dark we had the splendid sight of a great tract of forest on fire close to the sea. We landed here at a pier eight hundred feet long, accessible to launches at high water, where several peons and two inspectors of police met us. Our expedition has been the talk of the little foreign world of Malacca. We had an enthusiastic welcome at Government House, but Captain Shaw says he will never forgive himself for not writing to Captain Murray in time to arrange our transport, and for sending us off so hurriedly with so little food, but I hope by reiteration to convince him that thereby we gained the night on the Linggi river, which, as a traveling experience, is worth all the rest.

I. L. B.

A CHAPTER ON SELANGOR*

Selangor—Capabilities of Selangor—Natural Capabilities—Lawlessness in Selangor—British Interference in Selangor—A Hopeful Outlook

Selangor is a small State lying between 2 degrees 34', and 3 degrees 42' N. Its coast-line is about one hundred and twenty miles in length. Perak is its northern boundary, Sungei Ujong its southern, and some of the small States of the Negri Sembilan and unexplored jungle and mountains separate it from Pahang on the east. It is watered by the Selangor, Klang and Langat rivers, which rise in the hills of its eastern frontier. Its population is not accurately known, but the result of an attempt to estimate it, made by the Resident in 1876, is fifteen thousand Chinese and from two thousand to three thousand Malays. Mr. Douglas, the late Resident, puts the Malay population at a higher figure, and estimates the aboriginal population at one thousand, but this is probably largely in excess of their actual numbers.

[*In offering this very slight sketch of Selangor to my readers as prefatory to the letters which follow, I desire to express my acknowledgments specially to a valuable paper on "Surveys and Explorations of the Native States of the Malay Peninsula," by Mr. Daly, Superintendent of Public Works and Surveys, Selangor, read before the Royal Geographical Society on May 8, 1882. I have also made use of a brief account of the Native Malay States by Mr. Swettenham, Assistant Colonial Secretary to the Straits Settlements Government, published in the Journal of the Straits Branch of the*

ISABELLA LUCY BIRD

Royal Asiatic Society, and of "Our Malay Conquests" by Sir P. Benson Maxwell, late Chief Justice of the Straits Settlements.]

The wealth of Selangor lies in its apparently inexhaustible tin mines. The range of hills which forms the backbone of the Malay Peninsula rises in places to a height of seven thousand feet, and it is from this range that the alluvial detritus is washed down, beneath which is deposited the layer of ore or wash, which varies from four inches to ten feet in thickness. The supply of this ore is apparently inexhaustible, but no veins have as yet been found. The mine of Ampagnan only, near Kwala Lumpor, the capital, gives employment to over one thousand Chinamen, and each can extract in a year one thousand pounds weight of white smelted tin valued at 35 pounds sterling. This mineral wealth is the magnet which, according as the price of tin is higher or lower, attracts into Selangor more or fewer Chinamen. The chief source of the revenue of the State has been the export duty on tin.

The low lands on the coast are fringed with mangroves, which thrive in blue mud and heavy clays, and these lands, when drained, are well adapted for sugar. Wet rice grows well in the swampy valleys which separate the minor ranges, and dry rice on the rises; while tapioca, tobacco, pepper and gambier thrive on the medium heights. The sago palm flourishes on wet lands. The high hills are covered with primeval forests, and the Malays have neither settlements nor plantations upon them. It is believed that these hills, at a height of from two thousand five hundred to three thousand five hundred feet, are admirably adapted for the growth of Arabian coffee, cinchona and tea; and some Ceylon coffee planters are expecting an era of success in Selangor. At present, however, the necessary labor is not available. The soil in the interior on the mountain slopes consists of a light red and yellow clay, the product of a comparatively recent rock decomposition, covered with vegetable mould from eight to twelve inches thick. There are no droughts, and the rainfall, distributed pretty fairly over the year, averages about one hundred and thirty inches annually. The climate is remarkably healthy, and diseases of locality are unknown. Land can be purchased for eight shillings per acre on terms of deferred payments.

One curious feature of Selangor, as of Perak, is the occurrence of isolated hills of limestone varying from eighty to one thousand feet in height. At Batu there are magnificent limestone caves, richly adorned with stalactites and stalagmites. The dome of one cavern is three hundred and fifty-five feet from floor to roof. An important fact connected with these caverns is that they contain thousands of tons of bats' manure, which may be as valuable as guano to future planters. Between the heavy clays and blue mud of the mangrove swamps and the granite and sandstone of the mountain ranges, the undulating rises are mainly composed of red clay, sandstones, shales, and granitic and feldspathic rocks, with extensive deposits of laterite in red clays on the surface. In the valleys along the rivers the soil consists of rich alluvial deposits.

Undoubtedly Selangor has great capabilities, and if the difficulties of the labor question can be satisfactorily disposed of, it is likely that the new offer of leases for nine hundred and ninety-nine years, subject to improvement clauses, will attract a number of planters to its fertile soil and wholesome climate. Selangor includes three large districts, each on a considerable river of its own—Selangor, Klang, and Langat.

The Sultan was actually, as he is now nominally, supreme, but the story of disturbances under this government is a very old one, internal strife having been the normal condition of the State ever since Europeans have been acquainted with it. It seems to have been an undoubted fact that its rivers and island channels were the resort of pirates, and that its Rajahs devoted themselves with much success to harrying small vessels trading in the Straits of Malacca.

The name of this State is not found in the earlier Malayan records. Negri Calang, or the land of tin, was the designation of this part of the peninsula, and this depopulated region was formerly a flourishing dependency under the Malay sovereigns of Malacca. The population, such as it is, is chiefly composed of the descendants of a colony of Bugis from Goa in the Celebes, who settled in Selangor at the beginning of the eighteenth century under a Goa chief, who was succeeded by Sultan Ibrahim, an intense hater and sturdy opponent of the Dutch. He attacked Malacca, looted and burned its suburbs, and would have captured it but for the opportune arrival of a Dutch fleet. He surprised the Dutch garrison of Selangor by night, routed it, and captured all its heavy artillery and ammunition, but was afterward compelled to restore his plunder, and acknowledge himself a vassal of the Dutch East India Company. After this he attacked the Siamese, and was mainly instrumental in driving them out of Perak.

He was succeeded in 1826 by an ignoble prince, and under his weak and oppressive rule, and under the extortions and cruelties of his illegitimate brothers, the State lapsed into decay. Mr. Newbold, who had charge of a military post on the Selangor frontier in 1833, witnessed many of the atrocities perpetrated by these Bugis princes, who committed piracies, robbed, plundered, and levied contributions on the wretched Malays, without hindrance. In Mr. Newbold's day the whole population of Kwala Linggi, where he was stationed, fled by night into the Malacca territory, where they afterward settled to escape from the merciless exactions to which they were subjected. Slavery and debt slavery added to the miseries of the country, and it is believed that by emigration and other causes the Malay population was reduced to between two thousand and three thousand souls.

Only one event in the recent history of Selangor deserves notice. This miserable ruler, Sultan Mohammed, had no legitimate offspring, but it was likely that at his death his near relation, Tuanku Bongsu, a Rajah universally liked and respected by his countrymen, would have been elected to succeed him. Unfortunately for the good of the State this Rajah took upon himself the direction of the tin mines at Lukut, formerly worked by about four hundred Chinese miners on their own account, paying a tenth of their produce to the Sultan. One dark, rainy night in September, 1834, these miners rose upon their employers, burned their houses, and massacred them indiscriminately, including this enlightened Rajah; and his wife and children, in attempting to escape, were thrown into the flames of their house. The plunder obtained by the Chinese, exclusive of the jewels and gold ornaments of the women, was estimated at 3,500 pounds. This very atrocious business was believed to have been aided and abetted, if not absolutely concocted, by Chinese merchants living under the shelter of the British flag at Malacca. With the death of Tuanku Bongsu all hope of prosperity for Selangor under native rule was extinguished.

Matters became very bad in the years between 1867 and 1873, the fighting among the rival factions leading to a more complete depopulation of the country, not only by the loss in party fights, but by the exodus of peaceable cultivators. Lawlessness increased to such an extent that murders and robberies were of continual occurrence. Mr. Swettenham, the Assistant Colonial Secretary, affirms that it is hardly an exaggeration to say that every man above twenty years old had killed at least one man, and that even the women were not unaccustomed to use deadly weapons against each other.

The history of the way in which we gained a footing in Selangor is a tangled one, as the story is told quite differently by men holding high positions in the Colonial Government, who unquestionably are "all honorable men." Our first appearance on the scene was in 1871, when the Rinaldo destroyed Selangor, for reasons which will be found in the succeeding letter. In November, 1873, an act of piracy was committed on the Jugra river near the Sultan's residence. On this Sir A. Clarke, the Governor of the Straits Settlements, with a portion of H.B.M.'s China fleet, went to Langat and induced the Sultan to appoint a court to try the pirates, three of the ships and two Government Commissioners remaining to watch the trial. The prisoners were executed, the war-ships patroled the coast for a time, and everything became quiet.

In 1874, however, there were new disturbances and alleged piracies, and Tunku Dia Udin, the Sultan's son-in-law and viceroy, overmatched by powerful Rajahs, gladly welcomed an official, who was sent by Sir A. Clarke, "to remain with the Sultan should he desire it, and, by his presence and advice give him confidence, and assistance to carry out the promises which he had made," which were, in brief, to suppress piracy and keep good order in his dominions; not a difficult task, it might be supposed, for it is estimated that he had only about two thousand Malay subjects left, and the Chinese miners were under the efficient rule of their "Capitan," Ah Loi.

In January, 1875, at Tunku Dia Udin's request, a British Resident was sent to Selangor. Some time afterward the viceroy retired to Kedah, and the Sultan has been "advised" into a sort of pensioned retirement, the Resident levying, collecting, and expending the taxes. Sir Andrew Clarke was very fortunate in his selection of the Sultan's first adviser, for Mr. Davidson, according to all accounts, had an intimate knowledge of the Malays, as well as a wise consideration for them; he had a calm temper and much good sense, and is held in honorable remembrance, not only for official efficiency but for having gained the sincere regard of the people of Selangor. His legal training and high reputation in the colonial courts were of great value in the settlement of the many difficult questions which arose during his brief administration. He was succeeded in 1876 by Mr. Bloomfield Douglas, who has held the office of Resident for six years.

The revenue of Selangor amounted in 1881 to 47,045 pounds, derived mainly from the export duty on tin, the import duty on opium, and the letting of opium and other licenses and farms. The expenditure was 46,876 pounds, the heaviest items being for "establishments," "pensions," and "works and buildings." The outlook for Selangor appears to be a peaceful one, and it is to be hoped that, under the energetic administration of Sir F. A. Weld, its capabilities will be developed and its anomalies of law and taxation reformed, and that both Malays and foreigners may experience those advantages of good order and security which result from a just rule.

Letter XIV

The S.S. Rainbow—Sunset at Malacca—A Night at Sea—The Residency at Klang—Our "Next-of-Kin"—The Decay of Klang—A Remarkable Chinaman—Theatrical Magnificence—Misdeed of a "Rogue Elephant"—"A Cobra! A Cobra!"

S.S. "RAINBOW," MALACCA ROADS, February 1, 5 P.M.

I am once again on board this quaint little Chinese steamer, which is rolling on a lazy ground-swell on the heated, shallow sea. We were to have sailed at four P.M., but mat-sailed boats, with cargoes of Chinese, Malays, fowls, pine-apples, and sugar-cane, kept coming off and delaying us. The little steamer has long ago submerged her load-line, and is only about ten inches above the water, and still they load, and still the mat-sailed boats and eight-paddled boats, with two red-clothed men facing forward on each thwart, are disgorging men and goods into the overladen craft. A hundred and thirty men, mostly Chinese, with a sprinkling of Javanese and Malays, are huddled on the little deck, with goats and buffaloes, and forty coops of fowls and ducks; the fowls and ducks cackling and quacking, and the Chinese clattering at the top of their voices—such a Babel!

An hour later, "Easy ahead," shouts the Portuguese-Malay captain, for the Rainbow is only licensed for one hundred passengers, and the water runs in at the scuppers as she rolls, but five of the mat-sailed boats have hooked on. "Run ahead! full speed!" the captain shouts in English; he dances with excitement, and screams in Malay; the Chinamen are climbing up the stern, over the bulwarks, everywhere, fairly boarding us; and with about a hundred and fifty souls on board, and not a white man or a Christian among them, we steam away over the gaudy water into the gaudy sunset, and beautiful, dreamy, tropical Malacca, with its palm-fringed shores, and its colored streets, and Mount Ophir with its golden history, and the stately Stadthaus, whose ancient rooms have come to seem almost like my property, are passing into memories. A gory ball drops suddenly from a gory sky into a flaming sea, and

"With one stride comes the dark."

There is no place for me except on this little bridge, on which the captain and I have just had an excellent dinner, with hen-coops for seats. These noisy fowls are now quiet in the darkness, but the noisier Chinese are still bawling at the top of their voices. It is too dark for another line.

British Residency, Klang Selangor.—You will not know where Klang is, and I think you won't find it in any atlas or encyclopedia. Indeed, I almost doubt whether you will find Selangor, the Malay State of which Klang is, after a fashion, the capital. At present I can tell you very little.

Selangor is bounded on the north by the "protected" State of Perak, which became notorious in England a few years ago for a "little war," in which we inflicted a very heavy chastisement on the Malays for the assassination of Mr. Birch, the British Resident. It has on its south and southeast Sungei Ujong, Jelabu, and Pahang; but its boundaries in these directions are ill-defined. The Strait of Malacca bounds it on the west, and its coast-line is about a hundred and twenty miles long. From its slightly vague interior boundary to the coast, it is supposed to preserve a tolerably uniform depth of from fifty to sixty miles. Klang is on the Klang river, in lat. 3 degrees 3' N., and long. 101 degrees 29' 30" E. I call it "the Capital after a fashion," because the Resident and his myrmidons live here, and because vessels which draw thirteen feet of water can go no higher; but the true capital, created by the enterprise of Chinamen, is thirty-six miles farther inland, the tin-mining settlement of Kwala Lumpor. Selangor thrives, if it does thrive, which I greatly doubt, on tin and gutta; but Klang is a most misthriven, decayed, dejected, miserable-looking place.* The nominal ruler of Selangor is Sultan Abdul Samat, but he hybernates on a pension at Langat, a long way off, and must be nearly obliterated, I think.

*[*Kwala Lumpor is now the most important mining entrepot in Selangor, and in 1880 the British Resident and his staff were removed thither.]*

It is a great change from Malacca in every respect. I left it with intense regret. Hospitality, kindness, most genial intercourse, and its own semi-mediaeval and tropical fascinations, made it one of the brightest among the many bright spots of my wanderings. Mr. Hayward took me to the Rainbow in a six-oared boat, manned by six policemen, completing the list of "Government facilities" as far as Malacca is concerned. The mercury was 90 degrees in my little cabin or den, and it swarmed not only with mosquitoes, but with cockroaches, which, in the dim light, looked as large as mice. Of course, no one sleeps below in the tropics who can avoid it; so as the deck was thick with Chinamen, I had my mattress laid on a bench on the bridge, which was only occupied by two Malay look-out men. There is not very much comfort when one leaves the beaten tracks of travel, but any loss is far more than made up for by the intense enjoyment.

It was a delightful night. The moon was only a hemisphere, yet I think she gave more light than ours at the full. The night was so exquisite that I was content to rest without sleeping; the Babel noises of fowls and men had ceased, and there were only quiet sounds of rippling water, and the occasional cry of a sea-bird as we slipped through the waveless sea. When the moon set, the sky was wonderful with its tropic purple and its pavement and dust of stars. I have become quite fond of the Southern Cross, and don't wonder that the early navigators prostrated themselves on deck when they first saw it. It is not an imposing constellation, but it is on a part of the sky which is not crowded with stars, and it always lies aslant and obvious. It has become to me as much a friend as is the Plough of the northern regions.

At daybreak the next morning we were steaming up the Klang river, whose low shores are entirely mangrove swamps, and when the sun was high and hot we anchored in front of the village of Klang, where a large fort on an eminence, with grass embankments in which guns are mounted, is the first prominent object. Above this is a large wooden bungalow with an attap roof, which is the British Residency. There was no air, and the British ensign in front of the house hung limp on the flag-staff. Below there is a village, with clusters of Chinese houses on the ground, and Malay houses on stilts, standing singly, with one or two Government offices bulking largely among them. A substantial flight of stone steps leads from the river to a skeleton jetty with an attap roof, and near it a number of attap-roofed boats were lying, loaded with slabs of tin from the diggings in the interior, to be transhipped to Pinang. A dainty steam-launch, the Abdulsamat, nominally the Sultan's yacht, flying a large red and yellow flag, was also lying in the river.

Mr. Bloomfield Douglas, the Resident, a tall, vigorous, elderly man, with white hair, a florid complexion, and a strong voice heard everywhere in authoritative tones, met me with a four-oared boat, and a buggy with a good Australian horse brought me here. From this house there is a large but not a beautiful view of river windings, rolling jungle, and blue hills. The lower part of the house, which is supported on pillars, is mainly open, and is used for billiard-room, church, lounging-room, afternoon tea-room, and audience-room; but I see nothing of the friendly, easy-going to and fro of Chinese and Malays, which was a pleasant feature of the Residency in Sungei Ujong. In fact, there is here much of the appearance of an armed post amidst a hostile population. In front of the Residency there is a six-pounder flanked by two piles of shot. Behind it there is a guard-room, with racks of rifles and bayonets for the Resident's body-guard of twelve men, and quarters for the married soldiers, for soldiers they are, though they are called policemen. A gong hangs in front of the porch on which to sound the alarm, and a hundred men fully armed can turn out at five minutes' notice.

The family consists of the Resident, his wife, a dignified and gracious woman, with a sweet but plaintive expression of countenance, and an afflicted daughter, on whom her mother attends with a loving, vigilant, and ceaseless devotion of a most pathetic kind. The circle is completed by a handsome black monkey tied to a post, and an ape which they call an ouf, from the solitary monosyllable which it utters, but which I believe to be the "agile gibbon," a creature so delicate that it has never yet survived a voyage to England.

It is a beautiful creature. I could "put off" hours of time with it. It walks on its hind legs with a curious human walk, hanging its long arms down by its sides like B———-. It will walk quietly by your side like another person. It has nice dark eyes, with well-formed lids like ours, a good nose, a human mouth with very nice white teeth, and a very pleasant cheery look when it smiles, but when its face is at rest the expression is sad and wistful. It spends a good deal of its time in swinging itself most energetically. It has very pretty fingers and finger-nails. It looks fearfully near of kin to us, and yet the gulf is measureless. It can climb anywhere, and take long leaps. This morning it went into a house in which a cluster of bananas is hanging, leaped up to the roof, and in no time had peeled two, which it ate very neatly. It has not even a rudimentary tail. When it sits with its arms folded it looks like a gentlemanly person in a close-fitting fur suit.

The village of Klang is not interesting. It looks like a place which has "seen better days," and does not impress one favorably as regards the prosperity of the State. Above it the river passes through rich alluvial deposits, well adapted for sugar, rice, and other products of low-lying tropical lands; but though land can be purchased on a system of deferred payments for two dollars an acre, these lands are still covered with primeval jungle. Steam-launches and flattish-bottomed native boats go up the river eighteen miles farther to a village called Damarsara, from which a good country road has been made to the great Chinese village and tin mines of Kwala Lumpor. The man-eating tigers, which almost until now infested the old jungle track, have been driven back, and plantations of tobacco, tapioca, and rice have been started along the road. On a single Chinese plantation, near Kwala Lumpor, there are over two thousand acres of tapioca under cultivation, and the enterprising Chinaman who owns it has imported European steam machinery for converting the tapioca roots into the marketable article. Whatever enterprise I hear of in the interior is always in the hands of Chinamen. Klang looks as if an incubus oppressed it, and possibly the Chinese are glad to be as far as possible from the seat of what impresses me as a fussy Government. At all events, Klang, from whatever cause, has a blighted look; and deserted houses rapidly falling into decay, overgrown roads, fields choked with weeds, and an absence of life and traffic in the melancholy streets, have a depressing influence. The people are harassed by a vexatious and uncertain system of fees and taxes, calculated to engender ill feeling, and things connected with the administration seem somewhat "mixed."

You will be almost tired of the Chinese, but the more I see of them the more I am impressed by them. These States, as well as Malacca, would be jungles with a few rice clearings among them were it not for their energy and industry. Actually the leading man, not only at Kwala Lumpor (now the seat of government), but in Selangor, is Ah Loi, a Chinaman! During the disturbances before we "advised" the State, the Malays burned the town of Kwala Lumpor three times, and he rebuilt it, and, in spite of many disasters stuck to it at the earnest request of the native government. He has made long roads for the purpose of connecting the most important of the tin mines with the town. His countrymen place implicit confidence in him, and Mr. Syers, the admirable superintendent of police, tells me that by his influence and exertions he has so successfully secured peace and order in his town and district that during many years not a single serious crime has been committed. He employs on his estate—in mines, brickfields, and plantations—over four thousand men. He has the largest tapioca estate in the country and the best machinery. He has introduced the manufacture of bricks, has provided the sick with an asylum, has been loyal to British interests, has been a most successful administrator in the populous district intrusted to him, and has dispensed justice to the complete satisfaction of his countrymen. While he is the creator of the commercial interests of Selangor, he is a man of large aims and of an enlightened public spirit. Is there no decoration of St. Michael or St. George in reserve for Ah Loi?* So far, however, from receiving any suitable recognition of his services, it is certain that Ah Loi's claims for compensation for losses, etc., have not yet been settled.

> [*The months after my visit, Ah Loi received the Sultan of Selangor for several days with great magnificence, and in July, 1880, he entertained the Governor of the Straits Settlements and his suite with yet greater splendor, erecting for the occasion a fine banqueting-hall with open sides.]

Sir F. A. Weld writes of this visit—"At Kwala Lumpor, besides the reception and a dinner at the Capitan China's, a Chinese theatrical performance was given representing a sultan and great rajahs, quarreling, but laying aside their quarrels on the appearance of a 'governor,' who pacifies the country. Addresses and odes were also sung and recited to me from the stage, and the performers representing the great personages prostrated themselves and made obeisances. The dresses were all real hand-worked gold and silver embroidery on thick silks of the richest colors. The princes were attended by their warriors, some of whose helmets and arms were magnificent, with banners and feather standards, and coats of arms, or their equivalents, borne aloft by heralds; ladies also appeared, one a prima-donna, other actresses rode hobby-horses, only the head of the woman and hobby-horse being visible in the clouds of silk and gold. Jesters jested; and tumblers, in blue, loose tunics and wide scarlet trousers, shot across the stage when there was any room in front of the crowd of actors with the rapidity of meteors. The pace was too great to be even sure that they were human beings. I have seen Kean's Shakespearian revival pageants formerly in London, but I never realized what a mediaeval court pageant might have been till in the heart of the Malay Peninsula I saw the most gorgeous combination of color and picturesque effect that I have ever set eyes upon."

Klang does not improve on further acquaintance. It looks as if half the houses were empty, and certainly half the population is composed of Government employes, chiefly police constables. There is no air of business energy, and the queerly mixed population saunters with limp movements; even the few Chinese look depressed, as if life were too much for them. It looks too as if there were a need for holding down the population (which I am sure there isn't), for in addition to the fort and its barracks, military police stations are dotted about. A jail, with a very high wall, is in the middle of the village. The jungle comes so near to Klang that tigers and herds of elephants, sometimes forty strong, have been seen within half a mile of it. In Sungei Ujong there was some excitement about a "rogue elephant" (i.e., an elephant which for reasons which appear good to other elephants, has been expelled from the herd, and has been made mad and savage by solitude), which, after killing two men, has crossed the river into Selangor, and is man-killing here. A few days ago a man catching sight of him in the jungle took refuge in a tree, and the brute tore the tree down with its trunk, and trampled the poor fellow to death, his companion escaping during the process.

Yesterday evening we had service in the hall, the whole white population being "rounded up" for it; seven men and two women, three of whom are Roman Catholics. The congregation sat under one punkah and the Resident under another, both being worked by bigoted Mohammedans! Everything was "ship-shape," as becomes Mr. Douglas's antecedents; a union jack over the desk, from which the liturgy was read, and a tiger-skin over the tiles in front, the harmonium well played, the singing and chanting excellent. We had one of the most beautiful of the Ambrosian hymns, and possibly Dr. Bonar may like to hear that his hymn, "I heard the voice of Jesus say," was sung with equal enjoyment by Catholics and Protestants in the wilds of the Golden Chersonese.

There is an almost daily shower here, and it is lovely now, with a balmy freshness in the air. No one could imagine that we are in the torrid zone, and only 3 degrees from the equator. The mercury has not been above 83 degrees since I came, and the sea and land breezes are exquisitely delicious. I wish you could see a late afternoon here in its full beauty, with palms against a golden sky, pink clouds, a pink river, and a balm-breathing air, just strong enough to lift the heavy scented flowers which make the evenings delicious. There has been a respite from mosquitoes, and I am having a "real good time."

But I had a great fright yesterday (part of the "good time" though). I was going into the garden when six armed policemen leapt past me as if they had been shot, followed by Mr. Daly, the land-surveyor, who has the V.C. for some brave deed, shouting "a cobra! a cobra!" and I saw a hooded head above the plants, and then the form I most fear and loathe twisting itself toward the house with frightful rapidity, every one flying. I was up a ladder in no time, and the next moment one of the policemen, plucking up courage, broke the reptile's back with the butt of his rifle, and soon it was borne away, dead, by its tail. It was over four feet long. They get about three a day at the fort.

There is a reward of 20 cents per foot for every venomous snake brought in, 50 cents per foot for an alligator, and 25 dollars for every tiger. Lately the police have got two specimens of an ophiophagus, a snake-eating snake over eighteen feet long, whose bite they say is certain death. They have a horrible collection of snakes alive, half dead, dead, and preserved. There was a fright of a different kind late at night, and the two made me so nervous that when the moonlight glinted two or three times on the bayonet of the sentry, which I could see from my bed, I thought it was a Malay going to murder the Resident, against whom I fear there may be many a vendetta.

Letter XIV

Continued

Yachting in the Malacca Straits—A Tropic Dream—The Rajah Moussa —Tiger Stories—A Grand Excitement—A "Man-Eating Kris"—A Royal Residence—A Council of State—The Sultan's Attendants—The "Light of the Harem"—The Sultan's Offering

S.S. "ABDULSAMAT," LANGAT RIVER, SELANGOR

I was glad to get up at sunrise, when the whole heaven was flooded with color and glory, and the lingering mists which lay here and there over the jungle gleamed like silver. Before we left, Mrs. Douglas gave me tea, scones, and fresh butter, the first fresh butter that I have tasted for ten months. We left Klang in this beautiful steam-launch, the (so-called) yacht of the Sultan, at eight, with forty souls on board.

I am somewhat hazy as to where I am. "The Langat river" is at present to me only a "geographical expression." It is now past three o'clock, and we have been going about since eight, sometimes up rivers, but mostly on lovely tropic seas among islands. This is one of the usual business tours of the Resident, with the additional object of presenting a uniform to the Sultan. Besides Mr. Douglas there are his son-in-law, Mr. Daly; Mr. Hawley, who has lately been appointed to a collectorship, and who goes up to be presented to the Sultan; Mr. Syers, formerly a private in the 10th Regiment, now superintendent of the Selangor police force;

and thirty policemen, who go up to form the Sultan's escort to-morrow. Precautions, for some occult reason, seem to be considered indispensable here, and have been increased since the murder of Mr. Lloyd at the Dindings. The yacht has a complete permanent roof of painted canvas, and under this is an armament of boarding pikes. Round the little foremast four cutlasses and a quantity of ball cartridges are displayed. Six rifles are in a rack below, and the policemen and body-guard are armed with rifles and bayonets.

The yacht is perfection. The cabin, in which ten can dine, is high and airy, and, being forward, there is no vibration. Space is exquisitely utilized by all manner of contrivances. She is only 50 tons, and very low in the water, but we are going all the way to Prince of Wales island in her—200 miles. Everything is perfect on board, even to the cuisine, and I appreciate the low rattan chairs at the bow, in which one can sit in the shade and enjoy the zephyrs.

This day has been a tropic dream. I have enjoyed it and am enjoying it intensely. We steamed down the Klang river, and then down a narrow river-like channel among small palm-fringed islands which suddenly opened upon the sea, which was slightly green toward the coral-sanded, densely wooded, unpeopled shores, but westward the green tint merged into a blue tint, which ever deepened till a line of pure, deep, indescribable blue cut the blue sky on the far-off clear horizon. But, ah! that "many twinkling smile of ocean!" Words cannot convey an idea of what it is under this tropic sun and sky, with the silver-flashing wavelets rippling the surface of the sapphire sea, beneath whose clear warm waters brilliant fishes are darting through the coral groves. These are enchanted seas—

> "Where falls not rain, or hail, or any snow,
> Or ever wind blows loudly."

It is unseemly that the Abdulsamat should smoke and puff and leave a foamy wake behind her. "Sails of silk and ropes of sendal," and poetic noiseless movements only would suit these lovely Malacca Straits. This is one of the very few days in my life in which I have felt mere living to be a luxury, and what it is to be akin to seas and breezes, and birds and insects, and to know why nature sings and smiles.

  We had been towing a revenue cutter with stores for a new lighthouse, and cast her adrift at the point where we anchored, and the Resident and Mr. Daly went ashore with thirteen policemen, and I had a most interesting and instructive conversation with Mr. Syers. Afterward we steamed along the low wooded coast, and then up the Langat river till we came to Bukit Jugra, an isolated hill covered with jungle. The landing is up a great face of smooth rock, near the top of which is a pretty police station, and higher still, nearly concealed by bananas and cocoa-palms, is the large bungalow of the revenue officer and police magistrate of Langat. We saw Mr. Ferney, the magistrate, landed the police guard, and then steamed up here for a council.

  Mr. Syers went ashore, and returned with the Sultan's heir, the Rajah Moussa, a very peculiar-looking Malay, a rigid Mohammedan, who is known, the Resident says, to have said that when he becomes Sultan he "will drive the white men into the sea." He works hard, as an example to his people, and when working dresses like a coolie. He sets his face against cock-fighting and other Malay sports, is a reformer, and a *dour*, strong-willed man, and his accession seems to be rather dreaded by the Resident, as it is supposed that he will be something more than a mere figure-head prince. He is a Hadji, and was dressed in a turban made of many yards of priceless silk muslin, embroidered in silk, a white baju, and a long white sarong, and full white trousers—a beautiful dress for an Oriental. He shook hands with me. I wish that these people would not adopt our salutations, their own are so much more appropriate to their character.

  The yacht is now lying at anchor in a deep coffee-colored stream, near a picturesque Malay village on stilts, surrounded by very extensive groves of palms. Several rivers intersect each other in this neighborhood, flowing through dense jungles and mangrove swamps. The sun is still high. The four white men and the Rajah Moussa have gone ashore snipe shooting, the Malays on board are sleeping, and I am enjoying a delicious solitude.

February 4, 4 P.M.—We are steaming over the incandescent sapphire sea, among the mangrove-bordered islands which fringe the Selangor coast, under a blazing sun, with the mercury 88 degrees in the shade, but the heat, though fierce, is not oppressive, and I have had a delightful day. The men returned when they could no longer see to shoot snipes, with a well filled bag, and after sunset we dropped down to Bukit Jugra or Langat. Most of the river was as black as night with the heavy shadows of the forest, but along the middle there was a lane of lemon-colored water, the exquisite reflection of a lemon-colored sky. The Resident and Mr. Daly went down to the coast in the yacht to avoid the mosquitoes of the interior, but I with Omar, one of the "body guard," half Malay half Kling, as my attendant, and Mr. Syers, landed, to remain at the magistrate's bungalow. It was a lovely walk up the hill through the palms and bananas, and the bayonets of our escort gleamed in the intense moonlight, not with anything alarming about them either, for an escort is only necessary because the place is so infested by tigers. The bungalow is large but rambling, and my room was one built out at the end, with six windows with solid shutters, of which Mr. Ferney closed all but two, and half closed those, because of a tiger which is infesting the immediate neighborhood of the house, and whose growling, they say, is most annoying. He killed a heifer belonging to the Sultan two nights ago, and last night the sentry got a shot at him from the veranda outside my room as he was engaged in most undignified depredations upon the hen house.

There was a grand excitement yesterday morning. A tigress was snared in a pitfall and was shot. Her corpse was brought to the bungalow warm and limp. She measured eight feet two inches from her nose to her tail, and her tail was two feet six inches long. She had whelps, and they must be starving in the jungle tonight. Her beautiful skin is hanging up. All the neighborhood, Chinese and Malay, turned out. Some danced; and the Sultan beat gongs. Everybody seized upon a bit of the beast. The Sultan claimed the liver, which, when dried and powdered, is worth twice its weight in gold, as a medicine. The blood was taken, and I saw the Chinamen drying it in the sun on small slabs; it is an invaluable tonic! The eyes, which were of immense size, were eagerly scrambled for, that the hard parts in the centre, which are valuable charms, might be set in gold as rings. It was sad to see the terrible "glaring eyeballs" of the jungle so dim and stiff. The bones were taken to be boiled down to a jelly, which, when some mysterious drug has been added, is a grand tonic. The gall is most precious, and the flesh was all taken, but for what purpose I don't know. A steak of it was stewed, and I tasted it, and found it in flavor much like the meat of an ancient and overworked draught ox, but Mr. Ferney thought it like good veal. At dinner the whole talk was of the wild beasts of the jungle; and, as we were all but among them, it was very fascinating. I wanted to go out by moonlight, but Mr. Ferney said that it was not safe, because of tigers, and even the Malays there don't go out after nightfall.

Mr. Ferney has given me a stick with a snake-mark on it, which was given to him as a thing of great value. The Malay donor said that anyone carrying it would become invulnerable and invisible, and that if you were to beat anyone with it, the beaten man would manifest all the symptoms of snake poisoning! Mr. Ferney has also given me a kris. When I showed it to Omar this morning, he passed it across his face and smelt it, and then said, "This kris good—has ate a man."

I could not sleep much, there were such strange noises, and the sentry made the veranda creak all night outside my room; but this is a splendid climate, and one is refreshed and ready to rise with the sun after very little sleep. The tropic mornings are glorious. There is such an abrupt and vociferous awakening of nature, all dew-bathed and vigorous. The rose-flushed sky looks cool, the air feels cool, one longs to protract the delicious time. Then with a suddenness akin to that of his setting, the sun wheels above the horizon, and is high in the heavens in no time, truly "coming forth as a bridegroom out of his chamber, and rejoicing as a giant to run his course," and as truly "There is nothing hid from the heat thereof," for hardly is he visible than the heat becomes tremendous. But tropical trees and flowers, instead of drooping and withering under the solar fury, rejoice in it.

This morning was splendid. The great banana fronds under the still, blue sky looked truly tropical The mercury was 82 degrees at 7 A.M. The "tiger mosquitoes," day torments, large mosquitoes with striped legs, a loud metallic hum, and a plethora of venom, were in full fury from daylight. Ammonia does not relieve their bites as it does those of the night mosquitoes, and I am covered with inflamed and confluent lumps as large as the half of a bantam's egg. But these and other drawbacks, I know from experience, will soon be forgotten, and I shall remember only the beauty, the glory, and the intense enjoyment of this day.

Quite early the Rajah Moussa arrived in a baju of rich, gold-colored silk, which suited his swarthy complexion. He sat in the room pretending to look over the Graphic, but in reality watching me, as I wrote to you, just as I should watch an ouf. At last he asked how many Japanese I had killed!!!!

The succession is here hereditary in the male line, and this Rajah Moussa is the Sultan's eldest son. The Sultan receives 2,000 pounds a year out of the revenue, and this Rajah 960 pounds.

The Resident arrived at nine, wearing a very fine dress sword, and gold epaulettes on his linen coat; and under a broiling sun we all walked through a cleared part of the jungle, through palms and bananas, to the reception at the Sultan's, which was the "motive" of our visit. The Sultan, Abdulsamat, has three houses in a beautiful situation, at the end of a beautiful valley. They are in the purest style of Malay architecture, and not a Western idea appears anywhere. The wood of which they are built is a rich brown red. The roofs are very high and steep, but somewhat curved. The architecture is simple, appropriate, and beautiful The dwelling consists of the Sultan's house, a broad, open passage, and then the women's house or harem. At the end of the above passage is the audience-hall, and the front entrance to the Sultan's house is through a large porch which forms a convenient reception room on occasions like that of yesterday.

From this back passage or court a ladder, with rungs about two feet apart, leads into the Sultan's house, and a step-ladder into the women's house. Two small boys, entirely naked, were incongruous objects sitting at the foot of the ladder. Here we waited for him, two files of policemen being drawn up as a guard of honor. He came out of the women's house very actively, shook hands with each of us (obnoxious custom!), and passed through the lines of police round to the other side of his house into the porch, the floor of which was covered with fine matting nearly concealed by handsome Persian rugs.

The Sultan sat on a high-backed, carved chair or throne. All the other chairs were plain. The Resident sat on his right, I on his left, and on my left the Rajah Moussa, with other sons of the sultan, and some native princes. Mr. Syers acted as interpreter. Outside there were double lines of military police, and the bright adjacent slopes were covered with the Sultan's followers and other Malays. The balcony of the audience-hall, which has a handsome balustrade, was full of Malay followers in bright reds and cool white. It was all beautiful, and the palms rustled in the soft air, and bright birds and butterflies flew overhead, rejoicing in mere existence.

If Abdulsamat were not Sultan, I should pick him out as the most prepossessing Malay that I have seen. He is an elderly man, with iron-gray hair, a high and prominent brow, large, prominent, dark, eyes, a well-formed nose, and a good mouth. The face is bright, kindly, and fairly intelligent. He is about the middle height. His dress became him well, and he looked comfortable in it though he had not worn it before. It was a rich, black velvet baju or jacket, something like a loose hussar jacket, braided, frogged, and slashed with gold, trousers with a broad gold strip on the outside, a rich silk sarong in checks and shades of red, and a Malay printed silk handkerchief knotted round his head, forming a sort of peak. No Mohammedan can wear a hat with a rim or stiff crown, or of any kind which would prevent him from bowing his forehead to the earth in worship.

The Resident read the proceedings of the council of the day before, and the Sultan confirmed them. The nominal approval of measures initiated by the Resident and agreed to in council, and the signing of death-warrants, are among the few prerogatives which "his Highness" retains. Then a petition for a pension from Rajah Brean was read, the Rajah, a slovenly-looking man, being present. The petition was refused, and the Sultan, in refusing it, spoke some very strong words about idleness, which seems a great failing of Rajah Brean's but it has my strong sympathy, for—

"—Why
Should life all labor be?—
There is no joy but calm;
Why should we only toil, the roof and crown of things?"

During the reception a richly-dressed attendant sat on the floor with an iron tube like an Italian iron in his hand, in which he slowly worked an arrangement which might be supposed to be a heater up and down. I thought that he might be preparing betel-nut, but Mr. Douglas said that he was working a charm for the Sultan's safety, and it was believed that if he paused some harm would happen. Another attendant, yet more richly dressed, carried a white scarf fringed and embroidered with gold over one shoulder, and two vases of solid gold, with their surfaces wrought by exquisite workmanship into flowers nearly as delicate as filigree work. One of these contained betel-nut, and the other sirih leaves. Meanwhile the police, with their bayonets flashing in the sun, and the swarthy, richly-costumed throng on the palm-shaded slopes, were a beautiful sight. The most interesting figure to me was that of the reforming heir, the bigoted Moslem in his gold-colored baju, with his swarthy face, singular and almost sinister expression, and his total lack of all Western fripperies of dress. I think that there may be trouble when he comes to the throne, at least if the present arrangements continue. He does not look like a man who would be content to be a mere registrar of the edicts of "a dog of an infidel."

The Sultan has a "godown" containing great treasures, concerning which he leads an anxious life—hoards of diamonds and rubies, and priceless damascened krises, with scabbards of pure gold wrought into marvelous devices and incrusted with precious stones. On Mr. Douglas's suggestion (as I understood) he sent a kris with an elaborate gold scabbard to the Governor, saying: "It is not from the Sultan to the Governor, *but from a friend to a friend*." He seems anxious for Selangor to "get on." He is making a road at Langat at his own expense; and acting, doubtless, under British advice, has very cordially agreed that the odious system of debt slavery shall be quietly dropped from among the institutions of Selangor.

When this audience was over I asked to be allowed to visit the Sultana, and, with Mrs. Ferney as interpreter, went to the harem, accompanied by the Rajah Moussa. It is a beautiful house, of one very large, lofty room, part of which is divided into apartments by heavy silk curtains. One end of it is occupied by a high dais covered with fine mats, below which is another dais covered with Persian carpets. On this the Sultana received us, the Rajah Moussa, who is not her son, and ourselves sitting on chairs. If I understood rightly that this prince is not her son, I do not see how it is that he can go into the women's apartments. Two guards sat on the floor just within the door, and numbers of women, some of them in white veils, followers of the Sultana, sat in rows also on the floor.

It must be confessed that the "light of the harem" is not beautiful. She looks nearly middle-aged. She is short and fat, with a flat nose, open wide nostrils, thick lips, and filed teeth, much blackened by betel-nut chewing. Her expression is pleasant, and her manner is prepossessing. She wore a rich, striped, red silk sarong, and a very short, green silk kabaya with diamond clasps; but I saw very little of her dress or herself, because she was almost enveloped in a pure white veil of a fine woolen material spangled with gold stars, and she concealed so much of her face with it, in consequence of the presence of the Rajah Moussa, that I only rarely got a glimpse of the magnificent diamond solitaires in her ears. Our conversation was not brilliant, and the Sultana looked to me as if she had attained nirvana, and had "neither ideas nor the consciousness of the absence of ideas." We returned and took leave of the Sultan, and after we left I caught a glimpse of him lounging at ease in a white shirt and red sarong, all his gorgeousness having disappeared.

After we returned to the bungalow the Sultan sent me a gift. Eight attendants dressed in pure white came into the room in single file, and each bowing to the earth, sat down a brass salver, with its contents covered with a pure white cloth. Again bowing, they uncovered them, and displayed the fruitage of the tropics. There were young cocoa-nuts, gold-colored bananas of the kind which the Sultan eats, papayas, and clusters of a species of jambu, a pear-shaped fruit, beautiful to look at, each fruit looking as if made of some transparent, polished white wax with a pink flush on one side. The Rajah Moussa also arrived and took coffee, and the verandas were filled with his followers. Every Rajah goes about attended, and seems to be esteemed according to the size of his following.

We left this remote and beautiful place at noon, and after a delightful cruise of five hours down the Jugra, and among islands floating on a waveless sea, we reached dreary, decayed Klang in the evening.

I. L. B.

Letter XV

Tiger Mosquitoes—Insect Torments—A Hadji's Fate—Malay Custom —Oaths and Lies—A False Alarm

THE RESIDENCY, KLANG, February 7.

I have had two days of supposed quiet here after the charming expedition to Langat. The climate seems very healthy. The mercury has been 87 degrees daily, but then it falls to 74 degrees at night. The barometer, as is usual so near the equator, varies only a few tenths of an inch during the year. The rainfall is about 130 inches annually. It is most abundant in January, February and March, and at the change of the monsoon, and there is enough all the year round to keep vegetation in beauty. Here, on uninteresting cleared land with a featureless foreground and level mangrove swamps for the middle distance, it must be terribly monotonous to have no change of seasons, no hope of the mercury falling below 80 degrees in the daytime, or of a bracing wind, or of any marked climatic changes for better or worse all life through.

The mosquitoes are awful, but after a few months of more or less suffering the people who live here become inoculated by the poison, and are more bothered than hurt by the bites. I am almost succumbing to them. The ordinary pests are bad enough, for just when the evenings become cool, and sitting on the veranda would be enjoyable; they begin their foray, and specially attack the feet and ankles; but the tiger mosquitoes of this region bite all day, and they do embitter life. In the evening all the gentlemen put on sarongs over their trousers to protect themselves, and ladies are provided with sarongs which we draw over our feet and dresses, but these wretches bite through two "ply" of silk or cotton; and, in spite of all precautions, I am dreadfully bitten on my ankles, feet, and arms, which are so swollen that I can hardly draw on my sleeves, and for two days stockings have been an impossibility, and I have had to sew up my feet daily in linen! The swellings from the bites have become confluent, and are scarlet with inflammation. It is truly humiliating that "the crown of things" cannot defend himself against these minute enemies, and should be made as miserable as I am just now.

But it is a most healthy climate, and when I write of mosquitoes, land leeches, centipedes and snakes, I have said my say as to its evils. I will now confess that I was bitten by a centipede in my bath-house in Sungei Ujong, but I at once cut the bite deeply with a penknife, squeezed it, and poured ammonia recklessly over it, and in a few hours the pain and swelling went off.

I had been to the fort, the large barrack of the military police, and Mr. Syers showed me many things. In the first place, a snake about eight feet long was let out and killed. The Malays call this a "two-headed" snake, and there is enough to give rise to the ignorant statement, for after the proper head was dead the tail stood up and moved forward. The skin of this reptile was marked throughout with broad bands of black and white alternately. There was an ill-favored skull of a crocodile hanging up to dry, with teeth three inches long. One day lately a poor Hadji was carried off by one, and shortly afterwards this monster was caught, and on opening it they found the skull of the Hadji, part of his body, a bit of his clothing, and part of a goat. I brought away as spoils tiger's teeth and claws, crocodile's teeth, bear's teeth, etc.

I went also to the Government offices. The skin of a superb tiger, which was killed close to Klang after it had devoured six men, decorated the entrance. I heard two cases tried before the Resident. The first criminal was a Malay, who was "in trouble" for the very British crime of nearly beating his wife to death. She said she did not want to prosecute him, but to get a divorce. She was told to apply to the Imaum, and the man was bound over to keep the peace for six months. The next case was a very common one here, and the court was crowded with Chinese onlookers. A Chinaman had bought a girl (very nice-looking she was), and now a man wants to marry her, upon which her owner produces a promissory note from her, and demands $165 as her price! It was impossible to make him understand that the transaction is utterly illegal and immoral. The Resident addressed some very strong and just words to this man in reprobation of his conduct, which were translated for the benefit of the crowd.

I cannot elicit anything very definite, here or elsewhere, about the legal system under which criminals are tried in these States. Apparently, murder, robbery, forgery, and violent assault come under English criminal law, and must be equally punishable whether committed by a Briton, a Chinaman, or a Malay. But then nobody, except a Christian, can be punished for bigamy. So criminal law even undergoes modification by local custom; and the four wives of the Mussulman, and the subordinate wives of the Chinaman, have an equal claim to recognition with the one wife of the Englishman. Even Mohammedan law, by which the Malays profess to be ruled, is modified by Malay custom, which asserts itself specially in connection with marriage, its frequent attendant repudiation, and inheritance.

The "Malay custom" (adat Malayu) seems to have been originally a just and equitable code, though ofttimes severe in its punishments, as you will see if you can get Newbold's *Malacca*, and was probably suited to the people; but it has undergone such clippings and emendations by the successive Rajahs or Sultans of these native States, that the custom now in force bears a very faint resemblance to the original adat. It is said, indeed, that each alteration has been for the worse, and that now any chief who introduces anything of his own will, justifies it as "adat Malayu." Mr. Swettenham, the Assistant Colonial Secretary, says that the few upright Rajahs who exist say that there is no longer any "adat Malayu," but that everything is done by "adat Suka hate," i.e., the custom by which a man can best suit his own inclination.

THE GOLDEN CHERSONESE AND THE WAY THITHER (TRAVELS IN MALAYSIA)

So it seems that a most queerly muddled system of law prevails under our flag, Mohammedan law, modified by degenerate and evil custom, and to some extent by the discretion of the residents, existing alongside of fragments of English criminal law, or more perhaps correctly of "justice's justice," the Resident's notions of "equity," overriding all else.* Surely, as we have practically acquired those States, and are responsible for their good government, we ought to give them the blessing of a simple code of law, of which the residents shall be only the responsible interpreters, modified by the true "Malay custom" of course, but under the same conditions which are giving such growing satisfaction to the peoples of India and Ceylon.

[*A Colonial friend tells me that he asked an English magistrate in one of the native States, by what law—English, Colonial, or Malay—he had sentenced some culprits to three years' imprisonment, and that the reply was a shrug, and "The rascals were served right."]

The oaths are equally inscrutable, and probably no oath, however terrible in formula, would restrain a Chinese coolie witness from telling a lie, if he thought it would be to his advantage.*

[*Sir Benson Maxwell, late Chief Justice of the Straits Settlements, to whose kindness I am much indebted, wrote to me lately thus: "In China I believe an oath is rarely taken; when it is, it is in the form of an imprecation. The witness cuts off a cock's head, and prays that he may be so treated if he speaks falsely." "Would you cut off a cock's head to that?" I once asked a Chinese witness who had made a statement which I did not believe. "I would cut off an elephant's head to it," he replied. In the Colonial courts, Chinamen are sworn by burning a piece of paper on which is written some imprecation on themselves if they do not speak the truth.]

I went to see the jail, a tolerable building—a barred cage below, and a long room above—standing in a graveled courtyard, surrounded by a high wall. Formerly there were no prisons, and criminals were punished on the spot, either by being krissed, shot, or flogged. Here they have a liberal diet of rice and salt fish, and "hard labor" is only mild work on the roads. The prisoners, forty-two adult men, were drawn up in a row, and Mr. Syers called the roll, telling the crime of each man, and his conduct in prison; and most of those who had conducted themselves well were to be recommended to the Sultan for remission of part of their sentences. "Flog them if they are lazy," the Resident often said; but Mr. Syers says that he never punishes them except under aggravated circumstances. The prisoners are nearly all Chinamen, and their crimes are mostly murder, gang-robbery, assault, and theft. About half of them were in chains. There is an unusual mortality in the prison, attributed, though possibly not *attributable*, to the enforced disuse of opium. We went also to the hospital, mainly used by the police, a long airy shed, with a broad shelf on each side. Mr. Klyne, the apothecary, a half-caste, has a good many Malay dispensary patients.

On our return, four Malay women, including the Imaum's wife, came to see me. Each one would have made a picturesque picture, but they had no manners, and seized on my hands, which are coarsened, reddened, and swelled from heat and mosquito bites, all exclaiming, "chanti! chanti!"—pretty! pretty! I wondered at their bad taste, specially as they had very small and pretty hands themselves, with almond-shaped nails.

In the evening the "establishment" dined at the Residency. After dinner, as we sat in the darkness in the veranda, maddened by mosquito bites, about 9:30, the bugle at the fort sounded the "alarm," which was followed in a few seconds by the drum beating "to quarters," and in less than five minutes every approach to the Residency was held by men with fixed bayonets, and fourteen rounds of ball-cartridges each in their belts, and every road round Klang was being patrolled by pickets. I knew instinctively that it was "humbug," arranged to show the celerity with which the little army could be turned out; and shortly an orderly arrived with a note—"False alarm;" but Klang never subsided all night, and the Klings beat their tom-toms till daylight. I am writing at dawn now, in order that my letter may "catch the mail."

I. L. B.

Letter XVI

A Yachting Voyage—The Destruction of Selangor—Varieties of Slime—Swamp Fever—An Unprosperous Region—A "Deadly-Lively" Morning—A Waif and Stray—The Superintendent of Police

STEAM-LAUNCH "ABDULSAMAT" February 7.

You will certainly think, from the dates of my letters, that I am usually at sea. The Resident, his daughter, Mrs. Daly, Mr. Hawley, a revenue officer, and I, left Klang this morning at eight for a two days' voyage in this bit of a thing. Blessed be "the belt of calms!" There was the usual pomp of a body-guard, some of whom are in attendance, and a military display on the pier, well drilled, and well officered in quiet, capable, admirable, unobtrusive Mr. Syers; but gentle Mrs. Douglas, devoted to her helpless daughter, standing above the jetty, a lone woman in forlorn, decayed Klang, haunts me as a vision of sadness, as I think of her sorrow and her dignified hospitality in the midst of it.

Now, at half-past eleven, we are aground with an ebb-tide on the bar of the Selangor river; so I may write a little, though I should like to be asleep.

Bernam River, Selangor, February 8th.

"Chi-laka!" (worthless good-for-nothing wretch), "Bodo!" (fool). I hear these words repeated incessantly in tones of thunder and fury, with accompaniments which need not be dwelt upon. The Malays are a revengeful people. If any official in British service were to knock them about and insult them, one can only say what has been said to me since I came to the native States: "Well, some day—all I can say is, God help him!" But then if an official were to be krissed, no matter how deservedly in Malay estimation, a gunboat would be sent up the river to "punish," and would kill, burn, and destroy; there would be a "little war," and a heavy war indemnity, and the true bearings of the case would be lost forever.

Yesterday, after a detention on the bar, we steamed up the broad, muddy Selangor river, margined by bubbling slime, on which alligators were basking in the torrid sun, to Selangor. Here the Dutch had a fort on the top of the hill. We destroyed it in August, 1871. Some Chinese whose connection with Selangor is not traceable, after murdering nearly everybody on board a Pinang-owned junk, took the vessel to Selangor.

We demanded that the native chiefs should give up the pirates, and they gave up nine readily, but refused the tenth, against whom "it does not appear that there was any proof," and drew their krises on our police when they tried to arrest the man in defiance of them. The (acting) Governor of the Straits Settlements, instead of representing to the Sultan the misconduct, actual or supposed, of his officers, sent a war-ship to seize and punish them. This attempt was resented by the Selangor chiefs, and they fired on those who made it. The Rinaldo destroyed the town in consequence, and killed many of its inhabitants.

When the Viceroy, a brother of the Sultan of Kedah, retook Selangor two years afterward, he found that what had been a populous and thriving place was almost deserted, the few hovels which remained were in ruins, the plantations were overgrown with rank jungle growths, and their owners had fled; the mines in the interior were deserted, and the roads and jungle paths were infested by bands of half-starved robbers.*

[*This account of Selangor does not rest on local hearsay, but on the authority of two of the leading officials of the Colonial Government.]

Selangor is a most wretched place—worse than Klang. On one side of the river there is a fishing village of mat and attap hovels on stilts raised a few feet above the slime of a mangrove swamp; and on the other an expanse of slime, with larger houses on stilts, and an attempt at a street of Chinese shops, and a gambling-den, which I entered, and found full of gamblers at noonday. The same place serves for a spirit and champagne shop.

Slime was everywhere oozing, bubbling, smelling putrid in the sun, all glimmering, shining, and iridescent, breeding fever and horrible life; while land-crabs boring holes, crabs of a brilliant turquoise-blue color, which fades at death, and reptiles like fish, with great bags below their mouths, and innumerable armor-plated insects, were rioting in it under the broiling sun.

We landed by a steep ladder upon a jetty with a gridiron top, only safe for shoeless feet, and Mr. Hawley and I went up to the fort by steps cut in the earth. There are fine mango-trees on the slopes, said to have been planted by the Dutch two centuries ago. The fort is nearly oblong, and has a wall of stones and earth round it, in which, near the entrance, some of the Dutch brickwork is still visible.

The trees round it are much tattered and torn by English shell. In front of the entrance there is a large flat stone on a rude support. On this a young girl was sacrificed some years ago, and the Malay guns were smeared with her blood, in the idea that it would make them successful. I was told this story, but have no means of testing its accuracy.

Within the fort the collector and magistrate—a very inert-looking Dutch half-caste—has a wretched habitation, mostly made of attap. We sat there for some time. It looked most miserable, the few things about being empty bottles and meat-tins. A man would need many resources, great energy, and an earnest desire to do his duty, in order to save him from complete degeneracy. He has no better prospect from his elevation, than a nearly level plateau of mangrove swamps and jungle, with low hills in the distance, in which the rivers rise. It was hot—rather.

In the meantime the Resident was trying a case, and when it was concluded we steamed out to sea and hugged all day the most monotonous coast I ever saw, only just, if just, above high-water mark, with a great level of mangrove swamps and dense jungle behind, with high, jungle-covered hills in the very far distance, a vast area of beast-haunted country, of which nothing is known by Europeans, and almost nothing by the Malays themselves. So very small a vessel tumbles about a good deal even with a very light breeze, and instead of going to dinner I lay on the roof of the cabin studying blue-books. At nightfall we anchored at the mouth of the Bernam river, to avoid the inland mosquitoes, but we must have brought some with us, for I was malignantly bitten. Mrs. Daly and I shared the lack of privacy and comfort of the cabin. Perfect though the Abdulsamat is, there is very little rest to be got in a small and overcrowded vessel, and besides, the heat was awful. I think we were not far enough from the swampy shore, for Mrs. Daly was seized with fever during the night, and a Malay servant also. In the morning Mrs. Daly. who is comely and has a very nice complexion, looked haggard, yellow, and much shaken.

At daylight we weighed anchor and steamed for many miles up the muddy, mangrove-fringed river Bernam, the mangroves occasionally varied by the nipah palm. We met several palm-trees floating with their roots and some of their fruits above the water, like those we saw yesterday evening out on the Malacca Straits, looking like crowded Malay prahus with tattered mat-sails.

Before nine we anchored at this place, whose wretchedness makes a great impression on me, because we are to deposit Mr. Hawley here as revenue collector. I have seen him every day for a week; he is amiable and courteous, as well as intelligent and energetic, and it is shocking to leave him alone in a malarious swamp. This dismal revenue station consists of a few exceptionally poor-looking Malay houses on the river bank, a few equally unprosperous-looking Chinese dwellings, a police station of dilapidated thatch among the trees, close to it a cage in which there is a half-human looking criminal lying on a mat, a new house or big room, raised for Mr. Hawley, with the swamp all round it and underneath it, and close to it some pestiferous ditches which have been cut to drain it, but in which a putrid-looking brown ooze has stagnated.

There is a causeway about two hundred yards long on the river bank, but no road anywhere. The river is broad, deep, swift and muddy; on its opposite side is Perak, the finest State in the peninsula, and the cluster of mat houses on the farther shore is under the Perak Government.* Sampans are lying on the heated slime. Cocoa-nut trees fringe the river bank for some distance, and there are some large, spreading trees loaded with the largest and showiest crimson blossoms I ever saw, throwing even the gaudy Poinciana regia into the shade; but nothing can look very attractive here, with the swamp in front and the jungle behind, where the rhinoceros is said to roam undisturbed.

> [*The Bernam district has recently been handed over to Perak, and is now under Mr. Low's very capable administration.]

We landed in the police boat at a stilted jetty approached by a ladder with few and slippery rungs. At the top there was a primitive gridiron of loose nibong bars, and the river swirled so rapidly and dizzily below that I was obliged ignominiously to hold on to a Chinaman in order to reach the causeway safely. To add to the natural insecurity of the foothold, some men were killing a goat at the top of the ladder, and its blood made the whole gridiron slippery. The banks of the river are shining slime giving off fetid exhalations under the burning sun; there is a general smell of vegetable decomposition, and miasma fever (one would suppose) is exhaling from every bubble of the teeming slime and swamp.

In the veranda of Mr. Hawley's house a number of forlorn-looking Rajahs are sitting, each with his forlorn-looking train of followers, and in front of the police station a number of forlorn-looking Malays are sitting motionless hour after hour. The Chinese have a row of shops above the river bank, and even on this deadly-looking shore they display some purpose and energy. Mrs. Daly and I are sitting in Mr. Hawley's side veranda with the bubbling swamp below us. She reads a dull novel, I watch the dead life, pen in hand, and think how I can convey any impression of it to you. The Resident has gone snipe-shooting to replenish our larder. A boat now and then crosses from the Perak side, a sauntering Malay occasionally joins the squatting group, a fishing hawk now and then swoops down upon a fish, a policeman occasionally rouses up the wretch in the cage, and so the torrid hours pass.

I take this up again as the dew falls, and the sea takes on the coloring of a dying dolphin. The Resident returned with a good bag of snipe, and with Rajah Odoot, a gentle, timid-looking man, and another Rajah with an uncomfortable, puzzled face, took his place at a table, a policeman with a brace of loaded revolvers standing behind him. Policemen filed in; one or two cases were tried and dismissed, the Malay witnesses trembling from head to foot, and then the wretch from the cage was brought in looking hardly human, as, from under his shaggy, unshaven hair and unplaited pigtail which hung over his chest, he cast furtive, frightened glances at the array before him.

He was charged with being a waif. A Malay had picked him up at sea in a boat, of which he could give no account, neither of himself. So he is supposed to have been implicated in the murder of Mr. Lloyd, and we are bringing him, heavily ironed, and his boat up to Pinang. I wonder how many of the feelings which we call human exist in the lowest order of Orientals! It is certain that many of them only regard kindness as a confession of weakness. The Chinese seem specially inscrutable; no one seems really to understand them. Even the Canton missionaries said that they knew nearly nothing of them and their feelings. This wretched criminal, with his possible association with a brutal murder, is a most piteous object on deck, and comes between me and the enjoyment of this entrancing evening.

We reembarked late in the afternoon, and with the flood-tide in our favor have left Selangor behind. It has impressed me unfavorably as compared with Sungei Ujong. Of Kwalor Lumpor I cannot give any opinion, but I have seen no signs of progress or life anywhere else. The people of the State are harassed by vexatious imposts which yield very little, cost a great deal to collect, repress industry, and drive away population. Among such are taxes on individuals moving about the country up or down the rivers, cutting wood or in boats, oppressively heavy export duties on certain kinds of produce, and ad valorem duties on all articles of import and export not otherwise specially taxed. The costs of litigation are enormous, and the legal expenses to litigants are as great as in settlements where with the same money every advantage can be obtained. The stamps on all legal documents are also oppressive. The various departments are said to be in a state of "hugger-mugger."

With all this there is a good deal of display of military power on a small scale, and of such over-aweing implements as bayonets and revolvers, together with marching and counter-marching, body-guards and guards of honor. There must surely be a want of the right kind of vigor in the administration, and a "laisser aller" on the part of some of the minor officials, the result of which is that the great capabilities of the State are not developed, and its resources seem very little known. There has not been any disturbance in Selangor since 1874; and as neither the Sultan, the Malays, nor the Chinese have ever raised objections of any serious kind to the proposals of the British advisers, the "far back" state of things is very singular.

Mr. Syers, the superintendent of military police, appears a thoroughly efficient man, as sensible in his views of what would conduce to the advancement of the State as he is conscientious and careful in all matters of detail which concern his rather complicated position. He is a student of the people and of the country, speaks Malay fluently, and for a European seems to have a sympathetic understanding of the Malays, is studying the Chinese and their language, as well as the flora, fauna, and geology of the country, and is altogether unpretending. I have formed a very high opinion of him and should rely implicitly on anything which he told me as a fact. This is a great blessing, for conflicting statements on every subject, and the difficulty of estimating which one comes probably nearest the truth, are among the great woes of traveling!

I. L. B.

Letter XVII

The Dindings—The Tragedy on Pulu Pangkor—A Tropic Sunrise—Sir W. Robinson's Departure—"A Touch of the Sun"—Kling Beauty—A Question and Answer—The Bazaars of Georgetown—The Chinaman Goes Ahead—The Products of Pinang—Pepper-Planting

HOTEL DE L'EUROPE, PINANG, February 9.

In the evening we reached the Dindings, a lovely group of small islands ceded to England by the Pangkor Treaty, and just now in the height of an unenviable notoriety. The sun was low and the great heat past, the breeze had died away, and in the dewy stillness the largest of the islands looked unspeakably lovely as it lay in the golden light between us and the sun, forest-covered to its steep summit, its rocky promontories running out into calm, deep, green water, and forming almost land-locked bays, margined by shores of white coral sand backed by dense groves of cocoa-palms whose curving shadows lay dark upon the glassy sea. Here and there a Malay house in the shade indicated man and his doings, but it was all silent.

On a high, steep point there is a small clearing on which stands a mat bungalow with an attap roof, and below this there is a mat police station, but it was all desolate, nothing stirred, and though we had intended to spend the early hours of the night at the Dindings, we only lay a short time in the deep shadow upon the clear green water, watching scarlet fish playing in the coral forests, and the exquisite beauty of the island with its dense foliage in dark relief against the cool lemon sky. Peace brooded over the quiet shores, heavy aromatic odors of night-blooming plants wrapped us round, the sun sank suddenly, the air became cool, it was a dream of tropic beauty.

"Chalakar! Bondo!" Those jarring sounds seemed to have something linking them with the tragedy of which the peaceful-looking bungalow was lately the scene, and of which you have doubtless read. A Chinese gang swooped down upon the house from behind, beating gongs and shouting. Captain Lloyd got up to see what was the matter, and was felled by a hatchet, calling out to his wife for his revolver. This had been abstracted, and the locks had been taken off his fowling-pieces. The ayah fled to the jungle in the confusion, taking with her the three children, the youngest only four weeks old. The wretches then fractured, Mrs. Lloyd's skull with the hatchet, and having stunned Mrs. Innes, who was visiting her, they pushed the senseless bodies under the bed, and were preparing to set fire to it when something made them depart.

No more is likely to be known. The police must either have been cowardly or treacherous. The Pyah Pekket called the next day and brought the frightfully mangled corpse, Mrs. Lloyd, whose reason was overturned, and Mrs. Innes, on here. It is supposed that the Chinese secret societies have frustrated justice. A wretch is to be hanged here for the crime this morning on his own confession, but it is believed that he was doomed to sacrifice himself by one of these societies, in order to screen the real murderers. The contrast was awful between the island looking so lovely in the evening light, and this horrid deed which has desolated it.

The mainland approaches close to the Dindings, but the mangrove swamps of Selangor had given place to lofty ranges, forest covered, and a white coral strand fringed with palms. It was a lovely night. The northeast monsoon was fresh and steady, and the stars were glorious. It was very hot below, but when I went up on deck it was cool, and in the colored dawn we were just running up to the island-group of which Pinang is the chief, and reached the channel which divides it from Leper Island just at sunrise. All these islands are densely wooded, and have rocky shores. The high mountains of the native State of Kedah close the view to the north, and on the other side of a very narrow channel are the palm groves and sugar plantations of Province Wellesley. The Leper Island looked beautiful in the dewy morning with its stilted houses under the cocoa-palms; and the island of Pinang, with its lofty peak, dense woods, and shores fringed with palms sheltering Malay kampongs, each with its prahus drawn up on the beach, looked impressive enough.

The fierce glory of a tropic sunrise is ever a new delight. It is always the sun of the Nineteenth Psalm, with the prevailing yellow color of the eastern sky intensifying in one spot, a cool, lingering freshness, a deepening of the yellow east into a brilliant rose color, till suddenly, "like a glory, the broad sun" wheels above the horizon, the dew-bathed earth rejoices, the air is flooded with vitality, all things which rejoice in light and heat come forth, night birds and night prowlers retire, and we pale people hastily put up our umbrellas to avoid being shriveled in less than ten minutes from the first appearance of the sun.

"Pinang," from the Pinang or areca-palm, is the proper name of the island, but out of compliment to George IV, it was called Prince of Wales Island. Georgetown is the name of the capital, but by an odd freak we call the town Penang, and spell it with an e instead of an i.

There were a great many ships and junks at anchor, and the huge "P. and O." steamer Peking, and there was a state of universal hurry and excitement, for a large number of the officials of the Colonial Government and of the "protected" States are here to meet Sir W. Robinson, the Governor, who is on his way home on leave. There are little studies of human nature going on all round. Most people have "axes to grind." There are people pushing rival claims, some wanting promotion, others leave; some frank and above-board in their ways, others descending to mean acts to gain favor, or undermining the good reputation of their neighbors; everybody wanting something, and usually, as it seems, at the expense of somebody else!

Mr. Douglas, who had got up his men in most imposing costume, anchored the Abdulsamat close to the Peking, and at once went on board, with the kris with the gold hilt and scabbard presented by the

Sultan of Selangor. In the meantime the Governor sent for me to breakfast on board, and I was obliged to go among clean, trim people without having time to change my traveling dress. On deck I was introduced by the Governor to Mr. Low, the Resident in Perak, who has arranged for my transit thither, and to Mr. Maxwell, the Assistant Resident. I was so glad that I had no claims of my own to push when I saw the many perturbed and anxious faces. I sat next Sir William Robinson at breakfast, and found him most kind and courteous, and he interested himself in my impressions of the native States. No one could make out the flags on the Selangor yacht, four squares placed diagonally, two yellow and two red, in one of the red ones a star and crescent in yellow, and on the mizzenmast the same flag with a blue ensign as one of the squares! I wonder if the faineant Sultan who luxuriates at Langat knows anything of the sensationalism of his "yacht."

Mr. Douglas took me back to the launch in fierce blazing heat, which smote me just as I put down my umbrella in order to climb up her side, and caused me to fall forward with a sort of vertigo and an icy chill, but as soon as I arrived here I poured deluges of cold water on my head, and lay down with an iced bandage on, and am now much better. In nine months of tropical traveling, and exposure on horseback without an umbrella to the full force of the sun, I have never been affected before. I wear a white straw hat with the sides and low crown thickly wadded. I also have a strip four inches broad of three thicknesses of wadding, sewn into the middle of the back of my jacket, and usually wear in addition a coarse towel wrung out in water, folded on the top of my head, and hanging down the back of my neck.

Soon after I came into the salon Mr. Wood, the Puisne Judge, a very genial, elderly man, called and took me to his house, where I found a very pleasant party, Sir Thomas Sidgreaves, the Chief Justice, Mr. Maxwell, the Assistant Resident in Perak, Mr. Walker, appointed to the (acting) command of the Sikh force in Perak, and Mr. Kinnersley, a Pinang magistrate, with Mr. Isemonger, the police magistrate of the adjacent Province Wellesley. With an alteration in the names of places and people, the conversation was just what I have heard in all British official circles from Prince Edward Island to Singapore, who was likely to go home on leave, who might get a step, whether the Governor would return, what new appointments were likely to be created, etc., the interest in all these matters being intensified by the recent visit of Sir W. Robinson. It was all pleasant and interesting to me.

This evening the moonlight from the window was entrancingly beautiful, the shadows of promontory behind promontory lying blackly on the silver water amidst the scents and silences of the purple night.

As one lands on Pinang one is impressed even before reaching the shore by the blaze of color in the costumes of the crowds which throng the jetty. There are over fifteen thousand Klings, Chuliahs, and other natives of India on the island, and with their handsome but not very intellectual faces, their Turkey-red turbans and loin-cloths, or the soft, white muslins in which both men and women drape themselves, each one might be an artist's model. The Kling women here are beautiful and exquisitely draped, but the form of the cartilage of the nose and ears is destroyed by heavy rings. There are many Arabs, too, who are wealthy merchants and bankers. One of them, Noureddin, is the millionaire of Pinang, and is said to own landed property here to the extent of 400,000 pounds. There are more than twenty-one thousand Malays on the island, and though their kampongs are mostly scattered among the palm- groves, their red sarongs and white bajus are seen in numbers in the streets; but I have not seen one Malay woman. There are about six hundred and twelve Europeans in the town and on Pinang, but they make little show, though their large massive bungalows, under the shade of great bread-fruit and tamarind-trees, give one the idea of wealth and solidity.

The sight of the Asiatics who have crowded into Georgetown is a wonderful one, Chinese, Burmese, Javanese, Arabs, Malays, Sikhs, Madrassees, Klings, Chuliahs, and Parsees, and still they come in junks and steamers and strange Arabian craft, and all get a living, depend slavishly on no one, never lapse into pauperism, retain their own dress, customs, and religion, and are orderly. One asks what is bringing this swarthy, motley crowd from all Asian lands, from the Red to the Yellow Sea, from Mecca to Canton, and one of my Kling boatmen answers the question, "Empress good—coolie get money; keep it." This being interpreted is, that all these people enjoy absolute security of life and property under our flag, that they are certain of even-handed justice in our colonial courts, and that "the roll of the British drum" and the presence of a British iron-clad mean to them simply that security which is represented to us by an efficient police force. It is so strange to see that other European countries are almost nowhere in this strange Far East. Possibly many of the Chinese have heard of Russia, but Russia, France, Germany, and America, the whole lot of the "Great Powers" are represented chiefly by a few second-rate war-ships, or shabby consulates in back streets, while England is a "name to conjure with," and is represented by prosperous colonies, powerful protective forces, law, liberty, and security. These ideas are forced so strongly upon me as I travel westward, that I almost fear that I am writing in a "hifalutin" style, so I will only add that I think that our Oriental Grand Vizier knew Oriental character and the way of influencing Oriental modes of thinking better than his detractors when he added et Imperatrix to the much loved V. R.

This is truly a brilliant place under a brilliant sky, but Oh I weary for the wilds! There is one street, Chulia Street, entirely composed of Chulia and Kling bazaars. Each sidewalk is a rude arcade, entered by passing through heavy curtains, when you find yourself in a narrow, crowded passage, with deep or shallow recesses on one side, in which the handsome, brightly-dressed Klings sit on the floor, surrounded by their bright-hued goods; and over one's head and all down the narrow, thronged passage, noisy with business, are hung Malay bandannas, red turban cloths, red sarongs in silk and cotton, and white and gold sprinkled muslins, the whole length of the very long bazaar, blazing with color, and picturesque beyond description with beautiful costume. The Klings are much pleasanter to buy from than the Chinese. In addition to all the brilliant things which are sold for native wear, they keep large stocks of English and German prints, which they sell for rather less than the price asked for them at home, and for less than half what the same goods are sold for at the English shops.

I am writing as if the Klings were predominant, but they are so only in good looks and bright colors. Here again the Chinese, who number forty-five thousand souls, are becoming commercially the most important of the immigrant races, as they have long been numerically and industrially. In Georgetown, besides selling their own and all sorts of foreign goods at reasonable rates in small shops, they have large mercantile houses, and, as elsewhere, are gradually gaining a considerable control over the trade of the place. They also occupy positions of trust in foreign houses, and if there were a strike among them all business, not excepting that of the Post Office, would come to a standstill. I went into the Mercantile Bank and found only Chinese clerks, in the Post Office and only saw the same, and when I went to the "P. and O." office to take my berth for Ceylon, it was still a Chinaman, imperturbable, taciturn, independent, and irreproachably clean, with whom I had to deal in "pidjun English." They are everywhere the same, keen, quick-witted for chances, markedly self-interested, purpose-like, thrifty, frugal, on the whole regarding honesty as the best policy, independent in manner as in character, and without a trace of "Oriental servility."

Georgetown, February 11th.

I have not seen very much in my two days; indeed, I doubt whether there is much to see, in my line at least; nor has the island any interesting associations as Malacca has, or any mystery of unexplored jungle as in Sungei Ujong and Selangor. Pinang came into our possession in 1786, through the enterprise of Mr. Light, a merchant captain, who had acquired much useful local knowledge by trading to Kedah and other Malay States. The Indian Government desired a commercial "emporium" and a naval station in the far east, and Mr. Light recommended this island, then completely covered with forest, and only inhabited by two migratory families of Malay fishermen, whose huts were on the beach where this town now stands. In spite of romantic stories of another kind, to which even a recent encyclopedia gives currency, it seems that the Rajah of Kedah, to whom the island belonged, did not bestow it on Mr. Light, but sold it to the British Government for a stipulated payment of 2,000 pounds a year, which his successor receives at this day.

It is little over thirteen miles long; and from five to ten broad. It is a little smaller than the Isle of Wight, its area being one hundred and seven square miles.

The roads are excellent. After one has got inside of the broad belt of cocoa and areca palms which runs along the coast, one comes upon beautiful and fertile country, partly level, and partly rolling, with rocks of granite and mica-schist, and soil of a shallow but rich vegetable mould, with abundance of streams and little cascades, dotted all over with villas (very many of them Chinese) and gardens, and planted with rice, pepper and fruits, while cloves and nutmegs, which last have been long a failure, grow on the higher lands. The centre of Pinang is wooded and not much cultivated, but on the south and south-west coasts there are fine sugar, coffee and pepper plantations. The coffee looks very healthy. From the ridges in the centre of the island the ground rises toward the north, till, at the Peak, it reaches the height of two thousand nine hundred and twenty-two feet. There is a sanitarium there with a glorious view, and a delicious temperature ranging from 60 degrees to 75 degrees, while in the town and on the low lands it ranges from 80 degrees to 90 degrees. A sea breeze blows every day, and rain falls throughout the year, except in January and February. The vegetation is profuse, but less beautiful and tropical than on the mainland, and I have seen very few flowers except in gardens.

The products are manifold—guavas, mangoes, lemons, oranges, bananas, plantains, shaddocks, bread-fruit, etc.; and sugar, rice, sweet potatoes, ginger, areca, and cocoa-nuts, coffee, cloves, some nutmegs, and black and white pepper. My gharrie driver took me to see a Chinese pepper plantation—to me the most interesting thing that I saw on a very long and hot drive. Pepper is a very profitable crop. The vine begins to bear in three or four years after the cuttings have been planted, and yields two crops annually for about thirteen years. It is an East Indian plant, rather pretty, but of rambling and untidy growth, a climber, with smooth, soft stems, ten or twelve feet long, and tough, broadly ovate leaves. It is supported much as hops are. When the berries on a spike begin to turn red they are gathered, as they lose pungency if they are allowed to ripen. They are placed on mats, and are either trodden with the feet or rubbed by the hands to separate them from the spike, after which they are cleaned by winnowing. Black pepper consists of such berries wrinkled and blackened in the process of drying, and white pepper of similar berries freed from the skin and the fleshy part of the fruit by being soaked in water and then rubbed. Some planters bleach with chlorine to improve the appearance; but this process, as may be supposed, does not improve the flavor.

In these climates the natives use enormous quantities of pepper, as they do of all hot condiments, and the Europeans imitate them.

Although there are so many plantations, a great part of Pinang is uncleared, and from the peak most of it looks like a forest. It contains ninety thousand inhabitants, the Chinese more than equaling all the other nationalities put together. Its trade, which in 1860 was valued at 3,500,000 pounds, is now (1880) close upon 8,000,000 pounds, Pinang being, like Singapore, a great entrepot and "distributing point."

Now for the wilds once more!

I. L. B.

A CHAPTER ON PERAK

The Boundaries and Rivers of Perak—Tin Mining—Fruits and Vegetables—The Gomuti Palm—The Trade of Perak—A Future of Coffee—A Hopeful Lookout—Chinese Difficulties—Chinese Disturbances in Larut—The "Pangkor Treaty"—A "Little War"—The Settlement of Perak—The Resident and Assistant-Resident

The "protected" State of Perak (pronounced Payrah) is the richest and most important of the States of the Peninsula, as well as one of the largest. Its coast-line, broken into, however, by a bit of British territory, is about one hundred and twenty-five miles in length. Its sole southern boundary is the State of Selangor. On the north it has the British colony of Province Wellesley, and the native States of Kedah and Patani, tributary to Siam. Its eastern boundary is only an approximate one, Kelantan joining it in the midst of a vast tract of unexplored country inhabited solely by the Sakei and Semang aborigines. The State is about eighty miles wide at its widest part, and thirty at its narrowest, and is estimated to contain between four and five thousand square miles. The great artery of the country is the Perak river, a most serpentine stream. Ships drawing thirteen feet of water can ascend it as far as Durian Sabatang, fifty miles from its mouth, and boats can navigate it for one hundred and thirty miles farther. This river, even one hundred and fifty miles from its mouth at Kwala Kangsa, is two hundred yards wide, and might easily be ascended by "stern-wheel" boats drawing a foot of water, such as those which ply on the upper Mississippi. Next in size to the Perak is the Kinta, which falls into the Perak, besides which there are the Bernam and Batang Padang rivers, both navigable for vessels of light draught. Along the shores of these streams most of the Malay kampongs are built.

The interior of Perak is almost altogether covered with magnificent forests, out of which rise isolated limestone hills, and mountain ranges from five thousand to eight thousand feet in height. The scenery is beautiful. The neighborhood of the mangrove swamps of the coast is low and swampy, but as the ground rises, the earth which has been washed down from the hills becomes fertile, and farther inland the plains are so broken up by natural sand ridges which lighten the soil, that it is very suitable for rice culture.

Tin is the most abundant of the mineral products of Perak, and, as in the other States, the supply is apparently inexhaustible. So far it is obtained in "stream works" only. The export of this metal has risen from 144,000 pounds in 1876 to 436,000 pounds in 1881. Tin-mining continues to attract a steady stream of Chinese immigration, and the Resident believes that the number of Chinamen has increased from twenty thousand in 1879 to forty thousand in 1881. Wealth is reckoned in slabs of tin, and lately for an act of piracy a Rajah was fined so many slabs of tin, instead of so many hogsheads of oil, as he would have been on the West African coast.

Gold is found in tolerable quantities, even by the Malay easy-going manner of searching for it, and diamonds and garnets are tolerably abundant. Gold can be washed with little difficulty from most of the river beds, and from various alluvial deposits. The metal thus found is pure, but "rough and shotty." The nearer the mountains the larger the find. It is of a rich, red color. Iron ore is abundant; but though coal has been found, it is not of any commercial value. The methods of mining both for tin and gold are of the most elementary kind, and it is probable that Perak has still vast metallic treasures to yield up to scientific exploration and Anglo-Saxon energy.

Rice is the staple food of the inhabitants. Dry rice on the hillsides was the kind which was formerly exclusively cultivated, but from some Indians who came from Sumatra to Perak the Malays have learned the mode of growing the wet variety, and it is now largely practiced. Partly in consequence of a great lack of agricultural energy, and partly from the immense quantity of rice required by the non-producing Chinese miners, Perak imported in 1881 rice to the value of 70,000 pounds.

There is scarcely a tropical product which this magnificent region does not or may not produce, gutta-percha, india-rubber, sago, tapioca, palm-oil and fibre, yams, sweet potatoes, cloves, nutmegs, coffee, tobacco, pepper, gambier, with splendid fruits in perfection—the banana, bread-fruit, anona, cocoa-nut, mangosteen, durion, jak-fruit, cashew-nut, guava, bullock's heart, pomegranate, shaddock, custard-apple, papaya, pine-apple, with countless others. The indigenous fruits alone are so innumerable, that a description of the most valuable of them would fill a chapter.

Our homely vegetables do not flourish, but watermelons, cucumbers, gourds, capsicums, chilies, cocoa-nut cabbage, edible arums, and, where the Chinese have settled, coarse lettuces, radishes, and pulse, grow abundantly, with various other not altogether to be despised vegetables with Malay names.

The timber is magnificent, and under the unworthy name of "jungle produce" a large trade is done in it. Perak is the land of palms, and produces the invaluable cocoa-palm, most parts of which have their commercial value, the areca palm which produces the betel-nut, the gomuti palm from whose strong black fibres they make ropes, cordage, and strands for capturing the alligator; the jaggary-palm, from which sugar is made, as well as a fermented beverage; the nibong palm, which grows round the Malay kampong, and is used for their gridiron floors and for the posts of their houses; the dwarf-palms which serve no other purpose than to gladden the eyes by their beauty; and the nipah palm which fringes the rivers, and, under the name of attap, forms the thatch of both native and foreign houses.

Road-making has not made great strides in Perak, but railroads are being planned, and a good road extends from the port of Larut to the great Chinese mining town of Taipeng, and thence to the British residency at Kwala Kangsa, a distance of over thirty-three miles, the electric telegraph accompanying the road. Others are in course of construction, and there are numerous elephant and jungle tracks through the western parts of the State.

Still, the rivers form the natural highways. Perak has two ports—Teluk Anson on the Perak river, thirty-four miles from its mouth, and Teluk Kertang, a few miles up the Larut river, and eight miles from the great tin mines of Taipeng. The import and export trade is carried on mainly with Pinang, and at this time one of several small steamers leaves Larut for that port daily. A steamer calls at Teluk Anson once a fortnight on her voyage from and to Singapore and Pinang, and another calls at the same port every fourth day, as well as at the Dindings and the Bernam river.

Trade is rapidly advancing. The exports of the State, which were valued at 147,993 pounds in 1876, amounted to 513,317 pounds in 1881; and the imports which amounted to 166,275 pounds in 1876, had reached 488,706 pounds in 1881, the whole import and export trade of that year amounting to 1,002,023 pounds. The free population of Perak is now estimated at

Malays	56,000
Chinese	40,000
Other Asiatics	850
Europeans	90
Aborigines	1,000
	97,940

To which may be added a slave and bond debtor population of nearly four thousand souls.

The revenue of Perak has risen from 42,683 pounds in 1876 to 138,572 pounds in 1881; and the expenditure, keeping pace with it, has risen from 45,277 pounds in 1876 to 130,587 pounds in 1881. The chief sources of the Perak revenue are customs duties, opium and other farms and licenses, and land revenue; and the chief items of expenditure are for civil and police establishments, roads and bridges, and allowances and pensions to chiefs. It is worthy of remark that the military establishment—for so the magnificent Sikh armed police force may be called—costs more than the civil establishment. It may also be remarked that the revenue of Perak, thanks to the financial sagacity and wise discrimination of the Resident, is collected with little difficulty, and without inflicting any real vexations or hardships on the taxpayers.

Public works, such as the construction of good cart roads and bridges, the making of canals, the clearing rivers from impediments to navigation, the enlargement of experimental gardens, the introduction and breeding of sheep, cattle, and improved breeds of poultry, surveying wild land, and rebuilding and draining mining towns, are being carried on energetically. It has been found, after long and carefully-conducted experiments, that the lower mountains of Perak are admirably suited for the growth of tea, cinchona, and Arabian coffee, while Liberian coffee grows equally well on the lower lands. Coffee appears to be so nearly "played out" in Ceylon, that many coffee-planters have been "prospecting" in Perak; and now that the Government of India has consented to the importation of Indian coolie labor into the State, under certain restrictions, as an experimental measure, a future of coffee may be predicted with tolerable certainty. One of the causes for satisfaction in connection with this State is that the Malays themselves are undoubtedly contented with British rule, and are prospering under it. Crime of any kind in the Malay districts is very rare. The "village system" works well, and the courts of law conduct their business with an efficiency and economy which compare favorably with the transactions of our colonial courts; English law is being gradually introduced and gives general satisfaction, and the native Rajahs are being trained to administer even-handed justice according to its provisions, and at the same time without trenching upon Malay religion and custom. Slavery and debt bondage, which, as hitherto practiced in Perak, have involved evils and cruelties which are unknown to any but those who have actually lived in the State, will, it is hoped, be abolished by equitable arrangement in 1883. Various difficulties remain to be settled; the large Chinese element, with its criminal tendencies, requires great firmness of dealing, and the introduction of foreign capital and an additional form of alien labor may lead to new perplexities; but on the whole the outlook for Perak and its people is a favorable one, especially if the present Resident, Mr. Hugh Low, is able to remain to continue his task of developing the resources, settling the difficulties, and consolidating the well-being of the State.

Nothing is known of the early settlement of Perak. It was formerly tributary to the Malay sovereigns of Malacca, and afterward to those of Acheen, to whom the Perak Sultans sent gold and silver flowers as tribute. Siam has also at different times asserted sovereign rights and demanded tribute, but the Siamese were expelled in 1822 with the help of Rajah Ibrahim, the warlike chief of the neighboring State of Selangor. The Government was a despotism, administered during the last three centuries by Sultans who were connected with the ruling dynasties of Johore and Acheen.

Our connection with Perak began in 1818 by a commercial treaty between the East India Company and the Sultan, the chief object of which was to circumvent the Dutch on the subject of tin. By another treaty, in 1826, it was agreed that the Sultan should govern his country according to his own will; that no force should be sent either by Siam to "molest, attack, or disturb" Perak; and while it was stipulated that the Siamese should not attack or disturb Selangor, the English engaged not to allow Selangor to attack or disturb Perak.

So things jogged along till 1871, when the Sultan died, and the Rajahs, passing over two men who by blood were nearest to the throne, elected Ismail, an old and somewhat inoffensive man. Three years of intrigue followed, and many singular complications, which would be quite uninteresting to the general reader, and they furnished no excuse for English interference.

It is singular that the fall of Perak as an independent State was brought about by what may be called a civil war among the Chinese, who in 1871 were estimated at thirty thousand, and were principally engaged in tin-mining in Larut. These Chinamen were divided into two sections—the Go Kwans and the Si Kwans; and a few months after Sultan Ismail was elected, a dispute arose between the factions. Both parties flew to arms, and were aided with guns, ammunition, military stores, and food from Pinang, Pinang Chinese having previously supplied the capital needed for working the mines. The settlement was kept in perpetual hot water, its trade languished, and in return for military equipments the Chinese of Larut sent over two thousand wounded and starving men. The Mentri, the Malay "Governor" of Larut, although aided by Captain Speedy and a force of well-drilled troops recruited by him in India, and possessing four Krupp guns, was powerless to restore order, and Larut was destroyed, being absolutely turned into a wilderness, in which all but three houses had been burned, and, while the Malays had fled, the surviving Si Kwans were living behind stockades, while those of the faction opposed to that with which the Mentri and his Commander-in-Chief, Captain Speedy, had allied themselves, were living on the products of orchards from which their owners had been driven, and on booty, won by a wholesale system of piracy and murder, practiced not only on the Perak waters but on the high seas.

The war waged between the two parties threatened to become a war of extermination; horrible atrocities were perpetrated on both sides; and it is said and believed that as many as three thousand belligerents were slain on one day early in the disturbances. If the course of prohibiting the export of munitions of war had been persevered the strife would have died a natural death; but the Mentri made representations which induced the authorities of the Straits to accord a certain degree of support to himself and the Si Kwans, by limiting the prohibition to his enemies the Go Kwans. Things at last became so intolerable in Larut, and as a consequence in Pinang, that the Governor of the Straits Settlements, Sir A. Clarke, thought it was time to interfere. During these disturbances in Larut, Lower Perak and the Malays generally were living peaceably under Ismail, their elected Sultan. Abdullah, who was regarded as his rival, was a fugitive, with neither followers, money, nor credit. He had, however, friends in Singapore, to one of whom, Kim Cheng, a well-known Chinaman, he had promised a lucrative appointment if he would prevail on the Straits authorities to recognize him as Sultan. Lord Kimberley had previously instructed the Governor to consider the expediency of introducing the "Residential system" into "any of the Malay States," and the occasion soon presented itself.

An English merchant in Singapore and Kim Cheng drafted a letter to the Governor, which Abdullah signed, in which this chief expressed his desire to place Perak under British protection,* and "to have a man of sufficient abilities to show him a good system of government." Sir A. Clarke, thus appealed to, went to Pulo Pangkor, off the Perak coast, summoned the Chinese head men and the Malay chiefs to meet him there, and so effectively reconciled the former, who were bound over to keep the peace, that they were not again heard of. The Governor stated to the Malay chief and Abdullah that it was the duty of England to take care that the proper person in the line of succession was chosen for the throne. He inquired if there were any objection to Abdullah, and on none being made, the chiefs signed a paper dictated by Sir A. Clarke, since known as the "Pangkor Treaty." Its articles deposed Ismail, created Abdullah Sultan, ceded two tracts of territory to England, and provided that the new ruler should receive an English Resident and Assistant Resident, whose salaries and expenses should be the first charge on the revenue of the country, whose counsel must be asked and "acted upon" on all questions other than those of religion and custom, and under whose advice the collection and control of all revenues and the general administration should be regulated. After the signing of this treaty piracy ceased in the Perak waters, and Larut was repeopled and became settled and prosperous.

[*Abdullah informs "our friend" Sir W. Jervois, that his position and that of Perak are "in a most deplorable state," that there are two Sultans between whom no arrangement can be made, that the revenues are badly raised, and the laws are not executed with justice. "For these reasons," he says, "we see that Perak is in very great distress, and, in our opinion, the affairs of Perak cannot be settled except with strong, active assurance from our friend the representative of Queen Victoria, the greatest and most noble....We earnestly beg our friend to give complete assistance to Perak, and govern it, in order that this country may obtain safety and happiness, and that proper revenues may be raised, and the laws administered with justice, and all the inhabitants of the country may live in comfort."]*

So far, as regards the Sultanate, I have followed the account given by Sir Benson Maxwell. Mr. Swettenham, however, writes that Abdullah failed to obtain complete recognition of himself as Sultan, and instead of fulfilling the duties of his position, devoted himself to opium-smoking, cock-fighting, and other vices, estranging, by his overbearing manner and pride of position, those who only needed forbearance to make them his supporters. It may be remarked that Abdullah was not as yielding as had been expected to his English advisers.

The Pangkor Treaty was signed in January, 1874. On November 2d, 1875, Mr. Birch, the British Resident, who had arrived the evening before at the village of Passir Salah to post up orders and proclamations announcing that the whole kingdom of Perak was henceforth to be governed by English officers, was murdered as he was preparing for the bath.

On this provocation we entered upon a "little war," Perak became known in England, and the London press began to ask how it was that colonial officers were suffered to make conquests and increase Imperial responsibilities without the sanction of Parliament. Lord Carnarvon telegraphed to Singapore that he could not sanction the use of troops "for annexation or any other large political aims," supplementing his telegram by a despatch stating that the residential system had been only sanctioned provisionally, as an experiment, and declaring that the Government would not keep troops in a country "continuing to possess an independent jurisdiction, for the purpose of enforcing measures which the natives did not cheerfully accept."

As the sequel to the war and Mr. Birch's murder, Ismail, who had retained authority over a part of Perak, was banished to Johore; Abdullah, the Sultan, and the Mentri of Larut, who was designated as an "intriguing character," were exiled to the Seychelles, and the Rajah Muda Yusuf, a prince who, by all accounts, was regarded as exceedingly obnoxious, was elevated to the regency, Perak at the same time passing virtually under our rule.

A great mist of passion and prejudice envelops our dealings with the chiefs and people of this State, both before and after the war. Sir Benson Maxwell in "Our Malay Conquests," presents a formidable arraignment against the Colonial authorities, and Major M'Nair, in his book on Perak, justifies all their proceedings. If I may venture to give an opinion upon so controverted a subject, it is, that all Colonial authorities in their dealings with native races, all Residents and their subordinates, and all transactions between ourselves and the weak peoples of the Far East, would be better for having something of "the fierce light which beats upon a throne" turned upon them. The good have nothing to fear, the bad would be revealed in their badness, and hasty counsels and ambitious designs would be held in check. Public opinion never reaches these equatorial jungles; we are grossly ignorant of their inhabitants and their rights, of the manner in which our interference originated, and how it has been exercised; and unless some fresh disturbance and another "little war" should concentrate our attention for a moment on these distant States, we are likely to remain so, to their great detriment, and not a little, in one respect of the case at least, to our own.

When the changes in Perak were completed, Mr. Hugh Low, formerly administrator of the Government of Labuan, was appointed

Resident, and Mr. W. E. Maxwell, who had had considerable experience in Malay affairs, Assistant Resident. Both these gentlemen speak the Malay tongue readily and idiomatically, and Mr. Maxwell is an accomplished Malay scholar. Of both the superior and subordinate it may truly be said that, by tact, firmness, patience, and a uniformly just regard for both Malay and Chinese interests, they have not only pacified the State, but have conciliated the Rajahs, and in the main have reconciled the people to the new order of things.

Letter XVIII

Province Wellesley—Water Buffaloes—A Glorious Night—Perak Officials—A "Dismal Swamp"—Elephants at Home—An Epigrammatic Description—The British Residency at Taipeng—Sultan Abdulla's Boys—A Chinese Mining Town—The "Armed Police"—An Alligator's Victim—Major Swinburne—A Larut Dinner Party—A Morning Hymn

BRITISH RESIDENCY, LARUT, February 11.

I left Mr. Justice Wood's yesterday, and his servant dispatched me from the jetty in a large boat with an attap awning and six Kling rowers, whose oars worked in nooses of rope. The narrow Strait was very calm, and the hot, fiery light of the tropic evening resting upon it, made it look like oil rather than water.

In half an hour I landed on the other side in the prosperous Province Wellesley, under a row of magnificent casuarina trees, with gray, feathery foliage drooping over a beach of corals and, behind which are the solemn glades of cocoa-nut groves. On the little jetty a Sikh policeman waited for me; and presently Mrs. Isemonger, wife of the police magistrate of the Province, met me on the bright, green lawn studded with clumps of alamanda, which surrounds their lovely, palm-shaded bungalow.

Though the shadows were falling, Mr. Isemonger took me to see something of the back country in a trap with a fiery Sumatra pony. There are miles of cocoa-nut plantations belonging to Chinamen all along the coast, with the trees in straight lines forming long, broad avenues, which have a certain gloomy grandeur about them. Then come sugarcane and padi, and then palm plantations again.

The cocoa-nut palm grows best near salt water, no matter how loose and sandy the soil is, and in these congenial circumstances needs neither manure nor care of any kind. It bends lovingly toward the sea, and drops its ripe fruit into it. But if it is planted more than two hundred yards from the beach, it needs either rich or well-manured soil, or the proximity of human habitations.

It begins to bear fruit between its fourth and tenth years, according to soil, and a well-placed, generous tree bears from one hundred and forty to one hundred and fifty nuts a year. They are of wonderfully slow growth. It is three months from the time the blossom appears before the fruit sets, then it takes six months to grow, and three months more to ripen, and after that will hang two months on the tree before it falls—fourteen months from the first appearance of the flower!

It is certainly not beautiful as grown in Province Wellesley, and I am becoming faithless to my allegiance to it in this region of areca and other more graceful palms.

In returning we saw many Malay kampongs under the palms, each with a fire lighted underneath it, and there were many other fires for the water-buffaloes, with groups of these uncouth brutes gathered invariably on the leeward side, glad to be smoked rather than bitten by the mosquitoes.

These huge, thin-skinned animals have a strange antipathy to white people. They are petted and caressed by the Malays, and even small boys can do anything with them, and can ride upon their backs, but constantly when they see white people they raise their muzzles, and if there be room charge them madly. A buffalo is enormously strong, but he objects to the sun, and likes to bathe in rivers, and plaster himself with mud, and his tastes are much humored by his owners. A buffalo has often been known to vanquish a tiger when both have had fair play. Most of the drive back was accomplished by nearly incessant flashes of sheet lightning.

We had a most pleasant evening. Mrs. Isemonger, who is a sister of Mr. Maxwell, my present host, is gentle, thoughtful, well-informed, and studious, and instead of creating and living in an artificial English atmosphere which is apt to make a residence in a foreign country a very unproductive period, she has interested herself in the Malays, and has not only acquired an excellent knowledge of Malayan, but is translating a Malayan book.

I felt much humiliated by my ignorance of Province Wellesley, of which in truth I had never heard until I reached Malacca. It is a mere strip, however, only thirty-five miles long by about ten broad, but it is highly cultivated, fertile, rich, prosperous, and populous. From Pinang one sees its broad stretches of bright green sugar-cane and the chimneys of its sugar factories, and it grows rice and cocoa-nuts, and is actually more populous than Pinang or Malacca, and contains as many Malays as Sungei Ujong, Selangor and Pinang together—fifty-eight thousand! Mr. Maxwell had promised to bring the Kinta, a steam-launch, across from Georgetown by 8 P.M., and it shows how very pleasant the evening was, that though I was very tired, eight, nine, ten, and eleven came, and the conversation never flagged.

Soon after eleven the Kinta appeared, a black shadow on a silver sea, roaring for a boat, but the surf was so heavy that it was some time before the police boat was got off; and then Mr. Maxwell, whose cheery, energetic voice precedes him, and Mr. Walker landed, bullying everybody, as people often do when they know that they are the delinquents!

It was lovely in the white moonlight with the curving shadows of palms on the dewy grass, the grace of the drooping casuarinas, the shining water, and the long drift of surf. It was hard to get off, and the surf broke into the boat; but when we were once through it, the sea was like oil, the oars dripped flame, and, seen from the water, the long line of surf broke on the shore not in snow, but in a long drift of greenish fire.

The Kinta is a steam-launch of the Perak Government. Her boilers, to use an expressive Japanese phrase, are "very sick," and she is not nearly so fine as the Abdulsamat, but a quiet, peaceful boat, without any pretensions; and really any "old tub" is safe on the Straits of Malacca except in a "Sumatran." I stayed on deck for some time enjoying the exquisite loveliness of the night, and the vivacity of two of my companions, Mr. Maxwell, the Assistant Resident here, a really able and most energetic man, very argumentative, bright, and pleasant; and Captain Walker, A.D.C. to Sir W. Robinson, on his way from the ceaseless gayeties of Government House at Singapore to take command of the Sikh military police in the solitary jungles of Perak. The third, Mr. Innes, Superintendent of Lower Perak, whose wife so nearly lost her life in the horrible affair at Pulo Pangkor, was in dejected spirits, as if the swamps of Durion Sabatang had been too much for him.

The little cabin below was frightfully hot, and I shared it not only with two nice Malay boys, sons of the exiled Abdullah, the late Sultan, who are being educated at Malacca, but with a number of large and rampant rats. Finding the heat and rats unbearable, I went on deck in the rosy dawn, just as we were entering the Larut river, a muddy stream, flowing swiftly between dense jungles and mangrove swamps, and shores of shining slime, on which at low water the alligators bask in the sun—one of the many rivers of the Peninsula which do not widen at their mouths.

The tide was high and the river brimming full, looking as if it must drown all the forest, and the trestle-work roots on which the mangroves are hoisted were all submerged. It is a silent, lonely land, all densely green. Many an uprooted palm with its golden plumes and wealth of golden husked nuts came floating down on the swirling waters, and many a narrow creek well suited for murder, overarched with trees, and up which one might travel far and still be among mangrove swamps and alligators, came down into the Larut river; and once we passed a small clearing, where some industrious Chinamen are living in huts on some festering slime between the river and the jungle; and once a police station on stilts, where six policemen stood in a row and saluted as we passed, and at seven we reached Teluk Kartang, with a pier, a long shed, two or three huts, and some officialism, white and partly white, all in a "dismal swamp."

A small but very useful Chinese trading steamer, the Sri Sarawak, was lying against the pier, and we landed over her filthy deck, on which filthy Chinese swine, among half-naked men almost as filthy, were wrangling for decomposing offal. Dismal as this place looks, an immense trade in imports and exports is done there; and all the tin from the rich mines of the district is sent thence to Pinang for transhipment.

While my friends transacted business, I waited for an age in an empty office where was one chair, a table dark with years of ink splotches, a mouldy inkstand, a piece of an old almanac, and an empty gin bottle. Outside, cockle-shells were piled against the wall; then there were ditches or streamlets cutting through profuse and almost loathsome vegetation, and shining slime fat and iridescent, swarming with loathsome forms of insect and reptile life all rioting under the fierce sun, and among them, almost odious by proximity to such vileness, were small crabs with shells of a heavenly blue.

The strong vegetable stench was nearly overpowering, but I wrote to you and worked at your embroidery a little, and so got through this detention pleasantly, as through many a longer, though never a hotter one.

After a time three gharries arrived, and Mr. Innes and I went in one, the two other gentlemen in another, and Sultan Abdullah's boys in the third. No amount of world-wide practice in the getting in and out of strange vehicles is any help to the tortuous process necessary for mounting and dismounting from a Larut gharrie. A gharrie is a two- wheeled cart with a seat across it for two people and a board in front on which the driver sits when he is not running by his horse. This board and the low roof which covers the whole produce the complication in getting in and out.

The bottom of the cart is filled up with grass and leaves, and you put your feet on the board in front, and the little rats of fiery Sumatra ponies, which will run till they drop, jolt you along at great speed.

Klings, untroubled by much clothing, own and drive these vehicles, which are increasing rapidly. The traffic on the road of heavy buffalo carts, loaded with tin, cuts it up so badly that without care one might often be thrown upon the pony's back at the river end of it.

Near the port we met three elephants, the centre one of great size, rolling along, one of them with a mahout seated behind his great flapping ears. These are part of the regalia of the deposed Sultan, and were sent down from the interior for me and my baggage. The smallest of them would have carried me and my "Gladstone bag" and canvas roll. The first sight of "elephants at home" is impressive, but they are fearfully ugly, and their rolling gait does not promise well for the ease of my future journey.

We passed through a swampy, but busy-looking Chinese village, masculine almost solely, where Chinamen were building gharries and selling all such things as Chinese coolies buy, just the same there as everywhere, and at home there as everywhere; yellow, lean, smooth-shaven, keen, industrious, self-reliant, sober, mercenary, reliable, mysterious, opium-smoking, gambling, hugging clan ties, forming no others, and managing their own matters even to the post and money-order offices, through which they are constantly sending money to the interior of China.

I hope that it is not true that they look at us, as a singularly able and highly educated Chinaman lately said to me that they do, as "the incarnation of brute force allied to brute vices!" This is a Chinese region, so the degression is excusable.

It was bright and hot, the glorious, equable equatorial heat, and when we got out of the mangrove swamps through which the road is causewayed, there was fine tropical foliage, and the trees were festooned with a large, blue Thunbergia of great beauty. It is eight miles from the landing at Teluk Kartang to Taipeng, where the British Residency is.

The road crosses uninteresting level country, but every jolt brings one nearer to the Hijan mountains, which rise picturesquely from the plain to a height of over three thousand feet. In the distance there is an extraordinary "butte" or isolated hill, Gunong Pondok, a landmark for the whole region, and on the right to the east a grand mountain range, the highest peak of which cannot fall far short of eight thousand feet; and the blue-green ranges showing the foam of at least one waterfall almost helped one to be cool.

We reached Permatang, another Chinese village of some pretensions and population, near which are two very large two-storied Malay houses in some disrepair, in which the wife of the banished Mentri of Larut lives, with a number of slaves. A quantity of mirthful-looking slave girls were standing behind the window bars looking at us surreptitiously.

We alighted at the house of Mr. Wynne, the Government Agent, who at once said something courteous and hospitable about breakfast, which I was longing for; but after I had had a bath I found that we were to pursue our journey, I regretting for the second time already Mr. Maxwell's abstemiousness and power of going without food!

From this point we drove along an excellent road toward the mountains, over whose cool summits cloud mists now and then drifted; and near noon entered this important Chinese town, with a street about a mile long, with large bazaars and shops making a fine appearance, being much decorated in Chinese style; halls of meeting for the different tribes, gambling houses, workshops, the Treasury (a substantial dark wood building), large detached barracks for the Sikh police, a hospital, a powder magazine, a parade ground, a Government store-house, a large, new jail, neat bungalows for the minor English officials, and on the top of a steep, isolated terraced hill, the British Residency.

This hill is really too steep for a vehicle to ascend, but the plucky pony and the Kling driver together pulled the gharrie up the zigzags in a series of spasms, and I was glad to get out of the sunshine into a cool, airy house, where there was a hope of breakfast, or rather tiffin.

The Residency is large and lofty, and thoroughly draughty, a high commendation so near the equator. It consists of a room about thirty feet wide by sixty long, and about twenty feet high at its highest part, open at both ends, the front end a great bow window without glass opening on an immense veranda. This room and its veranda are like the fore cabin of a great Clyde steamer. It has a red screen standing partly across it, the back part being used for eating, and the front for sitting and occupation. My bedroom and sitting-room, and the room in which Sultan Abdullah's boys sleep are on one side, and Mr. Maxwell's room and office on the other.

Underneath are bath-rooms, and guard-rooms for the Sikh sentries. There are no ornaments or superfluities. There are two simple meals daily, with tea and bananas at 7 A.M., and afternoon tea at 5 P.M. Mr. Maxwell is most abstemious, and is energetically at work from an early hour in the morning. There is a perpetual coming and going of Malays, and an air of business without fuss. There is a Chinese "housemaid," who found a snake, four feet long, coiled up under my down quilt yesterday, and a Malay butler, but I have not seen any other domestic.

Those boys of Sultan Abdullah's are the most amusing children I ever saw. They are nine and twelve years old, with monkey-like, irrepressible faces. They have no ballast. They talk ceaselessly, and are very playful and witty, but though a large sum is being paid for their education at Malacca, they speak atrocious "pidjun," and never use Malayan, in my hearing at least. They are never still for one instant; they chatter, read snatches from books, ask questions about everything, but are too volatile to care for the answers, turn somersaults, lean over my shoulders as I write, bring me puzzles, and shriek and turn head over heels when I can't find them out, and jump on Mr. Maxwell's shoulders begging for dollars.

I like them very much, for, though they are so restless and mercurial, they are neither rude nor troublesome. They have kept the house alive with their antics, but they are just starting on my elephants for Kwala Kangsa, on a visit to the Regent. I wonder what will become of them? Their father is an exile in the Seychelles, and though it was once thought that one of them might succeed the reigning Rajah, another Rajah is so popular with the Malays, and so intelligent, that it is now unlikely that his claims will be set aside.

The steep little hill on which the Residency stands is planted with miserable coffee, with scanty yellow foliage. The house on my side has a magnificent view of the beautiful Hijan hills, down which a waterfall tumbles in a broad sheet of foam only half a mile off, and which breed a rampageous fresh breeze for a great part of the day. The front veranda looks down on Taipeng and other Chinese villages, on neat and prolific Chinese vegetable gardens, on pits, formerly tin mines, now full of muddy, stagnant water, on narrow, muddy rivulets bearing the wash of the tin mines to the Larut river, on all the weediness and forlornness of a superficially exhausted mining region, and beyond upon an expanse of jungle, the limit of which is beyond the limit of vision, miles of tree tops as level as the ocean, over which the cloud shadows sail in purple all day long. In the early morning the parade ground is gay with "thin red" lines of soldiers, and all day long with a glass I can see the occupations and bustle of Taipeng.

Taipeng is a thriving, increasing place, of over six thousand inhabitants, solely Chinese, with the exception of a small Kling population, which keeps small shops, lends money, drives gharries and bullock-carts, and washes clothes. This place was the focus of the disturbances in 1873, and the Chinese seem still to need to be held in check, for they are not allowed to go out at night without passes and lanterns.

They are miners, except those who keep the innumerable shops which supply the miners, and some of them are rich. Taipeng is tolerably empty during the day, but at dusk, when the miners return, the streets and gambling dens are crowded, and the usual Babel of Chinese tongues begins. There are scarcely any Malays in the town.

Mr. Maxwell walks and rides about everywhere unattended and without precautions, but Sikh sentries guard this house by night and day. They wear large blue turbans, scarlet coats and white trousers. There are four hundred and fifty of them, recruited in India from among the Sikhs and Pathans, and many of them have seen service under our flag. They are, to all intents and purposes, soldiers, drilled and disciplined as such, though called "Armed Police," and are commanded by Major

Swinburne of the 80th Regiment. There is a half battery of mountain train rifled guns, and many of these men are drilled as gunners. Their joy would be in shooting and looting, but they have not any scent for crime. They are splendid-looking men, with long moustaches and whiskers, but they plait the long ends of the latter and tuck them up under their turbans. They have good-natured faces generally, and are sober, docile and peaceable, but Major Swinburne says that they indulge in violent wordy warfare on "theological subjects." They are devoted to the accumulation of money, and very many of them being betrothed to little girls in India, save nearly all their pay in order to buy land and settle there. When off duty they wear turbans and robes nearly as white as snow, and look both classical and colossal. They get on admirably with the Malays, but look down on the Chinese, who are much afraid of them. One sees a single Sikh driving four or five Chinamen in front of him, having knotted their pigtails together for reins. I have been awoke each night by the clank which attends the change of guard, and as the moonlight flashes on the bayonets, I realize that I am in Perak.

The air is so bracing here and the nights so cool, that I have been out by seven each morning, and have been into Taipeng in the evening. This morning I went to see the hospital, mainly used by the Sikhs, who, though very docile patients, are most troublesome in other ways, owing to religious prejudices, which render it nearly impossible to cook for them. There was one wretched Chinaman there, horribly mangled. He was stealing a boat on one of the many creeks, when an alligator got hold of him, and tore both legs, one arm, and his back in such a way that it is wonderful that he lives. The apothecary is a young Madrassee. One or two cases of that terrible disease known in Japan as Kakke, and elsewhere as Beri-Beri, have just appeared.* We walked also to a clear mountain torrent which comes thundering down among great boulders and dense tropical vegetation at the foot of the mountains, as clear and cold as if it were a Highland stream dashing through the purple heather.

[*Since my visit there have been three fatal outbreaks of this epidemic, three thousand deaths having occurred among the neighboring miners and coolies. So firmly did the disease appear to have established itself, that a large permanent hospital was erected by the joint efforts of the chief mining adventurers and the Government, but it has now been taken over altogether by the Government, and is supported by an annual tax of a dollar, levied upon every adult Chinaman. Extensive hospital accommodation and sufficient medical attendance have also been provided in other stricken localities. In the jail, where the disease was very fatal, it has nearly died out, in consequence, it is believed, of supplying the prisoners with a larger quantity of nitrogenous food. It has been proposed to compel the employers of mining coolies to do the same thing, for the ravages of the disease are actually affecting the prosperity of Larut.]

There are "trumpeter beetles" here, with bright green bodies and membranous-looking transparent wings, four inches across, which make noise enough for a creature the size of a horse. Two were in the house tonight, and you could scarcely hear anyone speak. But there is a blessed respite from mosquitoes.

Major Swinburne and Captain Walker have dined here, and we had a simple dinner of roast mutton, the first that I have tasted for ten months. It is a great treat. One becomes tired of made dishes, consisting chiefly of impoverished fowls, disguised in about twenty different ways.

When I left Malacca, Captain Shaw said: "When you see Paul Swinburne you'll see a man you'll not see twice in a lifetime," so yesterday, when a tall, slender, aristocratic-looking man, who scarcely looks severable from the door-steps of a Pall Mall club, strode down the room and addressed me abruptly with the words: "The sooner you go away again the better; there's nothing to see, nothing to do, and nothing to learn," I was naturally much interested. He has a dash of acquired eccentricity of tone and manner, is very proud, but, unlike some proud people, appreciates the co-humanity of his inferiors, is a brilliant talker, dashing over art, literature, politics, society, tells stories brilliantly, never flags, is totally regardless of "the equities of conversation," and is much beloved by the Sikhs, to whom he is just.

At Pinang I heard an anecdote of him which is quite credible. The regent (it is said) wanted him to use the Sikhs to catch a female runaway slave, and on his refusing, the Rajah made use of a very opprobrious epithet, on which he drew himself up, saying: "You are a man of high birth in your country, but I'm a man of high birth in mine, and, so long as I bear Queen Victoria's commission, I refuse to accept insult. I take no future orders from your highness." Nor, it is said, has he.

My human surroundings have an unusual amount of piquancy. Mr. Maxwell is very pleasant, strong, both physically and mentally, clever and upright, educated at Oxford and Lincoln's Inn, but brought up in the Straits Settlements, of which his father was chief-justice. He is able, combative, dogmatic, well-read and well-informed, expresses himself incisively, is self-reliant, strong-willed, thoroughly just, thoroughly a gentleman, and has immense energy and business capacity, and a large amount of governing power. He, too, likes talking, and talks well, but with much perfectly good-natured vehemence. He is a man on whose word one may implicitly rely. Brought up among Malays, and speaking their language idiomatically, he not only likes them, but takes the trouble to understand them and enter into their ideas and feelings. He studies their literature, superstitions, and customs carefully, and has made some valuable notes upon them. I should think that few people understand the Malays better than he does. He dislikes the Chinese. I have the very pleasant feeling regarding him that he is the right man in the right place, and that his work is useful, conscientious, and admirable. As Assistant Resident he is virtually dictator of Larut, only subject to Mr. Low's interference. He is a judge, and can inflict the penalty of death, the Regent's signature, however, being required for the death-warrant. He rules the Chinese rigidly.

Captain Walker is a new comer, and does not know more about Perak than I do.

At this dinner of four there was as much noise as twenty stupid people would make! Something brought up the dead lock in Victoria, which excited violent feeling for some reason not obvious. Captain Walker threw off his somewhat suave A.D.C. manner, and looked dangerous, Mr. Maxwell fought for victory, and Major Swinburne to beat Mr. Maxwell, and the row was deafening.

I doubt whether such an argument could have been got up in moist, hot Singapore, or steamy Malacca! An energetic difference seems of daily occurrence, and possibly is an essential ingredient of friendship. That it should be possible shows what an invigorating climate this must be. Major Swinburne, in an aggravating tone, begins upon some peculiarity or foible, real or supposed, of his friend, with a deluge or sarcasm, mimicry, ridicule, and invective, torments him mercilessly, and without giving him time to reply, disappears, saying, Parthian-like, "Now, my dear fellow, its no use resenting it, you haven't such a friend as me in the world—you know if it were not for me you'd be absolutely intolerable!" All this is very amusing. How many differing characters are required to make up even the world that I know!

It is strange to be in a house in which there are no pets, for a small Malay bear which lives at the back can scarcely be called one. Sometimes in the evening a wild animal called a lemur rushes wildly through the house and out at the front veranda. I am always afraid of being startled by his tearing through my room in the depths of the night, for here, as in many other houses, instead of doors there are screens raised a foot from the ground.

This morning I got up before daylight, and went up a hill which is being cleared, to enjoy the sunrise, the loveliest time of the tropic day. It was all dew and rose color, with a delicious freshness in the air, prolonged unusually, because the sun was so slow to climb above the eastern mountain tops.

Then there was a sudden glory, and birds, beasts, and insects broke into a vociferous chorus, the tuneless hymn which ascends daily without a discord. There are sumptuously colored sunsets to be seen from this elevation, but one has no time to enjoy them, and they make one long for the lingering gold and purple of more northern latitudes. I have really been industrious since I came here, both in writing to you, and in "reading up" the native states in blue books, etc.

I. L. B.

Letter XIX

The Chinese in Larut—"Monkey Cups"—Chinese Hospitality—A Sikh Belle

BRITISH RESIDENCY, LARUT.

I am remaining here for another day or two, so have time to tell you a little about the surroundings.

Larut province is a strip of land about seventy miles long, and from twenty-five to forty-five broad. It was little known, and almost unexplored till 1848, when a Malay, while bathing, found some coarse, black sand, which, on being assayed, proved to be tin. He obtained twenty Chinese coolies, opened a mine which turned out lucrative, and the Chinese at home hearing that money was to be made, flocked into Larut, but after some years took to quarreling about the ownership of mines, and eventually to a war between the two leading clans, which threatened to be a war of extermination, and resulted in British interference, and the appointment of a Resident; and then Chinese merchants in Pinang made advances of money and provisions to such of their countrymen as were willing to work the abandoned mines. Very soon the population increased to such an extent that it became necessary to choose sites for mining towns, granting one to each faction; the Go Kwan town being called Taipeng, and the Si Kwan town Kamunting.

American mining enterprise could hardly go ahead faster. At the end of 1873 the population of Larut was four thousand, the men of the fighting factions only. Eleven months later these two mining towns contained nine thousand inhabitants, a tenth of whom were shopkeepers, and the district thirty-three thousand. Larut is level from the sea-shore to the mountain range, twenty miles inland, and is very uninteresting.

We have been in a gharrie to Kamunting, a Chinese mining town of four thousand people, three miles from here, approached through a pretty valley full of pitcher plants with purple cups and lids. You can imagine the joy of getting into my hands these wonderful nepenthes or "monkey cups" for the first time. I gathered five in the hope of finding one free from insects, but the cups of all were full of dried flies and ants, looking much as flies do when they have been clutched for a few days by the hairs of the "sun-dew." The lid has a quantity of nectar on its under side which attracts insects; but below the rolled rim of the cup, which is slightly corrugated, the interior is as smooth as glass, and the betrayed flies must fall at once into the water at the bottom and be drowned. As these ingenious arrangements are made for their destruction, doubtless the plant feeds upon their juices.*

[*I have since learned that this is an ascertained fact, and that nepenthes are among the insectiverous plants.]

We went first to a very large tin mine belonging to a rich and very pleasant-looking Chinaman, who received us and took us over it. The mine is like a large quarry, with a number of small excavations which fill with water, and are pumped by most ingenious Chinese pumps worked by an endless chain, but there are two powerful steam pumps at work also. About four hundred lean, leathery-looking men were working, swarming up out of the holes like ants in double columns, each man carrying a small bamboo tray holding about three pounds of stanniferous earth, which is deposited in a sluice, and a great rush of water washes away the sand, leaving the tin behind, looking much like "giant" blasting powder. The Chinese are as much wedded to these bamboo baskets as to their pigtails, but they involve a great waste of labor. A common hoe is the other implement used. The coolies are paid by piece-work, and are earning just now about one shilling and sixpence per day. Road-making and other labor is performed by Klings, who get one shilling a day.

The tin is smelted during the night in a very rude furnace, with most ingenious Chinese bellows, is then run into moulds made of sand, and turned out as slabs weighing 66 lbs. each. The export duty on tin is the chief source of revenue. Close to the smelting furnaces there are airy sheds with platforms along each side, divided into as many beds as there are Chinamen. A bed consists only of a mat and a mosquito-net. There are all the usual joss arrangements, and time is measured by the burning of joss-sticks. Several rain-cloaks, made of palm leaves, were hanging up. These, and nearly all the other articles consumed by this large population are imported from China.

Our Chinese host then took us to some rooms which he had built for a cool retreat, to which, in anticipation of our visit, he had conveyed champagne, sherry, and bitter beer! His look of incredulity when we said that we preferred tea, was most amusing; but on our persisting, he produced delicious tea with Chinese sweetmeats, and Huntley and Palmer's cocoa-nut biscuits. He then insisted on taking our hired gharrie and scrubby pony and sending us on in his buggy with a fine Australian horse, but Mr. Maxwell says that this was as much from policy as courtesy, as it gives him importance to be on obviously friendly terms with the Resident.

We went on to Kamunting, a forlorn town, mainly built of attap, with roads and ditches needing much improvement, and I bargained for some Chinese purses and visited a gambling saloon, the place in which one sees the peculiar expression of the Chinese face at its fullest development. There is nothing very shocking about it, nothing more than an intensified love of gain without a mask. Each coolie takes his pipe of opium after his day's work, and each has a pot of tea kept always hot in a thickly wadded basket, a luxury which no Chinaman seems able to do without.

We called at a Sikh guard-house, and the magnificent sergeant took me to see his wife, the woman of the regiment, who is so rigidly secluded that not even the commanding officer nor Mr. Maxwell have seen her. She is very beautiful, and has an exquisite figure, but was overloaded with jewelry. She wore a large nose-jewel, seven rings of large size weighing down her finely formed ears, four necklaces, and silver bangles on each arm from the wrist to the elbow, besides some on her beautiful ankles. She had an infant boy, the child of the regiment, in her arms, clothed only in a silver hoop, and the father took him and presented him to me with much pride. It was a pleasant family group.

The few days here have been a real rest, I have been so much alone. There are no women to twitter; and when Mr. Maxwell is not at work he talks of things that are worth talking about. The climate, too, is bracing and wholesome, and the boisterous afternoon wind, which sweeps letters and papers irreverently away, keeps off the mosquitoes.

I. L. B.

Letter XX

Novel Circumstances—The Excitements of the Jungle—Eternal Summer—The Sensitive Plant—The Lotus Lake of Matang—Elephant Ugliness—A Malay Mahout—A Novel Experience—Domestic Pets—Malay Hospitality-Land Leeches—"A Fearful Joy"—The End of My First Elephant Ride—Kwala Kangsa

BRITISH RESIDENCY, KWALA KANGSA, February 16.

This is rather exciting, for I have had an unusual journey, and my circumstances are unusual, for Mr. Low, the Resident, has not returned, and I am not only alone in his bungalow in the heart of the jungle, but so far as I can learn I am the only European in the region.

> "Of all my wild adventures past
> This frantic feat will prove the last,"

for in a fortnight I propose to be at Pinang on my way to conventional Ceylon, and the beloved "wilds" will be left behind.

At 4:30 this morning Mr. Maxwell's energetic voice roused me, and I got up, feeling for the first time in Larut very tired from the unwonted dissipation of another "dinner party," and from having been kept awake late by the frantic rushes of the lemur and the noise of the "trumpeter beetle," besides being awoke in a fright at 2 A.M., by the noise made in changing guard, from a dream that the Sikhs had mutinied and were about to massacre the Europeans, myself included! We had bananas and chocolate, and just at daybreak walked down the hill, where I got into a little trap drawn by a fiery little Sumatra pony, and driven by Mr. Gibbons, a worthy Australian miner who is here road-making, and was taken five miles to a place where the road becomes a quagmire not to be crossed. Elephants had been telegraphed for to meet me there, but the telegraph was found to be broken. Mr. Maxwell, who accompanied us on horseback, had sent a messenger on here for elephants, and was dismayed on getting to the quagmire to meet the news that they had gone to the jungle; so there was no means of conveyance but the small pachyderm which was bringing my bag, and which was more than two hours behind.

There was nothing for it but to walk, and we tramped for four miles. I could not have done the half of it had I not had my "mountain dress" on, the identical mud-colored tweed, in which I waded through the mud of Northern Japan. The sun had risen splendidly among crimson clouds, which, having turned gray, were a slight screen, and the air is so comparatively dry that, though within 5 degrees of the equator, it was not oppressively hot.

The drive had brought us out of the Chinese country into a region very thinly peopled by Malays only, here and there along the roadside, living in houses of all Malay styles, from the little attap cabin with its gridiron floor supported on stilts, to the large picturesque house with steep brown roofs, deep eaves and porches, and walls of matting or bamboo basket work in squares, light and dark alternately, reached by ladders with rungs eighteen inches apart, so difficult for shod feet.

The trees and plants of the jungle were very exciting. Ah! what a delight it is to see trees and plants at home which one has only seen as the exotics of a hothouse, or read of in books! In the day's journey I counted one hundred and twenty-six differing trees and shrubs, fifty-three trailers, seventeen epiphytes, and twenty-eight ferns. I saw more of the shrubs and epiphytes than I have yet done from the altitude of an elephant's back. There was one Asplenium nidus *[bird's nest fern]* which had thirty-seven perfect fronds radiating from a centre, each frond from three and a quarter to five and a half feet long, and varying from myrtle to the freshest tint of pea-green!

There was an orchid with hardly visible leaves, which bore six crowded clusters of flowers close to the branch of the tree on which it grew; each cluster composed of a number of spikes of red coral tipped with pale green. In the openings there were small trees with gorgeous erythrina-like flowers, glowing begonias, red lilies, a trailer with trumpet-shaped blossoms of canary yellow, and a smaller trailer, which climbs over everything that is not high, entwining itself with the blue Thunbergia, and bearing on single stalks single blossoms, primrose-shaped, of a salmon orange color with a velvety black centre. In some places one came upon three varieties of nepenthes or "monkey cups," some of their pitchers holding (I should think) a pint of fluid, and most of them packed with the skeletons of betrayed guests; then in moist places upon steel blue aspleniums and luxuriant selaginellas; and then came caelogynes with white blossoms, white flowered dendrobiums (crumentatum?), all growing on or clinging to trees, with scarlet-veined bauhinias, caladiums, ginger worts, and aroids, inclining one to make incessant exclamations of wonder and delight. You cannot imagine how crowded together this tropical vegetation is. There is not room for half of it on the ground, so it seeks and finds its home high up on the strong, majestic trees which bear it up into the sunshine, where, indeed one has to look for most of the flowers.

It is glorious to see the vegetation of eternal summer and the lavish prodigality of nature, and one revels among hothouse plants "at home," and all the splendor of gigantic leaves, and the beauty and grace of palms, bamboos, and tree-ferns; the great, gaudy flowers are as marvelous as the gaudy plumaged birds, and I feel that no words can convey an idea of the beauty and magnificence of an equatorial jungle; but the very permanence of the beauty is almost a fault. I should soon come to long for the burst of spring with its general tenderness of green, and its great broad splashes of sociable flowers, its masses of buttercups, or ox-eye daisies, or dandelions, and for the glories of autumn with its red and gold, and leagues of purple heather. These splendid orchids and other epiphytes grow singly. One sees one and not another, there are no broad masses of color to blaze in the distance, the scents are heavy and overpowering, the wealth is embarrassing. I revel in it all and rejoice in it all; it is intoxicating, yet I am haunted with visions of mossy banks starred with primroses and anemones, of stream sides blue with gentian, of meadows golden with buttercups, and fields scarlet with poppies, and in spite of my enjoyment and tropical enthusiasm, I agree with Mr. Wallace and others that the flowers of a temperate climate would give one more lasting pleasure.

On either side of the road the ground is densely carpeted with the sensitive plant, whose lovely tripartite leaves are green above and brown below. It is a fascinating plant, and at first one feels guilty of cruelty if one does more than look at it, but I have already learned, as all people do here, to take delight in wounding its sensibilities. Touch any part of a leaf ever so lightly, and as quick as thought it folds up. Touch the centre of the three ever so lightly, and leaf and stalk fall smitten. Touch a branch and every leaf closes, and every stalk falls as if weighted with lead. Walk over it, and you seem to have blasted the earth with a fiery tread, leaving desolation behind. Every trailing plant falls, the leaves closing, show only their red-brown backs, and all the beauty has vanished, but the burned and withered-looking earth is as fair as ever the next morning.

After walking for four miles we came upon a glorious sight at a turn of the road, a small lake behind which the mountains rise forest-covered, with a slope at their feet on which stand the cocoa-nut groves, and the beautiful Malay house of the exiled Mentri of Larut. I have written of a lake, but no water was visible, for it was concealed by thousands and thousands of the peltate leaves of the lotus, nearly round, attaining a diameter of eighteen inches, cool and dewy-looking under the torrid sun, with a blue bloom upon their intense green. Above them rose thousands of lotus flowers, buds, and seed-vessels, each one a thing of perfect beauty, and not a withered blossom was to be seen. The immense corollas varied in color from a deep rose crimson to a pink as pale as that of a blush rose. Some were just opening, others were half open, and others wide open, showing the crowded golden stamens and the golden disk in the centre. From far off the deep rose pink of the glorious blossoms is to be seen, and their beauty carried me back to the castle moats of Yedo, and to many a gilded shrine in Japan, on which the lotus blooms as an emblem of purity, righteousness, and immortality. Even here, where no such symbolism attaches to it, it looks a sacred thing. It was delightful to see such a sociable flower rejoicing in a crowd.

Beyond is the picturesque kampong of Matang, with many good houses and a mosque. Passing through a gateway with brick posts, we entered a large walled inclosure containing a cocoa-grove, some fine trees, and the beautiful dwellings of the Malay whom we have deported to the Seychelles. This is one of the largest Malay houses on the peninsula. It is built of wood painted green and white, with bold floral designs on a white ground round some of the circular windows, and a very large porch for followers to wait in, up a ladder of course. In a shed there were three gharries, and behind the house several small houses for slaves and others. A number of girls and children, probably mostly slaves, mirthfully peeped at us from under the tasteful mat blinds.

Really the upper class of Malay houses show some very good work. The thatch of the steep roof is beautifully put on, and between the sides of finely woven checked matting interspersed with lattice work and bamboo work, the shady inner rooms with their carved doorways and portieres of red silk, the pillows and cushions of gold embroidery laid over the exquisitely fine matting on the floors, the light from the half-shaded windows glancing here and there as the breeze sways the screens, there is an indescribable appropriateness to the region.

I waited for the elephant in a rambling empty house, and Malays brought pierced cocoa-nuts, buffalo milk, and a great bouquet of lotus blossoms and seed-vessels, out of which they took the seeds, and presented them on the grand lotus leaf itself. Each seed is in appearance and taste like a hazel-nut, but in the centre, in an oval slit, the future lotus plant is folded up, the one vivid green seed leaf being folded over a shoot, and this is intensely bitter.

The elephant at last came up and was brought below the porch. They are truly hideous beasts, with their gray, wrinkled, hairless hides, the huge ragged "flappers" which cover their ears, and with which they fan themselves ceaselessly, the small, mean eyes, the hideous proboscis which coils itself snakishly round everything; the formless legs, so like trunks of trees; the piggish back, with the steep slope down to the mean, bare tail, and the general unlikeness to all familiar and friendly beasts. I can hardly write, for a little wah-wah, the most delightful of apes, is hanging with one long, lean arm round my throat, while with its disengaged hand it keeps taking my pen, dipping it in the ink, and scrawling over my letter. It is the most winsome of creatures, but if I were to oppose it there is no knowing what it might do, so I will take another pen. The same is true of an elephant. I am without knowledge of what it may be capable of!

Before I came I dreamt of howdahs and cloth of gold trappings, but my elephant had neither. In fact there was nothing grand about him but his ugliness. His back was covered with a piece of raw hide, over which were several mats, and on either side of the ridgy backbone a shallow basket, filled with fresh leaves and twigs, and held in place by ropes of rattan. I dropped into one of these baskets from the porch, a young Malay lad into the other, and my bag was tied on behind with rattan. A noose of the same with a stirrup served for the driver to mount. He was a Malay, wearing only a handkerchief and sarong, a gossiping, careless fellow, who jumped off whenever he had a chance of a talk, and left us to ourselves. He drove with a stick with a curved spike at the end of it, which, when the elephant was bad, was hooked into the membranous "flapper," always evoking the uprearing and brandishing of the proboscis, and a sound of ungentle expostulation, which could be heard a mile off. He sat on the head of the beast, sometimes cross-legged, and sometimes with his legs behind the huge ear covers. Mr. Maxwell assured me that he would not send me into a region without a European unless it were perfectly safe, which I fully believed, any doubts as to my safety, if I had any, being closely connected with my steed.

This mode of riding is not comfortable. One sits facing forward with the feet dangling over the edge of the basket. This edge soon produces a sharp ache or cramp, and when one tries to get relief by leaning back on anything, the awkward, rolling motion is so painful, that one reverts to the former position till it again becomes intolerable. Then the elephant had not been loaded "with brains," and his pack was as troublesome as the straw shoes of the Japanese horses. It was always slipping forward or backward, and as I was heavier than the Malay lad, I was always slipping down and trying to wriggle myself up on the great ridge which was the creature's backbone, and always failing, and the mahout was always stopping and pulling the rattan ropes which bound the whole arrangement together, but never succeeding in improving it.

Before we had traveled two hours, the great bulk of the elephant, without any warning, gently subsided behind, and then as gently in front, the huge, ugly legs being extended in front of him, and the man signed to me to get off, which I did by getting on his head and letting myself down by a rattan rope upon the driver, who made a step of his back, for even when "kneeling," as this queer attitude is called, a good ladder is needed for comfortable getting off and on. While the whole arrangement of baskets was being re-rigged, I clambered into a Malay dwelling of the poorer class, and was courteously received and regaled with bananas and buffalo milk. Hospitality is one of the Malay virtues. This house is composed of a front hut and a back hut with a communication. Like all others it is raised to a good height on posts. The uprights are of palm, and the elastic, gridiron floor of split laths of the invaluable nibong palm (oncosperma filamentosum). The sides are made of neatly split reeds, and the roof, as in all houses, of the dried leaves of the nipah palm (nipa fruticans) stretched over a high ridge pole and steep rafters of bamboo. I could not see that a single nail had been used in the house. The whole of it is lashed together with rattan. The furniture consists entirely of mats, which cover a part of the floor, and are used both for sitting on and sleeping on, and a few small, hard, circular bolsters with embroidered ends. A musket, a spear, some fishing-rods, and a buffalo yoke hung against the wall of the reception room. In the back room, the province of the women and children, there were an iron pot, a cluster of bananas, and two calabashes. The women wore only sarongs, and the children nothing. The men, who were not much clothed, were lounging on the mats.

The Malays are passionately fond of pets, and are said to have much skill in taming birds and animals. Doubtless their low voices and gentle, supple movements never shock the timid sensitiveness of brutes. Besides this, Malay children yield a very ready obedience to their elders, and are encouraged to invite the confidence of birds and beasts, rather than to torment them. They catch birds by means of bird-lime made of gutta, by horse-hair nooses, and by imitating their call. In this small house there were bamboo cages containing twenty birds, most of them talking minas and green-feathered small pigeons. They came out of their cages when called, and perched in rows on the arms of the men. I don't know whether the mina can learn many words, but it imitates the human voice so wonderfully that in Hawaii when it spoke English I was quite deceived by it. These minas articulated so humanly that I did know whether a bird or a Malay spoke. There were four love-birds in an exquisitely made bamboo cage, lovely little creatures with red beaks and blue and green plumage. The children catch small grasshoppers for their birds with a shovel-shaped instrument of open rattan work. When I add that there were some homely domestic fowls and a nearly tailless cat, I think I have catalogued the visible possessions of this family, with the exception of a bamboo cradle with a small brown inmate hanging from the rafters, and a small shed, used, I believe, for storing rice.

The open floor, while it gives air and ventilation, has also its disadvantages, for solid and liquid refuse is thrown through it so conveniently that the ground under the house is apt to contain stagnant pools and heaps of decomposing matter, and men lying asleep on mats on these gridirons have sometimes been stabbed with a kris inserted between the bars from below by an enemy seeking revenge.

I must not, however, give the impression that the Malays are a dirty people. They wash their clothes frequently, and bathe as often as is possible. They try to build their houses near water, and use small bathing-sheds.

I went into another house, rather poorer than the former, and, with a touching hospitality, they made signs to me to know if I would like a cocoa-nut. I hinted that I would, and the man at once got up and called to him an ape or monkey about three feet high, which was playing with a child, and the animal went out with him, and in no time was at the top of a tall cocoa-nut tree. His master said something to him, and he moved about examining the nuts till he decided upon a green one, which he wrung off, using teeth and hands for the operation. The slightly acid milk was refreshing, but its "meat," which was of the consistency and nearly the tastelessness of the white of an egg boiled for five minutes, was not so good as that of the riper nuts.

I had walked on for some distance, and I had to walk back again before I found my elephant. I had been poking about in the scrub in search of some acid fruits, and when I got back to the road, was much surprised to find that my boots were filled with blood, and on looking for the cause I found five small brown leeches, beautifully striped with yellow, firmly attached to my ankles. I had not heard that these were pests in Perak, and feared that they were something worse; but the elephant driver, seeing my plight, made some tobacco juice and squirted it over the creatures, when they recoiled in great disgust. Owing to the exercise I was obliged to take, the bites bled for several hours. I do not remember feeling the first puncture. I have now heard that these bloodsuckers infest leaves and herbage, and that when they hear the rustling made by man or animal in passing, they stretch themselves to their fullest length, and if they can touch any part of his body or dress they hold on to it, and as quickly as possible reach some spot where they can suck their fill.

THE GOLDEN CHERSONESE AND THE WAY THITHER (TRAVELS IN MALAYSIA)

I am making my narrative as slow as my journey, but the things I write of will be as new to you as they were to me. New it was certainly to stand upon a carpet of the sensitive plant at noon, with the rays of a nearly vertical sun streaming down from a cloudless, steely blue sky, watching the jungle monster meekly kneeling on the ground, with two Malays who do not know a word of English as my companions, and myself unarmed and unescorted in the heart of a region so lately the scene of war, about which seven blue books have been written, and about the lawlessness and violence of which so many stories have been industriously circulated.

Certainly I always dreamed that there must be something splendid in riding on an elephant, but I don't feel the least accession of dignity in consequence. It is true, however, here, that though the trappings are mean and almost savage, a man's importance is estimated by the number of his elephants. When the pack was adjusted, the mahout jumped on the back, and giving me his hands hauled me up over the head, after which the creature rose gently from the ground, and we went on our journey.

But the ride was "a fearful joy," *if* a joy at all! Soon the driver jumped off for a gossip and a smoke, leaving the elephant to "gang his ain gates" for a mile or more, and he turned into the jungle, where he began to rend and tear the trees, and then going to a mud-hole, he drew all the water out of it, squirted it with a loud noise over himself and his riders, soaking my clothes with it, and when he turned back to the road again, he several times stopped and seemed to stand on his head by stiffening his proboscis and leaning upon it, and when I hit him with my umbrella he uttered the loudest roar I ever heard. My Malay fellow-rider jumped off and ran back for the driver, on which the panniers came altogether down on my side, and I hung on with difficulty, wondering what other possible contingencies could occur, always expecting that the beast, which was flourishing his proboscis, would lift me off with it and deposit me in a mud-hole.

On the driver's return I had to dismount again, and this time the elephant was allowed to go and take a proper bath in a river. He threw quantities of water over himself, and took up plenty more with which to cool his sides as he went along. Thick as the wrinkled hide of an elephant looks, a very small insect can draw blood from it, and, when left to himself, he sagaciously plasters himself with mud to protect himself like the water buffalo. Mounting again, I rode for another two hours, but he crawled about a mile an hour, and seemed to have a steady purpose to lie down. He roared whenever he was asked to go faster, sometimes with a roar of rage, sometimes in angry and sometimes in plaintive remonstrance. The driver got off and walked behind him, and then he stopped altogether. Then the man tried to pull him along by putting a hooked stick in his huge "flapper," but this produced no other effect than a series of howls; then he got on his head again, after which the brute made a succession of huge stumbles, each one of which threatened to be a fall, and then the driver, with a look of despair, got off again. Then I made signs that I would get off, but the elephant refused to lie down, and I let myself down his unshapely shoulder by a rattan rope, till I could use the mahout's shoulders as steps. The baskets were taken off and left at a house, the elephant was turned loose in the jungle; I walked the remaining miles to Kwala Kangsa, and the driver carried my portmanteau! Such was the comical end of my first elephant ride. I think that altogether I walked about eight miles, and I was not knocked up; this says a great deal for the climate of Perak. The Malay who came with me told the people here that it was "a wicked elephant," but I have since been told "that it was very sick and tired to death," which I hope is the true version of its most obnoxious conduct.

I have said nothing about the magnificence of the scenery for a part of the way, where the road goes through a grand mountain pass, where all the vegetable glories of the tropics seem assembled, and one gets a new idea of what scenery can be; while beneath superb tree-ferns and untattered bananas, and palms, and bright-flowered lianas, and graceful trailers, and vermilion-colored orchids, and under sun-birds and humming birds and the most splendid butterflies I ever saw, a torrent, as clear as crystal, dashes over the rocks, and adds the music of tumbling water to the enchantment of a scene whose loveliness no words can give any idea of. The pass of Bukit Berapit, seen in solitude on a glorious morning, is almost worth a journey round the world.

Another wonder of the route is Gunong Pondok, a huge butte or isolated mass of red and white limestone, much weather-stained and ore-stained with very brilliant colors, full of caverns, many of which are quite inaccessible, their entrances fringed with immense stalactites. Some of the accessible caves have roofs seventy feet in height. Gunong Pondok is shaped like the Bass Rock, and is about twelve hundred feet in height. Its irregular top is forest-crowned, but its nearly perpendicular walls of white or red rock afford scarcely roothold for trees, and it rises in comparatively barren solitude among the forest-covered mountains of the interior.

At the end of ten hours' traveling, as I was tramping along alone, I began to meet Malays, then I met nine elephants in groups of three, with men, women, and children on their backs, apparently taking "an airing," the beasts looking grand, as their fronts always do. But that part of the road passes through a lonely jungle region, tiger, elephant, and rhinoceros haunted, and only broken here and there by some rude Malay cultivation of bananas or sugar-cane. When the sun was low I looked down upon a broad and beautiful river, with hills and mountains on its farther side, a village on the shores of a promontory, and above that a grassy hill with a bungalow under cocoa-palms at its top, which I knew must be the Residency, from the scarlet uniforms at the door. There was a small bridge over the Kangsa, then a guard-room and some official residences on stilts, and at the top of a steep slope the bungalow, which has a long flight of stairs under a latticed porch, leading to a broad and comfortably furnished veranda used as the Resident's office and sitting-room, the centre part, which has a bed-room on each side of it and runs to the back of the house, serving for the eating-place. It is as unpretending a dwelling as can be. It keeps out the sun and rain, and gives all the comfort which is needed in this climate, but nothing more. My journey of thirty-three miles from the coast has brought me into the interior of the State, where the Kangsa river joins the Perak, at a distance of a hundred and fifty miles from its mouth, and I am alone in the wilds!

Letter XX

Continued

Mystification—A Grotesque Dinner-Party—Mahmoud and Eblis—Fun and Frolic—Mahmoud's Antics—A Perak Jungle—The Poetry of Tropical Life—Village Life—The Officials of the Mosques—A Moslem Funeral—The "Royal Elephant"—Swimming the Perak—The Village of Koto-lamah—A "Pirate's Nest"—Rajah Dris

I fear that the involvement and confusion of dates in this letter will be most puzzling. I was received by a magnificent Oriental butler, and after I had had a delicious bath, dinner, or what Assam was pleased to call breakfast, was "served." The word "served" was strictly applicable, for linen, china, crystal, flowers, cooking, were all alike exquisite. Assam, the Madrassee, is handsomer and statelier than Babu at Malacca; a smart Malay lad helps him, and a Chinaman sits on the steps and pulls the punkah. All things were harmonious, the glorious cocoa-palms, the bright green slopes, the sunset gold on the lake-like river, the ranges of forest-covered mountains etherealizing in the purple light, the swarthy faces and scarlet uniforms of the Sikh guard, and rich and luscious odors, floated in on balmy airs, glories of the burning tropics, untellable and incommunicable!

My valise had not arrived, and I had been obliged to redress myself in my mud-splashed tweed dress, therefore I was much annoyed to find the table set for three, and I hung about unwillingly in the veranda, fully expecting two Government clerks in faultless evening dress to appear, and I was vexed to think that my dream of solitude was not to be realized, when Assam more emphatically assured me that the meal was "served," and I sat down, much mystified, at the well-appointed table, when he led in a large ape, and the Malay servant brought in a small one, and a Sikh brought in a large retriever and tied him to my chair! This was all done with the most profound solemnity. The circle being then complete, dinner proceeded with great stateliness. The apes had their curry, chutney, pine-apple, eggs, and bananas on porcelain plates, and so had I. The chief difference was that, whereas I waited to be helped, the big ape was impolite enough occasionally to snatch something from a dish as the butler passed round the table, and that the small one before very long migrated from his chair to the table, and, sitting by my plate, helped himself daintily from it. What a grotesque dinner party! What a delightful one! My "next of kin" were so reasonably silent; they required no conversational efforts; they were most interesting companions. "Silence is golden," I felt; shall I ever enjoy a dinner party so much again?

My acquaintance with these fellow-creatures was made just after I arrived. I saw the two tied by long ropes to the veranda rail above the porch, and not liking their looks, went as far from them as I could to write to you. The big one is perhaps four feet high and very strong, and the little one is about twenty inches high.* After a time I heard a cry of distress, and saw that the big one, whose name is Mahmoud, was frightening Eblis, the small one. Eblis ran away, but Mahmoud having got the rope in his hands, pulled it with a jerk each time Eblis got to the length of his tether, and beat him with the slack of it. I went as near to them as I dared, hoping to rescue the little creature, and he tried to come to me, but was always jerked back, the face of Mahmoud showing evil triumph each time. At last Mahmoud snatched up a stout Malacca cane, and dragging Eblis near him, beat him unmercifully, the cries of the little semi-human creature being most pathetic. I vainly tried to get the Sikh sentry to interfere; perhaps it would have been a breach of discipline if he had left his post, but at the moment I should have been glad if he had run Mahmoud through with a bayonet. Failing this, and the case being clearly one of murderous assault, I rushed at the rope which tied Eblis to the veranda and cut it through, which so startled the big fellow that he let him go, and Eblis, beaten I fear to a jelly, jumped upon my shoulder and flung his arms round my throat with a grip of terror; mine, I admit, being scarcely less.

[*The sheet of my letter in which I afterward described the physique of these apes has unfortunately been lost, and I dare not trust to my memory in a matter in which accuracy is essential. The description of an ape (in Letter XIV) approaches near to my recollection of them.]

I carried him to the easy-chair at the other end of the veranda, and he lay down confidingly on my arm, looking up with a bewitching, pathetic face, and murmuring sweetly "Ouf! Ouf!" He has scarcely left me since, except to go out to sleep on the attap roof. He is the most lovable, infatuating, little semi-human creature, so altogether fascinating that I could waste the whole day in watching him. As I write, he sometimes sits on the table by me watching me attentively, or takes a pen, dips it in the ink, and scribbles on a sheet of paper. Occasionally he turns over the leaves of a book; once he took Mr. Low's official correspondence, envelope by envelope, out of the rack, opened each, took out the letters and held them as if reading, but always replaced them. Then he becomes companionable, and gently taking my pen from my hand, puts it aside and lays his dainty hand in mine, and sometimes he lies on my lap as I write, with one long arm round my throat, and the small, antique, pathetic face is occasionally laid softly against mine, uttering the monosyllable "Ouf! ouf!" which is capable of a variation of tone and meaning truly extraordinary. Mahmoud is sufficiently polite, but shows no sign of friendliness, I am glad to say. As I bore Eblis out of reach of his clutches he threw the cane either at him or me, and then began to dance.

That first night tigers came very near the house, roaring discontentedly. At 4 A.M. I was awoke by a loud noise, and looking out, saw a wonderful scene. The superb plumes of the cocoa-nut trees were motionless against a sky blazing with stars. Four large elephants, part of the regalia of a deposed Sultan, one of them, the Royal Elephant, a beast of prodigious size, were standing at the door, looking majestic; mahouts were flitting about with torches; Sikhs, whose great stature was exaggerated by the fitful light—some in their undress white robes, and others in scarlet uniforms and blue turbans—were grouped as onlookers, the torchlight glinted on peripatetic bayonets, and the greenish, undulating lamps of countless fireflies moved gently in the shadow.

I have now been for three nights the sole inhabitant of this bungalow! I have taken five meals in the society of apes only, who make me laugh with genuine laughter. The sentries are absolutely silent, and I hardly hear a human voice. It is so good to be away for a time from the "wearing world," from all clatter, chatter, and "strife of tongues," in the unsophisticated society of apes and elephants. Dullness is out of the question. The apes are always doing something new, and are far more initiative than imitative. Eblis has just now taken a letter of yours from an elastic band, and is holding it wide open as if he were reading it; an untamed siamang, which lives on the roof, but has mustered up courage to-day to come down into the veranda, has jumped like a demon on the retriever's back, and riding astride, is beating him with a ruler; and jolly, wicked Mahmoud, having taken the cushions out of the chairs, has laid them in a row, has pulled a table cover off the table, and having rolled it up for a pillow, is now lying down in an easy, careless attitude, occasionally helping himself to a piece of pine-apple. When they are angry they make a fearful noise, and if you hinder them from putting their hands into your plate they shriek with rage like children, and utter much the same sound as the Ainos do when displeased. They seem frightfully jealous of the sweet little wah-wah Eblis. Mahmoud beats it and teases it whenever it is not with me; he takes its food, and when it screams with rage he laughs and shows his white teeth. He upset all the chairs in the veranda this morning, and when I attempted to scold him he took a banana which he was peeling and threw it at me. I am sure that he would have a great deal of rough wit if he could speak our tongue.

The night I came, Mr. Low's clerk, a Singhalese, came to arrange an expedition, and early the next morning, after I had breakfasted with the apes, he arrived, bringing the Royal Elephant, as well-broken and stately an animal as I should wish to ride. He is such a height (they say ten feet!) that, though he lay down to be mounted, a good-sized ladder was needed for the climb upon his back. Assam put pillows and a good lunch into the baskets, and as the day was glorious from sunrise to sunset I had an altogether delightful expedition.

We turned at once into the jungle, and rode through it for seven hours on the left bank of the Perak river. The loveliness was intoxicating. The trees were lofty and magnificent; there were very many such as I have not seen before. Many run up a hundred feet or more before they branch. The twilight was green and dim, and ofttimes amidst the wealth of vegetation not a flower was to be seen. But as often, through rifts in the leafage far aloft, there were glimpses of the sunny, heavenly blue sky, and now and then there were openings where trees had fallen, and the glorious tropical sunshine streamed in on gaudy blossoms of huge trees, and on pure white orchids, and canary-colored clusters borne by lianas; on sun-birds, iridescent and gorgeous in the sunlight; and on butterflies, some all golden, others amber and black, and amber and blue, some with velvety bands of violet and green, others altogether velvety black with spots of vermilion or emerald-green, the under side of the wings corresponding to the spot, while sometimes a shoal of turquoise-blue or wholly canary-colored sprites fluttered in the sunbeams; the flash of sun-birds and the flutter of butterflies giving one an idea of the joy which possibly was intended to be the heritage of all animated existence. In these openings I was glad for the moment to be neither an ornithologist nor an entomologist, so that I might leave everyone of these daintily colored creatures to the enjoyment of its life and beauty.

It was not the trees and lianas only that were beautiful in these sunny openings, but the ferns, mosses, orchids, and selaginellas, with the crimson-tipped dracaena, and the crimson-veined caladium, and the great red nepenthe with purple blotches on its nearly diaphanous pitchers, and another pitcher-plant of an epiphytal habit, with pea-green pitchers scrambling to a great height over the branches of the smaller trees. The beautiful tree-ferns themselves were loaded with other ferns, orchids, and mosses; every fallen tree was draped with fresh green forms, every swampy bit was the home of mottled aroids, film ferns, and foliage plants, mostly green and gold, while in some places there were ginger-worts with noble shining leaves fully six feet long.

In the green twilight of the depths of the forest the dew gemmed the leaves till nearly 10 A.M., but in the openings the sun blazed with the heat of a furnace. The silence and colorlessness of the heart of the forest; and the color, vivacity, light, and movement in the openings, and among the tree-tops, contrast most curiously. Legions of monkeys inhabit the tree-tops, and seem to lead a completely aerial life. It is said that they never come down to earth, but that they cross the forests swinging themselves from tree to tree.

The Malays, if they can, build their kampongs near rivers, and during the day we passed several of these. Several had mosques more or less rude. Every village consists of such houses as I have described before, grouped, but not by any means closely, under the shade of cocoa-palms, jak, durion, bread-fruit, mango, nutmeg, and other fruit-trees. Plantations of bananas are never far off. Many of these people have "dug-outs" or other boats on the adjacent river, some have bathing-sheds, and others padi plantations. These kampongs have much of the poetry as well as inanity of tropical life about them. They are beautiful and appropriate, and food is above them and around them. "The primal curse" can hardly be known. A very little labor provides all that the Malay desires, and if the tenure of the land be secure (and the lack of security is one of the great evils), and he be not over-taxed, his life must be calm and easy, if not happy. The people were always courteous, and my Singhalese escort held long conversations in every kampong. These jungle dwellers raise their houses on very high posts, partly because tigers abound. The jak trees (artocarpus incisa), near of kin to the bread-fruit, and the durion, flourish round all the dwellings. The jak fruit, which may be called food rather than fruit, grows without a visible stem from the trunk and branches of the very handsome tree which bears it, and weighs from sixty to seventy pounds. The durion grows to the size of a man's head, and is covered closely with hard, sharp spines. The fall of either on one's head or shoulder is much to be deprecated, and the Malays stretch strong nets above their houses to secure themselves from accidents.

I saw for the first time the nutmeg growing in perfection. It was a great delight, as is the first sight of any tree or flower well known from description. It is a beautiful tree, from forty to fifty feet high when full grown, with shining foliage, somewhat resembling that of the bay, and its fruit looks like a very large nectarine. One fully ripe was gathered for me. It had opened, and revealed the nutmeg with its dark brown shell showing through its crimson reticulated envelope of mace, the whole lying in a bed of pure white, a beautiful object.

Each house in the kampong seemed to have all its inmates at home doing nothing but chewing betel-nut. In their home deshabilles the men wear only the sarong, and a handkerchief knotted round their heads, and I think that the women also dispense with an upper garment, for I noticed at the approach of two strange men they invariably huddled another sarong over their shoulders, heads, and faces, holding it so as to conceal all but their eyes. The young children, as usual, were only clothed in silver ornaments. This neglige dress in the privacy of their homes is merely a matter of custom and climate, for these people are no more savages than we are. These glimpses of a native tropic life, entirely uninfluenced by European civilization, are most interesting.

In these kampongs the people have music, singing, story-telling, games, and religious ceremonies, perhaps the most important of all. I have not heard that the Perak Malays differ in their religious observances from the other Malays of the Peninsula. It seems that before "a parish" can be formed there must be forty-four houses. The kampong may then have a properly constituted mosque in which every Friday the religious officer recites an oration in praise of God, the Prophet, and his vicegerents, from the steps of a rostrum. The same person performs the marriage ceremony. Another official performs sacrificial duties, and recites the service for the dead after the corpse has been lowered into the grave. There is an inferior official of the mosque who keeps it clean, and reports to the Imaum absentees from public worship, goes round the villages to give notice of public prayer, assists at burials, and beats the great drum of the mosque. The Imaum appears to be the highest functionary, and performs what are regarded as the most sacred rites of Islamism. There are regular fees paid to these persons for their services, and at sacrifices they receive part of the victim. I was afraid of going into any of the mosques. They are all conical buildings of wood and attap raised on wooden pillars, and are usually on small knolls a little way from the kampongs. They have no minarets, but the larger ones have a separate shed in which the drum or gong used for the call to prayer is kept.

Buffaloes are sacrificed on religious occasions, and at the births, circumcisions, marriages, and shaving of the heads of the children of wealthy people. The buffalo sacrificed for religious purposes must be always without blemish. Its bones must not be broken after death, neither must its horns be used for common purposes. It is slain near the mosque with solemn sacrificial ceremonies, and one-half is usually cooked and eaten on the spot by the "parishioners."

While I am on the subject of religious observances, I must tell you that I saw a Moslem funeral to-day from a respectful distance. The graves are decently placed together usually, though some of the pious rich have large isolated burial places. The grave is dug by rule—i.e., the digger continues his work till his ear and the surface are on a level. It is shaped like ours, with one important exception, that a chamber two feet high for the reception of the body is dug in the side.

The corpse, that of a man I believe, covered with a cloth and dressed in cotton clothing, was carried on a bier formed of two planks, with the male relations following. On reaching the grave the Imaum read a service in a monotonous tone, and then the body was lowered till it reached the level of the side chamber, in which it was placed, and inclosed with the planks on which it had been carried. Some leaves and flowers were then thrown in, and the grave was filled up, after which some water was sprinkled upon it, and a man, not the Imaum, sitting upon it, recited what the Singhalese said was a sort of confession of faith, turning toward Mecca. The relatives bowed in the same direction and then left the place, but on stated days afterward offerings of spices and flowers are made. It was reverential and decorous, perhaps even more so than the Buddhist funerals which I saw in Japan, but the tombs are not so carefully tended, and look more melancholy. The same dumpy, pawn-shaped pillars are placed at the head and feet of the raised mounds of earth which cover the graves, as in Malacca. It is believed that when the mourners have retired seven paces from the grave two angels enter upon inquisitorial functions. When death is seen to be approaching, the dying person is directed to repeat a short form of confession of his faith in the unity of God; and if he is unable, it is recited for him. The offices of washing and shrouding the dead are religious ceremonies, and are performed by one of the officials of the mosque. The influence of the great Prophet of Arabia is wonderfully enduring.

This letter, which began among sun-birds and butterflies, has got into a dismal groove, out of which I must rescue it, but it is difficult to give any consecutive account of anything when the fascinating Eblis murmurs ouf! ouf! sits on my writing book, takes my pen out of my hand, makes these scrawls which I fear will make my writing illegible, and claims constant attention.

The Royal Elephant is a noble animal. His docility is perfect. He climbed up and down places so steep that a good horse would have bungled at them, pulled down trees when he was told to do it, held others which were slanting dangerously across the track high above our heads till we had safely passed under them, lifted fallen trees out of his way, or took huge steps over them, and slid down a steep bank into the Perak with great dexterity. He was told to take a banana tree for his dinner, and he broke off the tough thick stem just above the ground as if it had been a stick, then neatly stripped the eight-foot leaves, and holding the thick end of each stalk under his foot, stripped off the whole leaf on each side of the midrib, and then, with the dexterity of a monkey peeling a banana, he peeled off the thick rind from the stem, and revelled in the juices of the soft inside. I was sitting on the ground in a place where there was scarcely room for him to pass, and yet he was so noble and gentle that I never thought of getting up, even though his ponderous feet just touched me, and I ate my lunch within the swing of his huge proboscis, but he stood quite still, except that he flapped his "ears" and squirted water over himself. Each elephant has his own driver, and there is quite a large vocabulary of elephant language. The mahout carried an invaluable knife-weapon, called a parang, broadest and heaviest at the point, and as we passed through the jungle he slashed to right and left to clear the track, and quite thick twigs fell with hardly an effort on his part.

After traveling for several hours we came upon a kampong under palms and nutmeg trees, and then dismounted and took our lunch, looking out from deep shadow down upon the beautiful river lying in the glory of the noonday sun, its banks bright with birds and butterflies. The mahout was here among friends, and the salutations were numerous. If nose-rubbing as a form of greeting is practiced I have never seen it. What I have seen is that when one man approaches another, or is about to pay a visit, he joins his hands as if in supplication, and the other touches them on both sides, and afterward raises his hands to his lips and forehead. It is a courteous looking mode of salutation.

At this point the Singhalese said that the natives told him that it was possible to ford the Perak, but that the mahout said that the elephant was a "diver," and would probably dive, but that there was no danger to us except of getting very wet. I liked the prospect of a journey on the other side, so we went down a steep bank into the broad, bright, river, and putting out from the shore, went into the middle, and shortly the elephant gently dropped down and was entirely submerged, moving majestically along, with not a bit of his huge bulk visible, the end of his proboscis far ahead, writhing and coiling like a water snake every now and then, the nostrils always in sight, but having no apparent connection with the creature to which they belonged. Of course we were sitting in the water, but it was nearly as warm as the air, and so we went for some distance up the clear, shining river, with the tropic sun blazing down upon it, with everything that could rejoice the eye upon its shores, with little beaches of golden sands, and above the forest the mountains with varying shades of indigo coloring.

There would have been nothing left to wish for if you had been there to see, though you would have tried to look as if you saw an elephant moving submerged along a tropical river every day with people of three races on his back!!

The Singhalese said, "I'm going to take you to Koto-lamah; no European has been there since the war. I've never been there, nor the Resident either." I have pored over blue books long enough to know that this is a place which earned a most unenviable notoriety during the recent troubles, and is described as "a stronghold of piracy, lawlessness, and disaffection." As we were making a diagonal crossing of the Perak, the Singhalese said, "A few months ago they would have been firing at us from both sides of the river." It was a beautiful view at that point, with the lovely river in its windings, and on the top of the steep bank a kampong of largish houses under palms and durions. A good many people assembled on the cliff, some with muskets and some with spears, and the Singhalese said, "I wish we had not come;" but as the elephant scrambled up the bank the people seemed quite friendly, and I dismounted and climbed up to a large house with a very open floor, on which fine mats were laid in several places. There were many women and children in the room when I went in, and one of the former put a fine mat over a rice sack for me. Presently the room filled up with people, till there were fifty-nine seated in circles on the floor, but some of the men remained standing, one a thorough villain in looks, a Hadji, with a dirty green turban and a red sarong. The rest of the men wore handkerchiefs and sarongs only.

These people really did look much like savages. They all carried parangs, or the short kris called a golo, and haying been told that the Malays were disarmed, I was surprised to see several muskets, a rifle, and about thirty spears on the wall. So I found myself in the heart of what has been officially described as "a nest of robbers and murderers," "the centre of disturbance and disaffection," etc. To make it yet more interesting, on inquiring whose house it was, the name of a notorious "rebel" leader was mentioned, and one of the women, I was told, is the principal wife or rather widow of the Maharajah Lela, who was executed for complicity in the assassination of Mr. Birch. However, though as a Briton I could not have been a welcome visitor, they sent a monkey for two cocoa-nuts, and gave me their delicious milk; and when I came away they took the entrance ladder from one of the houses to help me to mount the elephant.

Mr. Low was at first displeased that I had been to Koto-lamah, and said that my escort was "ignorant and foolish" for taking me; but now he says that though he would not have taken the responsibility of sending me, he is glad that the thing was done, as it affords a proof such as he has not yet had of the complete pacification of the district; but, he added, it would appear somewhat odd that the first European to test the disposition of the Koto-lamah people should be a lady.

Leaving this large kampong we traveled by a much-grown-up elephant track, needing the constant use of the parang and the strength and wisdom of the elephant to make it passable, saw several lairs and some recent tiger tracks, crossed a very steep hill, and, after some hours of hard riding, came down upon the lovely Perak, which we crossed in a "dugout" so nearly level with the water that at every stroke of the paddle of the native who crouched in the bow the water ran in over the edge. We landed at the village of Kwala Kangsa

THE GOLDEN CHERSONESE AND THE WAY THITHER (TRAVELS IN MALAYSIA)

"In the glory of the sunset,
In the purple mists of evening,"

in which the magnified purple mountains were piled like Alps against the flaming clouds. By the river bank lay the Dragon boat and the square bamboo floating bath, through the side of which Mr. Birch was mortally wounded.

On landing we met a very bright intelligent-looking young Malay with a train of followers, a dandy almost, in white trousers, short red sarong, black baju with gold buttons, gold watchguard, and red head dress. The expression of his face was keen and slightly scornful. This is Rajah Dris, a judge, and the probable successor to the Perak throne. The present Resident thinks highly both of his character and his abilities, and he is very popular among his countrymen. He walked with us as far as the mosque, and I heard him ask questions about me. The Mussulmen of the village, several of them being Hadjis, were assembling for worship, lounging outside the mosque till the call to prayer came. Ablutions before worshiping are performed in floating baths in the river. The trade of Kwala Kangsa seems in the hands of the Chinese, with a few Klings among them, and they have a row of shops.

Letter XX

Concluded

A Joyous Welcome—A Severe Mortification—The British Resident—Daily Visitors—Rajah Dris—A Tipsy Ape—Marriage Ceremonies—Marriage Festivities—Malay Children—The Rajah Muda Yusuf—A Dreary Funeral—Fascinating Companionship—A Cocoa-Nut Gatherer—The Argus Pheasant—An Opium Wreck—Rhinoceros Horns—Elephant-Taming—Petrifying Influences of Islamism—A Dwindling Race

February 17.

I was very glad that yesterday was Sunday, so that I had a quiet day, for nearly twelve hours of jungle riding on an elephant makes one very stiff and sleepy. Three days of solitude, meals in the company of apes, elephant excursions, wandering about alone, and free, open air, tropical life in the midst of all luxuries and comforts, have been very enchanting. At night, when the servants had retired to their quarters and the apes to the roof, and I was absolutely alone in the bungalow, the silent Oriental sentries motionless below the veranda counting for nothing, and without a single door or window to give one the feeling of restraint, I had some of the "I'm monarch of all I survey" feeling; and when drum beat and bugle blast, and the turning out of the Sikh guard, indicated that the Resident was in sight, I felt a little reluctant to relinquish the society of animals, and my "solitary reign," which seemed almost "ancient" also.

When Mr. Low, unattended as he always is, reached the foot of the stairs the retriever leapt down with one bound, and through the air over his head fled Mahmoud and Eblis, uttering piercing cries, the siamang, though keeping at a distance, adding to the jubilations, and for several minutes I saw nothing of my host, for these creatures, making every intelligent demonstration of delight, were hanging round him with their long arms; the retriever nearly wild with joy, but frantically jealous; all the creatures welcoming him more warmly than most people would welcome their relations after a long absence. Can it be wondered at that people like the society of these simple, loving, unsophisticated beings?

Mr. Low's arrival has inflicted a severe mortification on me, for Eblis, who has been absolutely devoted to me since I rescued him from Mahmoud, has entirely deserted me, takes no notice of me, and seems anxious to disclaim our previous acquaintance! I have seen children do just the same thing, so it makes the kinship appear even closer. He shows the most exquisite devotion to his master, caresses him with his pretty baby hands, murmurs ouf in the tenderest of human tones, and sits on his shoulder or on his knee as he writes, looking up with a strange wistfulness in his eyes, as if he would like to express himself in something better than a monosyllable.

This is a curious life. Mr. Low sits at one end of the veranda at his business table with Eblis looking like his familiar spirit, beside him. I sit at a table at the other end, and during the long working hours we never exchange one word. Mahmoud sometimes executes wonderful capers, the strange, wild, half-human face of the siamang peers down from the roof with a half-trustful, half-suspicious expression; the retriever lies on the floor with his head on his paws, sleeping with one eye open, always on the watch for a coveted word of recognition from his master, or a yet more coveted opportunity of going out with him; tiffin and dinner are silently served in the veranda recess at long intervals; the sentries at the door are so silently changed that one fancies that the motionless blue turbans and scarlet coats contain always the same men; in the foreground the river flows silently, and the soft airs which alternate are too feeble to stir the over-shadowing palm-fronds or rustle the attap of the roof. It is hot, silent, tropical. The sound of Mr. Low's busy pen alone breaks the stillness during much of the day; so silent is it that the first heavy drops of the daily tropical shower on the roof have a startling effect.

Mr. Low is greatly esteemed, and is regarded in the official circles of the Settlements as a model administrator. He has had thirty years' experience in the East, mainly among Malays, and has brought not only a thoroughly idiomatic knowledge of the Malay language, but a sympathetic insight into Malay character to his present post. He understands the Malays and likes them, and has not a vestige of contempt for a dark skin, a prejudice which is apt to create an impassable gulf between the British official and the Asiatics under his sway. I am inclined to think that Mr. Low is happier among the Malays and among his apes and other pets than he would be among civilized Europeans!

He is working fourteen hours out of the twenty-four. I think that work is his passion, and a change of work his sole recreation. He devotes himself to the promotion of the interests of the State, and his evident desire is to train the native Rajahs to rule the people equitably. He seems to grudge every dollar spent superfluously on the English establishment, and contents himself with this small and old-fashioned bungalow. In this once disaffected region he goes about unarmed, and in the daytime the sentries only carry canes. His manner is as quiet and unpretending as can possibly be, and he speaks to Malays as respectfully as to Europeans, neither lowering thereby his own dignity nor theirs. Apparently they have free access to him during all hours of daylight, and as I sit writing to you or reading, a Malay shadow constantly falls across my paper, and a Malay, with silent, cat-like tread glides up the steps and appears unannounced in the veranda, on which Mr. Low at once lays aside whatever he is doing, and quietly gives himself to the business in hand. The reigning prince, the Rajah Muda Yusuf, and Rajah Dris, are daily visitors; the former brings a troop of followers with him, and they remain outside, their red sarongs and picturesque attitudes as they lounge in the shade, giving to the place that "native" air which everywhere I love, at least where "natives" are treated as I think that they ought to be, and my requirements are pretty severe!

I am painfully aware of the danger here, as everywhere, of forming hasty and inaccurate judgments, and of drawing general conclusions from partial premises, and on my present tour there is the added risk of seeing things through official spectacles; but still certain things lie on the surface, and a traveler must be very stupid indeed if he does not come to an approximately just conclusion concerning them. As, for instance, it is easy to see that far in the interior of the Malay Peninsula, in regions rarely visited by Europeans, themselves without advisers, and away from the influence of public opinion, dealing with weak rulers to whom they represent preponderating brute force in the last resort, the position of "Resident" is very much what the individual man chooses to make it. Nor is it difficult to perceive whether the relations between the English official and the natives are hearty and cordial, or sullen and distrustful, or whether the Resident makes use of his position for purposes of self-aggrandizement, and struts tempestuously and swaggeringly before the Malays, or whether he devotes his time and energies to the promotion of prosperity, good order, and progress, in a firm and friendly spirit.

After a very quiet day we went at sunset, to see Rajah Dris, not taking the dog. The trifling matter of the dog being regarded as an abomination is one of the innumerable instances of the ingrained divergence between Moslem and Christian feeling. Rajah Dris lives in a good house, but it is Europeanized, and consequently vulgarized. He received us very politely on the stairs, and took us into a sitting- room in which there were various ill-assorted European things. His senior wife was brought in, a dull, heavy-looking woman, a daughter of the Rajah Muda Yusuf, and after her a number of slave women and babies, till the small room was well filled. The Rajah hospitably entertained us with tea, milk, and preserved bananas; but I noticed with regret that the white table-cloth was much soiled, and that the china and glass were in very bad taste. The house and its equipments are a distressing contrast to those of the Datu Bandar in Sungei Ujong, who adheres closely to Malay habits. Rajah Dris sent a servant the whole way back with us, carrying a table lamp.

To-day the mercury was at 90 degrees for several hours. The nights, however, are cool enough for sleep. I have lately taken to the Malay custom of a sleeping mat, and find it cooler than even the hardest mattress. I did not sleep much, however, for so many rats and lizards ran about my room. These small, bright-eyed lizards go up the walls in search of flies. They dart upon the fly with very great speed, but just as you think that they are about to swallow him they pause for a second or two and then make the spring. I have never seen a fly escape during this pause, which looks as if the lizard charmed or petrified his victim. The Malays have a proverb based upon this fact: "Even the lizard gives the fly time to pray." There were other noises; for wild beasts, tigers probably, came so near as to scare the poultry and horses, and roared sullenly in the neighborhood for a long time, and the sentries challenged two people, after which I heard a messenger tell Mr. Low of a very distressing death.

February. 18.

Major Swinburne and Captain Walker arrived in the morning, and we had a grand tiffin at twelve, and Mahmoud was allowed to sit on the table, and he ate sausages, pommeloe, bananas, pine-apple, chicken and curry, and then seizing a long glass of champagne, drank a good deal before it was taken from him. If drunkenness were not a loathsome human vice, it would have been most amusing to see it burlesqued by this ape. He tried to seem sober and to sit up, but could not, then staggered to a chair, trying hard to walk steadily, and nodding his head with a would-be witty but really obfuscated look; then, finding that he could not sit up, he reached a cushion and lay down very neatly, resting his head on his elbow and trying to look quite reasonable, but not succeeding, and then he fell asleep.

After tiffin a Rajah came and asked me to go with him to his house, and we walked down with his train of followers and my Malay attendant. It was a very nice house, with harmonious coloring and much deep shadow. It soon filled with people. There were two women, but not having an interpreter, I could not tell whether they were the chief's wives or sisters. He showed me a number of valuable krises, spears and parangs, and the ladies brought sherbet and sweetmeats, and they were altogether very jolly, and made me pronounce the Malay names of things, and the women laughed heartily when I pronounced them badly. They showed me some fine diamonds, very beautifully set in that rich, red "gold of Ophir" which makes our yellow western gold look like a brazen imitation, as they evidently thought, for they took off my opal ring, and holding the gold against their own ornaments, made gestures of disapproval. I think that opals were new to them, and they were evidently delighted with their changing colors.

Mussulman law is very stringent as to some of the rights of wives. In Malay marriage contracts it is agreed that all savings and "effects" are to be the property of husband and wife equally, and are to be equally divided in case of divorce. A man who insists on divorcing his wife not only has to give her half his effects, but to repay the sum paid as the marriage portion. It appears that polygamy is rare, except among the chiefs.

Marriage is attended with elaborate arrangements among these people, and the female friends of both parties usually make the "engagement," after which the bridegroom's friends go to the bride's father, talk over the dowry, make presents, and pay the marriage expenses. Commonly, especially among the higher classes, the bridegroom does not see the lady's face until the marriage day. Marriage is legalized by a religious ceremony, and then if the wife be grown up her husband takes her to his own home. Girls are married at fourteen or fifteen, and although large families are rare, they look old women at forty.

On the day before the marriage expenses are paid by the bridegroom, the bride-elect has her teeth filed. It is this process which gives the Malay women, who are very pretty as children, their very repulsive look. It produces much the same appearance of wreck and ruin as blackening the teeth does in Japan, and makes a smile a thing to be dreaded. Young girls are not allowed to chew betel, which stains badly, and have white, pearly teeth, but these are considered like the teeth of animals. The teeth are filed down to a quarter of their natural length by means of a hard Sumatran stone, or fine steel file. The operation lasts about an hour, and the gums continue swelled and painful for some days. After they have recovered, the blackening of the teeth by means of betel chewing is accelerated by means of a black liquid obtained by burning cocoa-nut shells on iron, Three days before the marriage ceremony henna is applied to the nails of the hands and feet, and also to the palms of the hands, and the hair is cut short over the forehead, something in the style of a "Gainsborough fringe."

The wedding feast is a very grand affair. Goats and buffaloes are killed, and the friends and relatives of the bride send contributions of food. The wedding decorations are family property, and descend from mother to daughter, and both bride and bridegroom are covered with flowers, jewels, and gay embroidery. The bride sits in state and receives the congratulatory visits of her relatives and friends, and after the actual ceremony is over, the newly-married couple sit on a seat raised above the guests, and the sirih and betel-nut are largely chewed. There are "floral decorations," music, and feasting; all strangers are made welcome; the young men spend the afternoon in games, among which cock-fighting usually plays a prominent part, and the maidens amuse themselves in a part of the house screened off from the rest of the guests by curtains, and made very gay.

As religious ceremonies attend upon marriage and death, so on the birth of a child the father puts his mouth to the ear of the infant and solemnly pronounces what is called the Azan or "Allah Akbar," the name of the one God being the first sound which is allowed to fall upon his ears on entering the world, as it is the last sound which he hears on leaving it. There is a form of prayer which is used at births, and another on the seventh day afterward, when the child's head is shaved. The sage femme remains for forty days with the mother, who on the fortieth day makes the ceremonial purifications and prayers which are customary, and then returns to her ordinary duties. The child, as soon as it can speak, learns to recite prayers and passages from the Koran, and is very early grounded in the distinctive principles of Islam.

The children of both sexes are very pretty, but with strangers they are very shy and timid. They look very innocent, and are docile, gentle and obedient, spending much of their time in taming their pets and playing with them, and in playing games peculiar to their age. Except in one or two cases in Sungei Ujong, I have not seen a child with eye or skin disease, or any kind of deformity.

There have been Rajahs all day in the veranda, and their followers sitting on the steps, all received by Mr. Low with quiet courtesy, and regaled with tea or coffee and cigarettes. A short time ago the reigning prince, who does not appear to be a cypher, came with a great train of followers, some of them only wearing sarongs, a grandson, to whom he is much attached, and the deposed Sultan's two boys, of whom I told you before. They are in Malay clothing, and seem to have lost their vivacity, or at least it is in abeyance. Before I came here, I understood from many people that "His Highness" is very generally detested. So, also, says Sir Benson Maxwell in *Our Malay Conquests*. Major M'Nair in his amusing book on Perak says: "He is a man over middle age, and is described as being of considerable ability, feared and hated by many of the chiefs, and as being of a fierce and cruel disposition, but he was a proved man as to his loyalty" (to British interests), "and there being no desire on the part of the Government to annex the State of Perak, his appointment was the wisest course that, under the circumstances, could be pursued." This is all that the greatest apologist for British proceedings in Perak has to say.

I was not prepossessed in his favor before I came, for among other stories of his cruel disposition, I was told that it was "absolutely true" that three years ago he poured boiling water down the back of a runaway female slave who had been recaptured, and then put a red ant's nest upon it. If "piracy" is to be the term applied to levying blackmail, he was certainly a pirate, for he exacted a tenth of the cargo of every boat which passed up his river, a Rajah higher up doing the same thing. He is said to have a very strong character, to be grasping, and to be a "brute;" but Mr. Low gets on very well with him apparently. He is an elderly man, wearing a sort of fez on a shaven head. He has a gray mustache. His brow is a fine one, and his face has a look of force, but the lower part of it is coarse and heavy. He was fanning himself with his fez, and when I crossed the veranda and gave him a fan, he accepted it without the slightest gesture of thanks, as if I had been a slave. When Mr. Low told him that I had been at Koto-lamah, he said that the chief in whose house I had rested deserved to be shot, and ought to be shot. He and Mr. Low talked business for an hour; but all important matters are transacted in what is called a native council.

I wrote that I believed myself to be the only European in Kwala Kangsa, but I find that there was another at the time when I wrote thus—a young man of good family, who came out here seeking an appointment. He was sun-stricken three days ago, and violent fever and delirium set in, during the height of which he overpowered four Sikhs who were taking care of him, rushed out of doors, fell down exhausted, was carried home, and died at four in the morning, his last delirious dreams being of gambling and losing heavily.

The lamentable burial took place in the evening as the shadows fell. This sums up the story—a career of dissipation, death at twenty-one, a rough, oblong box, no one to be sorry. It made my heart ache for the mother, who would have given much to be where I was, and see "the dreary death train" move slowly to the dreary inclosure on a hill-top, where the grass grows rank and very green round a number of white wooden crosses, which mark the graves of the officers and soldiers who fell in 1876. The Union Jack was thrown over the coffin, which was carried by six Sikhs, and Mr. Low, Major Swinburne, Rajah Dris and some followers, and Sultan Abdullah's two boys, who had nothing better to do, followed it. By the time the grave was reached torches were required, and the burial service was read from my prayer-book. It was all sad and saddening.

The weather is still glorious, the winding Perak still mirrors in scarcely rippled blue the intensely blue sky, "never wind blows loudly," but soft airs rustle the trees. One could not lead a more tropical life than this, with apes and elephants about one under the cocoa-palms, and with the mercury ranging from 80 degrees to 90 degrees! Gorgeous, indeed, are the birds and butterflies and flowers; but often when the erythrina and the Poinciana regia are strewing the ground with their flaming blossoms, I think with a passionate longing of the fragile Trientalis Europae, of crimson-tipped lichens, of faint odors of half-hidden primroses, of whiffs of honey and heather from purple moorlands, and of all the homely, fragrant, unobtrusive flowers that are linked with you! I should like a chance of being "cold to the bone!"

I have wasted too much of my time to-day upon the apes. They fascinate me more daily. They look exactly like familiar demons, and certainly anyone having them about him two hundred years ago would have been burned as a wizard. When Mr. Low walks down the veranda, these two familiars walk behind him with a stealthy tread. He is having a business conversation just now with some Rajahs, whose numerous followers are standing and lying about, and Eblis is sitting on his shoulder with one arm round his neck, while Mahmoud sits on the table opening letters, and the siamang, sitting on the rafter, is looking down with an unpleasant look. Eblis condescends to notice me to-day, and occasionally sits on my shoulder murmuring "Ouf! ouf!" the sweet sound which means all varieties of affection and happiness. They say wah-wah distinctly, and scream with rage like children, but have none of the meaningless chatter of monkeys. It is partly their silence which makes them such very pleasant companions. At sunrise, however, like their forest brethren, they hail the sun for some minutes with a noise which I have never heard them make again during the day, loud and musical, as if uttered by human vocal organs, very clear and pleasant. Doubtless the Malays like Mr. Low all the better for his love of pets.

At lunch they were both, as usual, sitting at the table. I am still much afraid of Mahmoud, but Captain Walker is infatuated with him, and likes his rough, jolly manners, and his love of fun and rough play. As Assam was bringing me a cup of coffee this creature put out his long arm, and with his face brimming over with frolic, threw the coffee over the mat. Then he took up a long glass of beer and began to drink it eagerly, but as Mr. Low disapproved of his being allowed to get tipsy a second time, it was taken from him, upon which he took up the breast of a fricasseed chicken and threw it at the offender. The miscreant did every kind of ludicrous thing, finishing by pulling everyone to go out with him, as he always does at that hour; and when he had succeeded in getting us all out was in a moment at the top of a high tree, leaping from branch to branch, throwing himself on coffee shrubs below, swinging himself up again in a flash, leaping, bounding! a picture of agility, strength, and happiness. The usual morning gathering of Rajahs and their followers, with Klings and Sikhs, was there, and I suspect that they thought adult Europeans very foolish for being amused with these harum-scarum antics.

A follower had brought a "baboon," an ape or monkey trained to gather cocoa-nuts, a hideous beast on very long legs when on all fours, but capable of walking erect. They called him a "dog-faced baboon," but I think they were wrong. He has a short, curved tail, sable-colored fur darkening down his back, and a most repulsive, treacherous, and ferocious countenance. He is fierce, but likes or at all events obeys his owner, who held him with a rope fifty feet long. At present he is only half tame, and would go back to the jungle if he were liberated. He was sent up a cocoa-nut tree which was heavily loaded with nuts in various stages of ripeness and unripeness, going up in surly fashion, looking round at intervals and shaking his chain angrily. When he got to the top he shook the fronds and stalks, but no nuts fell, and he chose a ripe one, and twisted it round and round till its tenacious fibers gave way, and then threw it down and began to descend, thinking he had done enough, but on being spoken to he went to work again with great vigor, picked out all the ripe nuts on the tree, twisted them all off, and then came down in a thoroughly bad, sulky, temper. He was walking erect, and it seemed discourteous not to go and thank him for all his hard toil.

As I write I see a fascinating sight: three black apes sitting under the roof in such a position that I can only see their faces, and they are all leaning their chins on a beam, and with their wrinkled faces and gray beards are looking exactly like ——-. It is most interesting to be among wild beasts, which, though tame, or partly so, are not in captivity, and to see their great sagacity and their singular likeness and unlikeness to us. I could dispense with the reptiles, though. Last night there were seventeen lizards in my room and two in my slippers. During the profound stillness of about 3 A.M., a crowd, hooting, yelling, and beating clappers, passed not far off in the darkness, and there was a sound of ravaging and rending caused by a herd of elephants which had broken into the banana grounds.

Besides apes, elephants, dogs, and other pets, there are some fine jungle-fowls, a pheasant, a "fire-back," I think, and an argus pheasant of glorious beauty; but glorious is not quite the word either, for the hundred-eyed feathers of its tail are painted rather in browns than colors. These birds are under the charge of a poor Chinaman, who once had money, but has gone to complete ruin from opium-smoking. His frame is reduced to a skeleton covered with skin. I never saw such emaciation even in an advanced stage of illness.

Just now I saw Mahmoud and Eblis walk into my room, and shortly following them, I found that Mahmoud had drawn a pillow to the foot of the bed, and was lying comfortably with his head upon it, and that Eblis was lying at the other end. I do hope that you will not be tired of the apes. To me they are so intensely interesting that I cannot help writing about them. Eblis has been feverish for some days. I think he has never recovered from the thrashing he got the day I came. He is pining and growing very weak; he eats nothing but little bits of banana, and Mr. Low thinks he is sure to die. It is a curious fact that these apes, which are tamed by living with Europeans, acquire a great aversion to Malays.

February 19.

Eblis became much worse while I was out yesterday, and I fear will surely die. He can hardly hold anything in his cold, feeble hands, and eats nothing. He has a strangely human, faraway look, just what one sees in the eyes of children who have nearly done with this world.

The heat is much greater to-day, there is less breeze, and the mercury has reached 90 degrees, but in the absence of mosquitoes, and with pine-apples and bananas always at hand, one gets on very well. But mosquitoes do embitter existence and interfere with work. Apparently, people never become impervious to the poison, as I thought they did, and there is not a Malay in his mat hut, or a Chinese coolie in his crowded barrack, who has not his mosquito curtains; and I have already mentioned that the Malays light fires under their houses to smoke them away. Last night a malignant and hideous insect, above an inch long, of the bug species, appeared. The bite of this is as severe as the sting of a hornet.

The jungle seems to be full of wild beasts, specially tigers, in this neighborhood, and the rhinoceros is not uncommon. Its horn is worth $15, but Rajah Muda Yusuf, who desires to have a monopoly of them, says that there are horns with certain peculiar markings which can be sold to the Chinese for $500* each to be powdered and used as medicine. Wild elephants are abundant, but, like the rhinoceros, they ravage the deep recesses of the jungle. All the tame elephants here, however, were once wild, including the fifty which, with swords, dragons, bells, krises with gold scabbards, and a few other gold articles, formed the Perak regalia. The herds are hunted with tame, steady elephants, and on a likely one being singled out, he is driven by slow degrees into a strong inclosure, and there attached by stout rattan ropes to an experienced old elephant, and fed on meager diet for some weeks, varied with such dainties as sugar-cane and sweet cakes. The captive is allowed to go and bathe, and plaster himself with mud, all the while secured to his tame companion, and though he makes the most desperate struggles for liberty, he always ends by giving in, and being led back to his fastenings in the corral. At times a man gets upon him, sits on his head, and walks upon his back. It is here generally about two years before an elephant is regarded as thoroughly broken in and to be trusted; and, as elsewhere, stories are told of elephant revenge and keepers being killed. A full-grown elephant requires about 200 lbs. of food a day. These animals are destructive to the cocoa-nut trees, and when they get an opportunity they put their heads against them, and then, with a queer swaying movement throw the weight of their bodies over and over again against the stem till the palm comes down with a crash, and the dainty monster regales himself with the blossoms and the nuts. The Malays pet and caress them, and talk to them as they do to their buffaloes. Half a ton is considered a sufficient load for a journey if it be metal or anything which goes into small compass, but if the burden be bulky, from four to six hundred weight is enough. Except where there are rivers or roads suitable for bullock-carts or pack bullocks, they do nearly all the carrying trade of Perak, carrying loads on "elephant tracks" through the jungle. An elephant always puts his foot into the hole which another elephant's foot has made, so that a frequented track is nothing but a series of pits filled with mud and water. Trying to get along one of these I was altogether baffled, for it had no verge. The jungle presented an impassable wall of dense vegetation on either side, the undergrowth and trees being matted together by the stout, interminable strands of the rattan and other tenacious creepers, including a thorn-bearing one, known among the Malays as "tigers' claws," from the curved hook of the thorn. I think I made my way for about seven feet. This was a favorable specimen of a jungle track, and I now understand how the Malays, by felling two or three trees, so that they lay across similar and worse roads, were able to delay the British troops at a given spot for a day at a time.

> [*It is possible that this was an exaggeration, and that the real price is $50.]

One might think that elephants roaming at large would render cultivation impossible, but they have the greatest horror of anything that looks like a fence, and though they are almost powerful enough to break down a strong stockade, a slight fence of reeds usually keeps them out of padi, cane, and maize plantations.

Malays are gradually coming into Perak. It is said that there has been recently a large immigration from Selangor. The Malay population is fifty-seven thousand nearly, with a large preponderance of males, but fifty-eight thousand have crowded into the little strip of land called Province Wellesley, which is altogether under British rule, and sixty-seven thousand into Malacca, which has the same advantage. I suppose that slavery and polygamy have had something to do with the diminution of the population, as well as small-pox. Formerly large armies of fighting men could be raised in these States. Islamism is always antagonistic to national progress. It seems to petrify or congeal national life, placing each individual in the position of a member of a pure theocracy, rather than in that of a patriotic citizen of a country, or member of a nationality. In these States law, government and social customs have no existence apart from religion, and, indeed, they grow out of it.

It is strange that a people converted from Arabia, and partly, no doubt, civilized both from Arabia and Persia, should never have constructed anything permanent. If they were swept away to-morrow not a trace of them except their metal work would be to be found. Civilized as they are, they don't leave any more impress on the country than a Red Indian would. They have not been destroyed by great wars, or great pestilences, or the ravages of drink, nor can it be said that they perish mysteriously, as some peoples have done, by contact with Europeans;

yet it is evident that the dwindling process has been going on for several generations.

I. L. B.

Letter XXI

A Malay Interior—Malay Bird-Scaring—Rice Culture—Picturesque Dismalness—A Bad Spell—An Alarm—Possibilities of Peril—Patience and Kindness—Masculine Clatter

KWALA KANGSA, February 20.

Yesterday afternoon I had an expedition which I liked very much, though it ended a little awkwardly owing to a late start. Captain Walker was going on a shooting excursion to a lotus lake at some distance, and invited me to join him. So we started after tiffin with two Malays, crossed the Perak in a "dug-out," and walked for a mile over a sandy, grassy shore, which there lies between the bright water and the forest, then turned into the jungle, and waded through a stream which was up to my knees as we went, and up to my waist as we returned. Then a tremendous shower came on, and we were asked to climb into a large Malay house, of which the floor was a perilously open gridiron. At least three families were in it, and there were some very big men, but the women hid themselves behind a screen of matting. It looked forlorn. A young baboon was chained to the floor, and walked up and down restlessly like a wild beast in a menagerie; there were many birds in cages, and under the house was much rubbish, among which numerous fowls were picking. There was much fishing-tackle on the walls, both men and women being excessively fond of what I suppose may be called angling. They brought us young cocoa-nuts, and the milk, drank as it always ought to be, through one of the holes in the nut, was absolutely delicious.

THE GOLDEN CHERSONESE AND THE WAY THITHER (TRAVELS IN MALAYSIA)

Where the Malays are not sophisticated enough to have glass or china, they use dried gourds for drinking-vessels. The cocoa-nut is an invaluable product to them. Besides furnishing them with an incomparable drink, it is the basis of the curries on which they live so much, and its meat and milk enter into the composition of their sweet dishes. I went to see the women behind their screen, and found one of them engaged in making a dish which looked like something which we used to call syllabub. It was composed of remarkably unbleached sago, which they make from the sago-palm, boiled down with sugar to nearly a jelly. It was on an earthenware plate, and the woman who was preparing it mixed sugar with cocoa-nut milk, and whipping it with a bunch of twigs to a slight froth, poured it over the jelly.

When the rain ceased we got through the timber belt into a forlorn swamp of wet padi, where the water was a foot deep, and in some places so unintelligibly hot that it was unpleasant to put one's feet into it. It was truly a dismal swamp, and looked as if the padi were coming up by accident among the reeds and weeds. Indeed, I should have thought that it was a rice fallow, but for a number of grotesque scarecrows, some mere bundles of tatters, but others wearing the aspect of big birds, big dolls, or cats. I could not think how it was that these things made spasmodic jerking movement, as there was not a breath of air, and they were all soaked by the shower, till I saw that they were attached by long strings to a little grass hut raised on poles, in which a girl or boy sat "bird-scaring." The sparrows rob the rice-fields, and so do the beautiful padi-birds, of which we saw great numbers.

The Malays are certainly not industrious; they have no need to be so, and their cultivation is rude. They plow the rice-land with a plow consisting of a pole eight feet long, with a fork protruding from one end to act as a coulter, and a bar of wood inserted over this at an oblique angle forms a guiding handle. This plow is drawn by the great water buffalo. After plowing, the clods are broken by dragging a heavy beam over them, and are harrowed by means of a beam set with iron spikes The women do the sowing and planting. The harvest succeeds the planting in four months. The rice ears are cut short off, sometimes by a small sickle, and sometimes by an instrument which produces the effect of shears. Threshing consists in beating the ears with thick sticks to loosen the husks, after which the padi is carried in baskets to platforms ten feet above the ground, and is allowed to fall on mats, when the chaff is driven away by the wind. It is husked by a pestle, and it requires some skill to avoid crushing the grain. All these operations are performed by women.

The Perak Malays don't like working for other people, but some of them cultivate sugar-cane and maize for sale. Even for clearing jungle-land foreign labor has to be resorted to.

Ah, that swamp is a doleful region! One cannot tell where it ends and where the jungle begins, and dark, heavy, ominous-looking clouds generally concealed the forest-covered hills which are not far off. I almost felt the redundancy of vegetation to be oppressive, and the redundancy of insect and reptile life certainly was so; swarms of living creatures leaped in and out of the water, bigger ones hidden from view splashed heavily, and a few blackish, slug-like looking reptiles, which drew blood, and hung on for an hour or two, attached themselves to my ankles. I was amused when Captain Walker congratulated himself on the absence of leeches, for these blood-suckers were at least their next of kin. I fell down into the water twice from the submerged ridge that I tried to walk upon, but there is no risk of cold from a hot bath in a stove.

Then we came to a smothered, reedy, ditch-like stream, in which was an old "dug-out" half full of water, in which we managed to stow ourselves, and by careful balancing contrived to keep its edges just above the water. Our impeded progress down this ditch startled myriads of whirring, splashing creatures. The ditch opened into a reedy swamp where hideous pink water buffaloes were wallowing and enjoying themselves, but on the report of a gun they all plunged into deep water and swam away, except for their big horns, looking more like hippopotami than bovine quadrupeds. They are nearly as ugly as a rhinoceros; all albino animals are ugly, and when these are wet their hides are a bright salmon pink.

The swamp merged itself into a lotus lake, covered over much of its extent with thousands of noble leaves and rose-pink blossoms. It seemed almost sacrilege to tear and bruise and break them and push rudely through them in our canoe. A sadder and lonelier scene could not be. I have seldom been more powerfully affected by nature. The lake lying in hot mist under dark clouds, with the swamp and jungle on one side and an absolutely impenetrable wall of entangled trees and trailers on the other, so dense and matted that before putting one's feet on shore space would have to be cut for them with a parang, seemed as if it must be a hundred miles from the abodes of men, and as if nobody had ever been there before or ever would be there again. The heavy mist lifted, showing mountains, range beyond range, forest-covered, extending back into the heart of the peninsula; and though the highest may be under five thousand feet in height, yet from their shape, and from rising so near the sea-level, and from the woolly mists which hung round their bases, and from something in the gray, sad atmosphere, they looked fully ten thousand feet high.

Captain Walker climbed into a low tree which overhung the lake to look out for teal and widgeon, which were perfectly innumerable, while the Malays, never uttering a word, silently poled the boat over the dreary lake in the dreary evening to put up the birds. There they went high over our heads in long flights, and every time there was the report of a gun there were screams and shrieks and squawks, and myriads of birds rose out of their reedy covers, and fish splashed, and the smoke lay heavily on the water, and then all was silent again. Any place more solitary and apparently isolated could not be imagined—it was a most pathetic scene. Hazy visions of the mere near which King Arthur lay dying came before my eyes. If I had seen the solemn boat with "the three fair queens," in "robes of samite, mystic, wonderful," I should not have been surprised, nor would it have been odd if the lake had changed into the Styx, across which I was being ferried, a cold, colorless shade. To and fro, up and down, we poled over the tragic waters till I actually felt a terror far beyond eeriness taking possession of me.

It grew grayer and darker, and we went back for Captain Walker, who, with the absorption of a true sportsman, had hardly noticed the falling shadows. It was a relief to hear the human voice once more. It broke the worst spell I was ever bound by. As he came out on the branch to get into the canoe it gave way, and he fell into the water up to his chin. Then the boat pole broke, so that when we got back to the padi it was obvious that "the dark" was coming "at one stride," and I suggested that, as we had two miles to walk and a river to cross at night, and we should certainly be very late for dinner; Mr. Low might become uneasy about us, as we were both strangers and unable to speak the language; but Captain Walker thought differently.

There had been so much rain that it was heavy wading through the padi, and it was quite dark when we reached the jungle, in which the rain had made the footing very precarious, and in darkness we forded the swollen stream, and stumbled along the shore of the Perak, where fireflies in thousands were flashing among the bushes—a beautiful sight. When we reached the bank of the river where we had left the canoe we found several Malays, who laughed and seemed singularly pleased to see us, and talked vociferously to our men, i.e., vociferously for Malays, who are in the habit of speaking quietly. It was very difficult to get down the steep, slippery bank, into a precarious canoe which I could not see, and so thick was the darkness that I sat down in the water between the two gridirons, and had to remain there during the crossing, which took a long time, being against the stream.

When we landed, a Sikh sergeant met us, very much excited. He spoke Malayan, and I guessed from a few words that I knew that there was a hue and cry at the Residency. You know how all pleasure is at once spoiled when, after you have been enjoying yourself very much, you find that people at home have been restless and uneasy about you; and as it is one of my traveling principles to avoid being a bother to people, I was very sorry. We found a general state of perturbation. Major Swinburne, who was leaning over the veranda, received us with some very pungent objurgations, and told us that Mr. Low was out and very anxious. I was covered with mire, and wet from head to foot, and disappeared, but when we sat down to the long-delayed dinner I saw from Mr. Low's silence and gloomy manner that he had been really much annoyed; however, he recovered himself, and we had a very lively evening of conversation and discussion, though I had a good deal of pain from the inflamed bites of the bloodsuckers in the swamp. Malay scouting parties had been sent in various directions. Rajah Dris was away with one, and the Sikh police were all ready to do nobody knows what, as there were no dogs. Major Swinburne said that his fears did not travel farther than the river, which he thinks is dangerous to cross at night in a "dug-out;" but Mr. Low had before him the possibility of our having been assailed by bad characters, or of our having encountered a tiger in the jungle, and of my having been carried off from my inability to climb a tree!

Eblis is surely dying. He went to the roof, where the half-tamed siamang was supporting him hour after hour as gently as a mother would support a sick child. This wild ape has been very gentle and good to Eblis ever since he became ill. I went out for a short time with Mr. Low, and on returning he called Eblis, but the little thing was too weak to come, and began to cry feebly, on which the wild ape took him by one of his hands, put an arm round him, gently led him to a place from which he could drop upon Mr. Low's chair, and then darted away, but while daylight lasted was looking anxiously at Eblis, and at 6 A.M. had so far conquered his timidity that he sat on the window-sill behind Mr. Low, that he might watch his sick friend. The little bewitching thing, which is much emaciated, clings to its master now the whole time, unlike other animals, which hide themselves when they are ill, puts out its feeble little arms to him with a look of unspeakable affection on its poor, pinched face, and murmurs in a feeble voice ouf! ouf! Mr. Low pours a few drops of milk down its throat every half hour, and if he puts it down for a moment, it screams like a baby and stretches out its thin hands.

It is very interesting and pleasant to see the relations which exist between Mr. Low and the Malays. At this moment three Rajahs are lying about on the veranda, and their numerous followers are clustered on and about the stairs. He never raises his voice to a native, and they look as if they like him, and from their laughter and cheeriness they must be perfectly at ease with him. He is altogether devoted to the interests of Perak, and fully carries out his instructions,* which were, "to look upon Perak as a native State ultimately to be governed by native Rajahs," whom he is to endeavor to educate and advise "without interfering with the religion or custom of the country." He obviously attempts to train and educate these men in the principles and practice of good government, so that they shall be able to rule firmly and justly. Perak is likely to become the most important State of the Peninsula, and I earnestly hope that Mr. Low's wise and patient efforts will bring forth good fruit, at all events in Rajah Dris. [*See Appendix A.]

Mr. Low is only a little over fifty now, and when he first came the Rajahs told him that they were "glad that the Queen had sent them an *old* gentleman!" He is excessively cautious, and, like most people who have had dealings with Orientals, is possibly somewhat suspicious, but his caution is combined with singular kindness of heart, and an almost faulty generosity regarding his own concerns, as, for instance, he refuses to send his servants to prison when they rob him, saying: "Poor fellows! they know no better." He is just as patiently forbearing to the apes. Mr. ——- told me that he had made a very clean and careful copy of a dispatch to Lord Carnarvon, when Mahmoud dipped his fingers in the ink and drew them over a whole page, and he only took him in his arms and said: "Poor creature, you've given me a great deal of trouble, but you know no better."

This is my last evening here, and I am so sorry. It is truly "the wilds." There is rest. Then the apes are delightful companions, and there are all sorts of beasts, and birds, and creeping things, from elephants downward. The scenery and vegetation of the neighborhood are beautiful, the quiet Malay life which passes before one in a series of pictures is very interesting, and the sight of wise and righteous rule carried on before one's eyes, with a total absence of humbug and red-tapeism, and which never leaves out of sight the training of the Malays to rule themselves, is always pleasing. I like Kwala Kangsa better than any place that I have been at in Asia, and am proportionately sorrier to leave it. Mr. Low would have sent me up the Perak in the Dragon boat, and over the mountains into Kinta on elephants, if I could have stayed; but I cannot live longer without your letters, and they, alas! are at Colombo. Mr. Low kindly expresses regret at my going, and says he has got quite used to my being here, and added: "You never speak at the wrong time. When men are visiting me they never know when to be quiet, but bother one in the middle of business." This is most amusing, for it would be usually said: "Women never know when to be quiet." Mr. Maxwell one day said, that when men were with him he could "get nothing done for their clatter." I wished to start at 4 A.M. to-morrow, to get the coolness before sunrise, but there are so many tigers about just now in the jungle through which the road passes, that it is not considered prudent for me to leave before six, when they will have retired to their lairs.

I. L. B.

Letter XXII

*A Pleasant Canter—A Morning Hymn—The Pass of Bukit Berapit—
The "Wearing World" Again!—A Bad Spirit—Malay Demon-
ology—"Running Amuck"—An Amok-Runner's Career—The Supposed
Origin of Amok—Jungle Openings in Perak—Debt-Slavery—The Fate
of Three Runaway Slaves—Moslem Prayers—"Living Like
Leeches"—Malay Proverbs—A "Ten-Thousand-Man Umbrella"*

BRITISH RESIDENCY, TAIPENG, February 21.

I am once again on this breezy hill, watching the purple cloud-shadows sail over the level expanse of tree-tops and mangroves, having accomplished in about four hours the journey, which took nearly twelve in going up. The sun was not up when I left the bungalow at Kwala Kangsa this morning. I rode a capital pony, on Mr. Low's English saddle, a Malay orderly on horseback escorting me, and the royal elephant carried my luggage. It was absurd to see this huge beast lie down merely to receive my little valise and canvas roll, with a small accumulation of Malacca canes, mats, krises, tigers' teeth and claws, and an elephant's tusk, the whole not weighing 100 lbs.

Mr. Low was already at his work, writing and nursing Eblis at the same time, the wild ape sitting on a beam looking on. I left, wishing I were coming instead of going, and had a delightful ride of eighteen miles. The little horse walked very fast and cantered easily. How peaceful Perak is now, to allow of a lady riding so far through the jungle with only an unarmed Malay attendant! Major M'Nair writes: "The ordinary native is a simple, courteous being, who joins with an intense love of liberty a great affection for his simple home and its belongings," and I quite believe him. Stories of amok running, "piracies," treachery, revenge, poisoned krises, and assassinations, have been made very much of, and any crime or slight disturbance in the native States throws the Settlements into a panic. It must have been under the influence of one of these that such a large sea and land force was sent to Perak three years ago. Crime in the Malay districts in these States is so rare, that were it not for the Chinese, a few policemen would be all the force that would be needed. The "village system," the old Malay system with its head man and village officials, though formerly abused, seems under the new regime to work well, and by it the Malays have been long accustomed to a species of self-government, and to the maintenance of law and order. I notice that all the European officials who speak their language and act righteously toward them like them very much, and this says much in their favor.

I met with no adventures on the journey. I had a delightful canter of several miles before the sun was above the tree-tops, the morning mists, rose-flushed, rolled grandly away, and just as I reached the beautiful pass of Bukit Berapit, the apes were hooting their morning hymn, and the forests rang with the joyous trills and songs of birds. "All Thy works praise Thee, O Lord!"

There were gorgeous butterflies. Among them I noticed one with the upper part of its body and the upper side of its wings of jet black velvet, and the lower half of its body and the under side of its wings of peacock-blue velvet, spotted; another of the same "make," but with gold instead of blue, and a third with the upper part of the body and wings of black velvet with cerise spots, the lower part of the body cerise, and the under side of the wings white with cerise spots. All these measured fully five inches across their expanded wings. In one opening only I counted thirty-seven varieties of these brilliant creatures, not in hundreds but in thousands, mixed up with blue and crimson dragon-flies and iridescent flies, all joyous in the sunshine.

The loud-tongued stream of crystal water was very full, and through the deep greenery, and among the great, gray, granite boulders, it flung its broad drifts of foam, rejoicing in its strength; and every green thing leaned lovingly toward it or stooped to touch it, and all exquisite things which love damp, all tender mosses and selaginellas, all shade-loving ferns and aroids, flourish round it in perennial beauty; while high above, in the sunshine, amid birds and butterflies, the graceful areca palm struggles with the feathery bamboo for precarious root-hold on rocky ledges, and spikes of rose-crimson blossoms, and dark green fronds of bananas, and all the leafy wealth born of moisture and sunshine, cling about it tenderly. And lower down the great forest trees arch over it, and the sunbeams trickle through them, and dance in many a quiet pool, turning the far-down sands to gold, brightening majestic tree-ferns, and shining on the fragile polypodium tamariscinum which clings tremblingly to the branches of the graceful waringhan, on a beautiful lygodium which adorns the uncouth trunk of an artocarpus, on glossy ginger-worts and trailing yams, on climbers and epiphytes, and on gigantic lianas which, climbing to the tops of the tallest trees, descend in vast festoons, many of them with orange and scarlet flowers and fruitage, passing from tree to tree, and interlacing the forest with a living network, while selaginellas and lindsayas, and film ferns, and trichomanes radicans drape the rocks in feathery green, along with mosses scarcely distinguishable from ferns. Little rivulets flash out in foam among the dark foliage, and mingle their musical warble with the deep bass of the torrent, and there are twilight depths of leafy shade into which the sunshine never penetrates, damp and cool, in which the music of the water is all too sweet, and the loveliness too entrancing, creating that sadness hardly "akin to pain" which is latent in all intense enjoyment.

Gunong Pondok, the limestone butte, twelve hundred feet in nearly perpendicular height, showed all its brilliancy of color, and Gunong Bubu, one of the highest mountains in Perak, reared his granite crest above the forest. The lotus lake at Bukit Gantang was infinitely more beautiful than under the grayer sky of Friday; a thousand rosy vases were drinking in the sunshine, and ten thousand classic leaves were spreading their blue-green shields below them; all nature smiled and sang. I was loath to exchange my good horse for a gharrie, with a Kling driver draped slightly in Turkey-red cotton sitting on the shafts, who, statuesque as he was, had a far less human expression than Mahmoud and Eblis. In the noonday the indigo-colored Hijan hills, with their swollen waterfall coming down in a sheet of foam, looked cool, but as we dashed through Taipeng I felt overpowered once more by what seems the "wearing world," after beautiful, silent Kwala Kangsa, for there are large shops with gaudy sign-boards, stalls in the streets, tribal halls, buffalo-carts with buffaloes yoked singly, for the spread of their huge horns is so great that they cannot be yoked in pairs; trains of carts with cinnamon-colored, humped bullocks yoked in pairs standing at shop doors, gharries with fiery Sumatra ponies dashing about, crowds of Chinese coolies, busy and half-naked, filling the air with the din of their ceaseless industry, and all the epitomized stir of a world which toils, and strives, and thirsts for gain.

But I must give these coolies their due, for in some ways they show more self-respect than the ordinary English laborer, inasmuch as in bad times they don't become chargeable to anyone, and when the price of the commodity which they produce falls, as that of tin has done, instead of "striking" and abusing everybody all round, they accept the situation, keep quiet, live more frugally, and work for lower wages till things mend. But I don't intend to hold up the Taipeng Chinese as patterns of the virtues in other respects, for they are not. They are turbulent; and crime, growing chiefly out of their passion for gain, is very rife among them. The first thing I heard on arriving here was that a Chinese gang had waylaid a revenue officer in one of the narrow creeks, and that his hacked and mutilated body had drifted down to Permatang this morning.

Mr. Maxwell tells me that, as he returned from escorting me to Bukit Gantang, he overtook a gharrie with a Malay woman in it, and dismounting joined her husband who was walking, but did not speak to the woman. to-day the man told him that his wife woke the following night with a scream which was succeeded by a trance; and that, knowing that a devil had entered into her, he sent for a pawan (a wise man or sorcerer), who on arriving asked questions of the bad spirit, who answered with the woman's tongue. "How did you come?" "With the tuan," i.e., Mr. Maxwell. "How did you come with him?" "On the tail of his gray horse." "Where from?" "Changat-Jering." The husband said that these Changat-Jering devils were very bad ones. The pawan then exorcised the devil, and burned strong-smelling drugs under the woman's nose, after which he came out of her, and she fell asleep, the "wise man" receiving a fee.

I never heard of any country of such universal belief in devils, familiars, omens, ghosts, sorceries, and witchcrafts. The Malays have many queer notions about tigers, and usually only speak of them in whispers, because they think that certain souls of human beings who have departed this life have taken up their abode in these beasts, and in some places, for this reason, they will not kill a tiger unless he commits some specially bad aggression. They also believe that some men are tigers by night and men by day!

The pelisit, the bad spirit which rode on the tail of Mr. Maxwell's horse, is supposed to be the ghost of a woman who has died in childbirth. In the form of a large bird uttering a harsh cry, it is believed to haunt forests and burial-grounds and to afflict children. The Malays have a bottle-imp, the polong, which will take no other sustenance than the blood of its owner, but it rewards him by aiding him in carrying out revengeful purposes. The harmless owl has strange superstitions attaching to it, and is called the "specter bird;" you may remember that the fear of encountering it was one of the reasons why the Permatang Pasir men would not go with us through the jungle to Rassa.

A vile fiend called the penangalan takes possession of the forms of women, turns them into witches, and compels them to quit the greater part of their bodies, and flyaway by night to gratify a vampire craving for human blood. This is very like one of the ghoul stories in the *Arabian*

Nights Entertainments. Then they have a specter huntsman with demon dogs who roams the forests, and a storm fiend who rides the whirlwind, and spirits borrowed from Persia and Arabia. It almost seems as if the severe monotheism to which they have been converted compels them to create a gigantic demonology.

They have also many odd but harmless superstitions: For instance, that certain people have the power of making themselves invulnerable by the agency of spirits; that the regalia of the States are possessed of supernatural powers; that the wearing of a tiger claw prevents disease; that rude "Aeolian harps" hung up in trees will keep the forest goblins from being troublesome; that charms and amulets worn or placed about a house ward off many evils; that at dangerous rapids, such as those of Jerom Pangong on the Perak river, the spirits must be propitiated by offerings of betel-nut and bananas; that to insure good luck a betel-chewer must invariably spit to the left; that it is unlucky either to repair or pull down a house; that spirits can be propitiated and diseases can be kept away by hanging up palm leaves and cages in the neighborhood of kampongs, and many others. They also believe as firmly as the Chinese do in auspicious and inauspicious days, spells, magic, and a species of astrology. I hope that Mr. Maxwell will publish his investigations into these subjects.

"Running amuck" (amok) is supposed by some to be the result of "possession;" but now, at least, it is comparatively uncommon in these States. A Malay is on some points excessively sensitive regarding his honor, and to wipe out a stain upon it by assassinating the offender is considered as correct and in accordance with etiquette as dueling formerly was in our own country. In cases, however, in which the offender is of higher rank than the injured man, the latter in despair sometimes resorts to opium, and, rushing forth in a frenzy, slays all he can lay hands upon. This indiscriminate slaying is the amok proper. In certain cases, such as those arising out of jealousy, the desire for vengeance gains absolute possession of a Malay. Mr. Newbold says that he has seen letters regarding insults in which the writers say, "I ardently long for his blood to clean my face," or "I ardently long for his blood to wash out the pollution of the hog's flesh with which he has smeared me!"

Considering how punctilious and courteous the Malays are, how rough many of the best of us are, how brutal in manner many of us are, and how inconsiderate our sailors are of the customs of foreign peoples, especially in regard to the seclusion of their women, it is wonderful that bloody revenge is not more common than it is.

"Amok" means a furious and reckless onset. When Mr. Birch was murdered, the cry "amok! amok!" was raised, and the passion of murder seized on all present. Only about a year ago one of the sons of the Rajah Muda Yusuf, a youth of twenty, was suddenly seized with this monomania, drew his kris, and rushing at people killed six, wounded two, and then escaped into the jungle. Major M'Nair says that a Malay, in speaking of amok, says: "My eyes got dark, and I ran on."

In Malacca Captain Shaw told me that "running amuck" was formerly very common, and that on an expedition he made, one of his own attendants was suddenly seized with the "amok" frenzy. He mentioned that he had known of as many as forty people being injured by a single "amok" runner. When the cry "amok! amok!" is raised, people fly to the right and left for shelter, for after the blinded madman's kris has once "drank blood," his fury becomes ungovernable, his sole desire is to kill; he strikes here and there; men fall along his course; he stabs fugitives in the back, his kris drips blood, he rushes on yet more wildly, blood and murder in his course; there are shrieks and groans, his bloodshot eyes start from their sockets, his frenzy gives him unnatural strength; then all of a sudden he drops, shot through the heart, or from sudden exhaustion, clutching his bloody kris even in the act of rendering up his life.

As his desire is to kill everybody, so, as he rushes on, everybody's desire is to kill him, and gashed from behind or wounded by shots, his course is often red with his own blood. Under English rule the great object of the police is to take the "amok" runner alive, and have him tried like an ordinary criminal for murder; and if he can be brought to bay, as he sometimes is, they succeed in pinning him to the wall by means of such a stout two-pronged fork as I saw kept for the purpose in Malacca. Usually, however the fate of the "amok" runner is a violent death, and men feel no more scruple about killing him in his frenzy than they would about killing a man-eating tiger. I hear that this form of frenzy affects the Malays of all the islands of the Archipelago. Some people attribute it to the excessive use of opium by unprepared constitutions, and others to monomania arising from an unusual form of digestive disturbance; but from it being peculiar to Malays, I rather incline to Major M'Nair's view: "There can be no doubt that the amok had its origin in the deed of some desperate Malay, that tradition handed it down to his highly-sensitive successors, and the example was followed and continues to be followed as the right thing to do by those who are excited to frenzy by apprehension, or by some injury that they regard as deadly, and only to be washed out in blood."

I have been interrupted by a visit from two disconsolate-looking Ceylon planters, who have come "prospecting" for coffee. An enterprising son of an Edinburgh "Bailie" has been trying coffee-planting beyond the Perak, but he has got into difficulties with his laborers, and is "getting out of it." This difficulty about labor will possibly have to be solved by the introduction of coolies from India, for the Malays won't work except for themselves; and the Chinese not only prefer the excitement of mining, and the evening hubbub of the mining towns, but in lonely places they are not always very manageable by people unused to them.

Even for clearing the jungle foreign labor must be employed. Perak is a healthy and splendid State, and while the low grounds are suited for sugar, tapioca, and tobacco, the slopes of the hills will produce coffee, cinchona, vanilla, tea, cloves, and nutmegs. It is a land of promise, but at present of promise only! I understand that to start a plantation a capital of from 2,500 pounds to 3,500 pounds would be required. Jungle is cleared at the rate of 25s. per acre. The wages of Javanese coolies are 1s. a day, and a hut which will hold fifty of them can be put up for 5 pounds. Land can be had for three years free of charge. It is then granted in perpetuity for a dollar an acre, and there is a tax of 2-1/2 per cent. on exported produce. These arrangements are not regarded as altogether satisfactory, and will probably be improved upon. Tell some of our friends who have sons with practical good sense, but more muscle than brains, that there are openings in the jungles of Perak! Good sense, perseverance, steadiness, and a degree of knowledge of planting, are, however, preliminary requisites.

The two "prospectors" look as if they had heard couleur de rose reports, and had not "struck ile." Possibly they expected to find hotels and macadamized roads. Roads must precede planting, I think, unless there are available lands near the rivers.

I have mentioned slavery and debt-slavery more than once. The latter is a great curse in Perak, and being a part of "Malay custom" which our treaties bind us to respect, it is very difficult to deal with. In the little States of Sungei Ujong and Selangor, with their handful of Malays, it has been abolished with comparative ease. In Perak, with its comparatively large Malay population, about four thousand are slaves, and the case seems full of complications.

Undoubtedly the existence of slavery has been one cause of the decay of the native States, and of the exodus of Malays into the British settlements. Some people palliate the system, and speak of it as "a mild form of domestic servitude;" but Mr. Birch, the late murdered Resident, wrote of it in these strong terms: "I believe that the system as practiced in Perak at the present time involves evils and cruelties which are unknown to any but those who have actually lived in these States."

From the moment a man or woman becomes a debtor, he or she, if unable to pay, may be taken up by the creditor, and may be treated as a slave, being made to work in any way that the creditor chooses, the debtor's earnings belonging to the creditor, who allows no credit toward the reduction of the debt. To make the hardship greater, if a relative or friend comes forward to pay the debt, the creditor has the right to refuse payment, and to keep his slave, whose only hope of bettering himself is in getting his owner to accept payment for him from a third party, so that he may become the slave of the person who has ransomed him.

But there are worse evils still, for in cases where a married man contracts a debt, his wife and existing children, those who may hereafter be born, and their descendants, pass into slavery; and all, male and female, are compelled as slaves to work for their master, who in very many cases compels the women and girls to live a life of degradation for his benefit, and even the wives of a creditor are well satisfied to receive the earnings of these poor creatures. If a debt be contracted by an unmarried man or woman, and he or she marry afterwards, the person so taken in marriage and all the offspring become slave debtors. The worst features of the system are seen where a Rajah is the creditor, for he is the last man to be willing to receive payment of a debt and free the debtor, for the number of his followers, even if they are but women and girls, increases his consequence, and debtors when once taken into a Rajah's household are looked upon as being as much a part of his property as his cattle or elephants. Mr. Swettenham, the Assistant Colonial Secretary of the Straits Settlements, writes that "in Perak the cruelties exercised toward debtors are even exclaimed at by Malays in the other States."* In Selangor, where it is said that slavery has been quietly abolished, only five years ago the second son of that quiet-looking Abdul Samat killed three slave debtors for no other reason than that he willed it; and when two girls and a boy, slave debtors of the Sultan's, ran away, this same bloodthirsty son caught them, took the boy into a field, and had him krissed. His wife, saying she was going to bathe in the Langat river, told the two girls to follow her to a log which lay in the water a few yards from her house, where they were seized, and a boy follower of her husband took them successively by the hair and held their heads under the water with his foot till they were dead, when their corpses were left upon the slimy bank. The Sultan, to do him justice, was very angry when his son went to him and said, "I have thrown away those children who ran away."

[*For Mr. Swettenham's Report on Slavery in the Native States, see Appendix B.]

In Perak it has been the custom to hunt and capture the Jakun women and make them and their children slaves.

Instances of cruelty have greatly diminished since British influence has entered Perak, and I should think that Mr. Low will ere long mature a scheme for the emancipation of all persons held in bondage.* I heard of a curious case this morning. The aunt of a Malay policeman in Larut, passing near a village, met an acquaintance, and taking a stone from the roadside sat down upon it while she stopped to talk, and on getting up forgot to remove it. An hour later a village child tripped over the stone and slightly cut its forehead. The placing the stone in the pathway was traced to the woman, who was arrested and sentenced to pay a fine of $25, and being unable to pay it she and her children became slave-debtors to the father of the child which had been hurt. In this case, though Captain Speedy lent the policeman money wherewith to pay his aunt's fine, the creditor repeatedly refused to receive it, preferring to exercise his prerogative of holding the family as his rightful slaves. [*Such a scheme is now under consideration. See Appendix C.]

Slavery and polygamy, the usual accompaniments of Islamism, go far to account for the decay of these States.

I wish it were possible to know to what extent the Malays are a "religious" people as Moslems. That they are bigots and have successfully resisted all attempts to convert them to Christianity there is no doubt, as well as that they are ignorant and grossly superstitious. Their prayers, so far as I can hear anything about them, consist mainly of reiterated confessions of belief in the Divine unity, and of simple appeals for mercy now and at the last day.

The pilgrimage to Mecca is made not only once, but twice and thrice by those who can afford it, and at much cost earthen jars containing water from the holy well of Zem-zem, the well said to have been shown to Hagar in the wilderness, are brought home by the pilgrims for themselves and their friends for use in the hour of death, when Eblis, the devil, is supposed to stand by offering a bowl of the purest water with which to tempt the soul to abjure its faith in the unity of God. One of the declarations most commonly used is, "There is no God but God alone, whose covenant is truth and whose servant is victorious. There is no God but God without a partner. His is the kingdom, to Him be praise, and He over all things is Almighty." There is a grand ring of Old Testament truth about these words, though of a melancholy half truth only.

The men who make the Mecca pilgrimage are not regarded by the English who know them as a "holy lot"; in fact, they are said to lead idle lives, and to "live like leeches on the toil of their fellow-men," inciting the people "to revolt or to make amok." Doubtless it adds to a man's consequence for life to be privileged to wear the Arab costume and to be styled Tuan hadji. Yet they may have been stirred to devotion and contrition at the time as they circled the Kaabeh reciting such special prayers as, "O God, I extend my hands to Thee, great is my longing towards Thee. Oh accept Thou my supplications, remove my hindrances, pity my humiliation, and mercifully grant me Thy pardon;" and "O my God, verily I take refuge with Thee from idolatry, and disobedience, and every hypocrisy, and from evil conversation, and evil thoughts concerning property, and children, and family;" or, "O God, I beg of Thee that faith which shall not fall away, and that certainty which shall not perish, and the good aid of Thy prophet Mohammed—may God bless and preserve him! O God, shade me with Thy shadow in that day when there is no shade but Thy shadow, and cause me to drink from the cup of Thy apostle Mohammed—may God bless him and preserve him! that pleasant draught after which is no thirst to all eternity. O Lord of honor and glory."*

> [*I have preferred to give, instead of the translation of these prayers which I obtained in Malacca, one introduced by Canon Tristram into a delightful paper on Mecca in the Sunday at Home for February, 1883.]

As I write, I look down upon Taipeng on "a people wholly given to idolatry." This is emphatically "The dark Peninsula," though both Protestants and Romanists have made attempts to win the Malays to Christianity. It may be that the relentless crusade waged by the Portuguese against Islamism has made the opposition to the Cross more sullen and bigoted than it would otherwise have been. Christian missionary effort is now chiefly among the Chinese, and by means of admirable girls' schools in Singapore, Malacca, and Pinang.

In Taipeng five dialects of Chinese are spoken, and Chinamen constantly communicate with each other in Malay, because they can't understand each other's Chinese. They must spend large sums on opium, for the right to sell it has been let for 4,000 pounds a year!

Mr. Maxwell tells me that the Malay proverbs are remarkably numerous and interesting. To me the interest of them lies chiefly in their resemblance to the ideas gathered up in the proverbs of ourselves and the Japanese.*

> [*Mr. Maxwell has since published a paper on Malay proverbs in the Transactions of the Straits branch of the Royal Asiatic Society. I have not been able to obtain it, but I understand that it contains a very copious and valuable collection of Malay proverbial philosophy.]

Thus, "Out of the frying-pan into the fire" is, "Freed from the mouth of the alligator to fall into the tiger's jaws." "It's an ill wind that blows nobody good," is, "When the junk is wrecked the shark gets his fill." "The creel tells the basket it is coarsely plaited" is equivalent to "The kettle calling the pot black." "For dread of the ghost to clasp the corpse," has a grim irony about it that I like.

Certain Scriptural proverbial phrases have their Malay counterparts. Thus, the impossibility of the Ethiopian changing his skin or the leopard his spots is represented by "Though you may feed a jungle-fowl off a gold plate, it will make for the jungle all the same." "Casting pearls before swine" by "What is the use of the peacock strutting in the jungle?" "Can these stones become bread?" by "Can the earth become grain?" "Neither can salt water yield sweet," by a very elaborate axiom, "You may plant the bitter cucumber in a bed of sago, manure it with honey, water it with molasses, and train it over sugar cane, but it will be the bitter cucumber still," and "Clear water cannot be drawn from a muddy fountain."

Some of their sayings are characteristic. In allusion to the sport of cock-fighting, a coward is called "a duck with spurs." A treacherous person is said to "sit like a cat, but leap like a tiger;" and of a chatterer it is said, "The tortoise produces a myriad eggs and no one knows it; the hen lays one and tells the whole word." "Grinding pepper for a bird on the wing" is regarded as equivalent to "First catch you hare before you cook it." "To plant sugar-cane on the lips" is to be "All things to all men." Fatalism is expressed by a saying, "Even the fish which inhabit the seventh depth of the sea sooner or later enter the net." "Now it is wet, now it is fine," is a common way of saying that a day of revenge is not far off. Secrecy is enjoined by the cynical axiom, "If you have rice, hide it under the unhusked grain." "The last degree of stinginess is not to disturb the mildew," is a neat axiom; and "The plantain does not bear fruit twice," tells that the Malays have an inkling that "There is a tide in the affairs of men," etc.

I have found it very interesting to be the guest of a man who studies the Malays as sympathetically as Mr. Maxwell does. I hope he will not get promotion too soon!*

> [*As I copy this letter I hear that Mr. Maxwell has been removed to a higher and more highly paid post, but that he leaves the Malays with very sincere regret, and that they deeply deplore his loss, because they not only liked but trusted him. During the time in which he was Assistant Resident, and living in the midst of a large Chinese population, it was necessary to be very firm, and at times almost severely firm, but the Chinese have shown their

appreciation of official rectitude by presenting him with a gorgeous umbrella of red silk, embroidered with gold, which they call "A ten-thousand-man umbrella," i.e., an offering from a community which is not only unanimous in making it, but counts at least that number of persons.]

I. L. B.

Letter XXIII

"Gang Murders"—Malay Nicknames—A Persecuted Infant—The Last of the Golden Chersonese

MR. JUSTICE WOOD'S, THE PEAK, PINANG, February 24.

However kind and hospitable people are, the process of "breaking in" to conventionalities again is always a severe one, and I never feel well except in the quiet and freedom of the wilds, though in the abstract nothing can be more healthy than the climate of this lofty Peak. The mercury has been down at 68 degrees for two nights, and blankets have been a comfort!

Shortly after finishing my last letter I left Taipeng with Mr. Maxwell, calling on our way to the coast at Permatang, to inquire if there were any scent of the murderers of the revenue officer, but there was none. The inspector said that he had seen many murdered bodies, but never one so frightfully mutilated. These Chinese "gang-murders" are nearly always committed for gain, and the Chinese delight in cruel hackings and purposeless mutilations. The Malay assassinations are nearly all affairs of jealousy—a single stab and no more.

The last part of the drive on a road causewayed through the endless mangrove swamp impresses the imagination strongly by its dolefulness. Here are hundreds of square miles all along the coast nothing but swamp and slime, loaded with rank and useless vegetation, which has not even beauty to justify its existence, teeming with alligators, serpents, and other vengeful creatures. There is a mournfulness in seeing the pointed fruit of the mangrove drop down through the still air into the slime beneath, with the rootlet already formed of that which never fails to become a tree.

A Sikh guard of honor of fifty men in scarlet uniforms lined the way to the boat as a farewell to Major Swinburne, whose feet they had embraced and kissed with every Oriental demonstration of woe two hours before. We asked him what his farewells were, and he says that he said, "You are a lot of unmitigated scoundrels; half of you deserve hanging; but keep out of scrapes if you can till I come back, that I may have the pleasure of hanging you myself." He really likes them though, and called after Captain Walker, who is to act as his substitute, "Now, old man, don't knock those fellows about!" The chief dread of the "fellows" is that they will be at the mercy of an interpreter under the new regime. The Malays give sobriquets to all Europeans, founded upon their physical or mental idiosyncrasies. Thus they call Major Swinburne "The Mad One" and "The Outspoken One." Captain Walker they have already dubbed "The Black Panther." They call Mr. Maxwell "The Cat-eyed One," and "The Tiger Cub."

Just before sailing I had the satisfaction of getting this telegram from Kwala Kangsa: "Eblis is a little better this morning. He has eaten two grasshoppers and has taken his milk without trouble, but he is very weak."*

> [*Those of my readers who have become interested in this most bewitching ape will be sorry to hear that, after recovering and thriving for a considerable time, he died, to the great grief of his friends.]

We embarked at 5:30 P.M. along with a swarm of mosquitoes, and after a beautiful night anchored at Georgetown at 2 A.M., but it was a ludicrously uncomfortable voyage. An English would-be lady, i.e., a "fine lady," a product of imperfect civilization with which I have little sympathy, had demanded rather than asked for a passage in the Kinta, and this involved not only a baby, but an ayah and man-servant. The little cabin of the launch can hold two on two coaches, but the lady, after appropriating one, filled up most of the other with bags and impediments of various kinds. The floor was covered with luggage, among which the ayah and infant slept, and the man sat inside on the lowest rung of the ladder. Thus there were five human beings, a host of mosquitoes, and a lamp in the stifling den, in which the mercury stood all night at 88 degrees. Then a whole bottle of milk was spilt and turned sour, a vial of brandy was broken and gave off its disgusting fumes, and the infant screamed with a ferocious persistency, which contrasted with the patient wistfulness of the sick Eblis and his gentle murmur of "ouf! ouf!" Before we anchored the lady asked me to go and wake the gentlemen and get a teaspoonful of brandy for her, at which request, though made with all due gravity, they laughed so tremendously that I was hardly able to go back to her with it. Major Swinburne, who professes to be a woman and child hater, was quite irrepressible, and whenever the infant cried outrageously, called to his servant, "Wring that brat's neck," the servant, of course, knowing not a word of English, and at 2 A.M., when there was chocolate on deck, and the unfortunate baby was roaring and kicking, he called down to me, "Will you come and drink some chocolate to King Herod's memory?" Mr. Maxwell, who has four children, did not behave much better; and it was a great exertion to me, by overdone courtesy and desperate attempts at conversation, to keep the mother as far as possible from hearing what was going on!

At 6 A.M., in the glory of the tropic sunrise, Mr. Maxwell and I landed in Province Wellesley, under the magnificent casuarina trees which droop in mournful grace over the sandy shore. The somberness of the interminable groves of cocoa-palms on the one side of the Strait, the brightness of the sun-kissed peaks on the other, and the deep shadows on the amber water, were all beautiful. Truly in the tropics "the outgoings of the morning rejoice."

We found Mrs. Isemonger away, no one knew where, so we broke open the tea-chest, and got some breakfast, at the end of which she returned, and we had a very pleasant morning. At noon a six-oared gig, which was the last of the "Government facilities," took us over to Georgetown, spending an hour in crossing against an unfavorable tide, under a blazing sun. This was the last of the Malay Peninsula.

S.S. Malwa, February 25.

We sailed from Pinang in glorious sunshine at an early hour this afternoon, and have exchanged the sparkling calms of the Malacca Straits for the indolent roll of the Bay of Bengal. The steamer's head points northwest. In the far distance the hills of the Peninsula lie like mists upon a reddening sky. My tropic dream is fading and the "Golden Chersonese" is already a memory.

I. L. B.

APPENDIX A: RESIDENTS

A policy of advice, and that alone, was contemplated by the Colonial Office; but without its orders or even cognizance affairs were such that the government of those Malayan States to which Residents have been accredited has been from the first exercised by the Residents themselves, mainly because neither in Perak, Selangor, or Sungei Ujong has there ever been a ruler powerful enough to carry out such an officer's advice, the Rajahs and other petty chiefs being able to set him at defiance. Advice would be given that peace and order should be preserved, justice administered without regard to the rank of the criminal, the collection of revenue placed upon a satisfactory footing, and good administration generally secured, but had any reigning prince attempted to carry out these recommendations he would have been overborne by the Rajahs, whose revenues depended on the very practices which the Resident denounced, and by the piratical bands whose source of livelihood was the weakness and mal-administration of the rulers. The Pangkor Treaty contained the words that the Resident's advice *"must be acted upon,"* and consequently the Residents have taken the direction of public affairs, organizing armed forces, imposing taxes, taking into their own hands the collection of the revenues, receiving all complaints, executing justice, punishing evil-doers, apprehending criminals, and repressing armed gangs of robbers. These officers are, in fact, far more the agents of the Governor of the Straits Settlements than the advisers of the native princes, and though paid out of native revenues are the virtual rulers of the country in all matters, except those which relate to Malay religion and custom. As stated by Lord Carnarvon, "Their special objects should be the maintenance of peace and law, the initiation of a sound system

APPENDIX A: RESIDENTS

of taxation, with the consequent development of the general resources of the country, and the supervision of the collection of the revenue so as to insure the receipt of funds necessary to carry out the principal engagements of the Government, and to pay for the cost of British officers and whatever establishments may be found necessary to support them." Lord Carnarvon in the same dispatch states: "Neither annexation nor the government of the country by British officers in the name of the Sultan [a measure very little removed from annexation] could be allowed;" and elsewhere he says: "It should be our present policy to find and train up some chief or chiefs of sufficient capacity and enlightenment to appreciate the advantages of a civilized government, and to render some effectual assistance in the government of the country."

The treaty of Pangkor provides "that the Resident's advice must be asked and acted upon (in Perak) on all questions other than those relating to Malay religion and custom, and that the collection and control of all revenue and the general administration of the country must be regulated under the advice of these Residents." It was on the same terms that Residents were appointed at Selangor and Sungei Ujong.

APPENDIX B: SLAVERY IN THE MALAY STATES

Langat, 30th June, 1875.

Sir—When on board the Colonial steamer Pluto last week, accompanying His Excellency the Governor in a tour to some of the native States, His Excellency made inquiry of me with regard to the present state of debt-slavery in the Peninsula.

This was a subject so large and important as hardly to admit of thorough explanation in a conversation; I therefore asked His Excellency's leave to report upon it.

I now beg to give you a detailed account of the circumstances of debt-slavery as known to me personally.

In treating the question under its present condition—I mean under Malay rule—it is necessary to consider the all-but slavery of the debtors and the difficulty of making any arrangement between debtor and creditor which while it frees the one will satisfy the other, and still be in keeping with the "adat Malayu," as interpreted in these States.

The relative positions of debtor and creditor in the Western States, more especially in Perak, involve evils which are, I believe, quite unknown to Europeans, even those living so near as Singapore.

The evils to which I refer have hitherto been regarded as unavoidable, and a part of the ordinary relations between Rajahs and subjects.

APPENDIX B: SLAVERY IN THE MALAY STATES

I may premise by saying that though the system of "debt-slavery," as it has been called, exists to some extent in all the States, it is only seen in its worst light where a Rajah or chief is the creditor and a subject the debtor.

Few subjects in a Malay country are well off. The principal reason of this is, that as soon as a man or woman is known to be in possession of money, he or she would be robbed by the Rajah; or the money would be borrowed with no intention of future payment, whether the subject wished to lend or not.

Thus, when a Ryot (or subject) is in want of money, he goes to his Rajah or chief to lend it him, because he alone can do so. Either money or goods are then lent, and a certain time stipulated for payment. If at the expiration of that time the money is not paid, it is usual to await some time longer, say two or three, or even six months.

Should payment not then be made, the debtor, if a single man, is taken into the creditor's house; he becomes one of his followers, and is bound to execute any order or do any work the Rajah as creditor may demand, until the debt is paid, however long a time that may be.

During this time the Rajah usually provides the debtor with food and clothing, but if the creditor gives him money, that money is added to the debt.

Often, however, the Rajah gives nothing, and the debtor has to find food and clothing as he can.

Should the debtor marry—and the Rajah will in all probability find him a wife—then the debtor's wife, his children, his grandchildren, all become equally bound with himself to the payment of this debt.

APPENDIX B: SLAVERY IN THE MALAY STATES

Should the debtor be originally married, then not only he, but his wife and children, are taken into the Rajah's house, and are his to order until the debt is paid.

Should the debtor be a woman, unmarried, or a widow, the same course is taken, and whoever marries her becomes jointly responsible for the debt; and this goes on through generations—the children and grandchildren of the debtor being held in the same bondage by the children and grandchildren of the creditor.

Should at any time the debtor succeed in raising the amount of the debt and proffer it to the creditor, then it would be customary to accept it. If, however, a large family were in bondage for the debt, one whose numbers seemed to the Rajah to add to his dignity, then he would probably refuse to accept payment, not absolutely, but would say "wait," and the waiting might last for years.

Debtors once absorbed into the Rajah's household are looked upon as his property, just as his bullocks or his goats, and those who alone would have the power to interfere look on and say nothing, because they do the same themselves.

In different States this debtor-bondage is carried to greater or less extremities, but in Perak the cruelties exercised toward debtors are even exclaimed against by Malays in other States.

Many chiefs in Perak have a following principally composed of young men and girls, for the most part debtors.

The men are treated as I have already described—either food and clothes are found for them or not; they are usually found—for the Rajah's power and his pride consists in the number of arms-bearing followers he has at his beck and call; men, too, are useful to him in many other ways. Those who have grown old in their bondage, whether men or

APPENDIX B: SLAVERY IN THE MALAY STATES

women, either for very shame the Rajah provides for, or he compels their children to support them.

The men either (1) follow because they like it (a very small percentage indeed); or (2) they are debtors, or the children of debtors; or (3) they are real slaves from Sumatra or Abyssinia, or the children of slaves.

The girls are treated differently; they are (1) either slaves or the daughters of slaves; or (2) debtors, the daughters or granddaughters of debtors; or (3) the Rajah has simply taken them from their houses into his own house because he wanted them; or (4) they follow him for pleasure.

In Perak some of the chiefs do not provide their girls with food or clothing, but they tell them to get these necessaries of life as best they can, i.e., by prostitution—for the labor of the debtor being the property of the creditor, prostitution is in this case a necessity and not a choice.

Each Rajah in his own district claims the privilege of fining, either for a capital offence or for a trifling misdeed. Should, then, a man be fined and not pay the fine, he and his family, if he has one, are at once taken into this debt-bondage, not to work out the fine, but to toil away their lives amid blows and upbraidings—the daughters driven to prostitution, the sons to thieving, and even greater crimes.

This is no exaggerated statement, but the plain truth.

When the Rajah gives nothing, neither food nor clothes, or when he is a passionate man, and threatens to kill one or other of his followers for some trivial offence, or for no offence at all, it often happens that one will seek refuge in flight. If caught, though, it may be said to be the received custom to inflict only some slight punishment; yet that would not deter a Rajah from punishing such an offence even with death should it seem good to him.

APPENDIX B: SLAVERY IN THE MALAY STATES

Bond-debtors are handed about from one Rajah to another without a thought of consulting them. If one runs away and is caught, it is at great risk of being put to death, while probably no one would move a finger to save him, his master excusing himself on the plea that it is necessary to frighten others from running away also.

These Rajah-creditors would tell you smilingly that they knew by Mohammedan law the creditors can take and sell all their debtor's property for an overdue debt, and that then the debtor is free; but they never act on that principle.

Many men and women, however, rarely incur debts, knowing well what lies before them in case of non-payment.

Malays, by their laws, are allowed to buy and sell slaves, and if, having for years lost sight of a slave, the owner finds him or her, he takes the slave with his wife and family, if he has one, as his lawful property.

There is one other phase of debtor-bondage, and that a common one, where the father or mother places one or more of their own children as security with the creditor for a debt; thus in reality selling their own flesh and blood into often a life-long bondage. If these children die on the creditor's hands, the parents supply their places by others, or the Rajah, should he wish it, can at any time after the debt is due, take the whole family into his house.

Only the other day a man here, for a debt of $40, placed his daughter in a Rajah's hands and ran away. Probably he will never return; meanwhile the girl must obey her master in all things like the veriest slave. Such a state of things as this is only brought about by the custom which allows it.

Another common practice in the States, more especially in Perak, is to capture, as you might wild beasts, the unoffending Jakun women, and make them and their children slaves through generations.

APPENDIX B: SLAVERY IN THE MALAY STATES

In April I was in Ulu Selangor, and the headmen there complained that a chief from Slim had a fortnight before caught 14 Jakuns and one Malay in Ulu Selangor, had chained them and driven off to Slim. Arrived there, the Malay was liberated and he returned.

Letters were written to Slim and Perak, but though we ascertained the party had reached Slim, they did not remain there, and they have not yet been discovered.

I have already stated that the Rajah looks to the number of his following as the gauge of his power, and other Rajahs will respect and fear him accordingly. Thus he tries to get men into his service in this way, and is rather inclined to refuse payment should the debtor be so fortunate as to raise the requisite amount of his debt.

Almost the only chance the debtor has of raising this amount is by successful gambling. Of course it hardly ever happens that he is successful; but, like all gamblers, he always thinks he will be, and thus gambling becomes a mania with him, which he will gratify at all costs, caring little by what means he gets money for play so long as he does obtain it.

These are the general facts relating to the position of the slave-debtor, and these things which I have described, seemingly so difficult of belief, are done almost daily; looked upon by those who do them as a right divine; by the victims as a fate from which there is no reprieve.

To compel his followers to obey him implicitly, the Rajah treats them with a severity which sometimes makes death the punishment of the slightest offence to him. These followers he thus holds to do whatever he bids them, even to the commission of the gravest crimes.

They again, having to provide themselves with food and clothes, and yet having to work for him, are led to prey on the defenceless population, from whom, in the name of their Rajah-master, they extort whatever

APPENDIX B: SLAVERY IN THE MALAY STATES

there is to get, and on whom they sometimes visit those cruelties which they have themselves already experienced.

This system of debtor bondage influences, then, the whole population, not slightly but deeply, in ways it is hardly possible to credit except when seen in a constant intercourse with all classes of Malay society.

The question at issue seems to be; how to deprive the Rajah of this great power—an unscrupulous instrument in unscrupulous hands—how to free the debtors from their bondage, the women from lives of forced prostitution, the unoffending population from the robberies and murderous freaks of Rajahs and their bondsmen.* [*Some of these remarks apply specially to Selangor, in which State slavery is now abolished. I. L. B.]

In Perak it is different; the debtor-bondage is one of the chief customs —one of the "pillars of the State"—an abuse jealously guarded by the Perak Rajahs and Chiefs, and especially by those who make the worst uses of it.

I have often discussed this question of debt-slavery with the Malays themselves, but they say they see no way under the rule of their Rajahs to put down this curse of their country, with all the evils that follow in its train. I have, etc.

(Signed)
Frank A. Swettenham,
(Now Asst. Colonial Secretary at Singapore.)
The Honorable the Secretary for Native States,
Singapore, Straits Settlements.

APPENDIX C: TWO LETTERS

No. I

From H.B.M.'s Resident, Perak, to Colonial Secretary, Straits Settlements Residency, Kwala Kansa, December 14, 1878.

Sir—In reference to your letter of the 28th June last, directing, by command of His Excellency the Governor, my particular attention to the plan adopted in Selangor for the extinction of the claims against slave-debtors, by a valuation of their services to their creditors according to a fixed scale, and directing me to consider to His Excellency with a view to its being afterward submitted for the consideration of the Council of State:

1. I have the honor to state in reply that a copy of that letter and its inclosure was supplied to the Assistant Resident of Perak, and its contents communicated to the other magistrates, with instructions on all occasions in which such cases should be brought before them, to endeavor, with the consent of the creditors, to come to a settlement on such a basis.

2. The Toh Puan Halimah, daughter of the exiled Laxamana of Perak, and chief wife of the banished Mentri of the State, had invested most of her private money in advances of this description, which, up to the time of British interference, was the favorite form of security, and she is now the largest claimant in the country for the repayment of her money. Another, Wan Teh Sapiah, has also claims of a like nature on several families, and

APPENDIX C: TWO LETTERS

both these ladies willingly undertook to accept of liquidation by such an arrangement.

3. In the former case it has, I am sorry to say, fallen through, from the impossibility of inducing the debtors to work regularly, and from very many of them, who are living in entire freedom in different parts of the country, declining to come into the arrangement, though acknowledging their debts.

4. In many other cases the creditors from the first put forward the certainty of the failure of such a system from the above-mentioned cause; others have objected that they had no regular employment in which to place their debtors; others, that they are utterly ruined by the events of recent years, and that they would accede to the proposal if fairly carried out on the other part, provided the Government would advance money as the native Rajahs did to enable them to open mines or gardens in which they could employ their debtors; nearly all have declared themselves willing, and even anxious, to accept a just amount in payment of their debts, several suggesting that the State might conveniently undertake to do this, employing the labor in public works until the debtor should be free.

5. I cannot undertake to say what may have been the practice in former times, as to the treatment, in Perak, of this class of persons; but no case of cruelty or any great hardship has been brought to my notice since I came into the country. By far the larger number of the slave-debtors live with their families apart and often at great distances from their masters, enjoying all the fruits of their labor, rendering occasional assistance to them when called upon to do so, which, in the majority of cases, is of rare occurrence.

6. The circumstances of Perak would probably be found to differ from those of Selangor, which I understand has a much smaller

APPENDIX C: TWO LETTERS

population; was governed by an enlightened ruler under the advice of British Residents, who succeeded in introducing the present regulation immediately after the conquest of the district.

7. To introduce such a measure into Perak at the present time would, in my opinion, have a very disturbing effect, and although I do not think that it would lead to any extensive or organized armed resistance, I am sure that it would so shake the confidence which has arisen between the European officers and principal people that years would be required to restore it.

8. I confess that I am not able to devote all my sympathy to the weaker class in this question. I concur with the principal natives that the introduction of a measure which formed no part of the original contract would practically amount to a confiscation of their property, the value of the labor of this class of persons being scarcely more than nominal; and I adhere to the opinion that the just and politic course is, as has been done, to prohibit any extension or renewal of the practice either of slave indebtedness or slavery; to secure good treatment for the servile classes under penalty of enforced manumission; to reduce claims when they come before the magistrates to the minimum which justice to the creditor will permit; to await the increased means of freeing themselves which must develop for the poorer classes upon the extensive introduction of European capital into agricultural industries; and, finally, to purchase at a rate which, in consequence of the notorious discouragement with which every case is treated by the European officers and the courts, and the pressure of other influences, will, in time, be much diminished from what would probably be considered a fair equivalent. I have, etc.,

(Signed) Hugh Low, Resident.
The Hon. the Colonial Secretary, Straits Settlements,
Singapore.

APPENDIX C: TWO LETTERS

No. II

From H.B.M.'s Resident, Perak, to the Honorable the Colonial Secretary

Teluk Anson, April 26, 1882.

Sir—I have the honor to acknowledge the receipt of your letter of the 14th instant, calling upon me for information as to the progress made toward the extinction of debt slavery in this State since 1879, for transmission to Her Majesty's Secretary of State.

In reply I have the honor to report that the policy explained in my letters to your predecessor, dated 28th May and 14th December, 1878, has been steadily pursued in Perak; all slave debtors who have appealed to the protection of the courts having their cases adjudicated upon on the most liberal terms consistent with justice to the creditors, and a considerable number have availed themselves of the facilities presented to them and bought up the claims upon them.

Further and more intimate knowledge of the people has confirmed the impression that whatever may have been the case in former times, cruelty to slaves or slave debtors has been very rare since the establishment of settled government, and in every instance in which such has come to my knowledge or to that of the British officers, manumission without compensation was carried out.

Three such cases have occurred in the families of two very high officers of State, and these, with one other case, are all the instances of cruelty which have been reported to me.

An attempt was made in 1879 to procure a census of the population through the chiefs of the village communities. Each of these chiefs recorded the name of every householder in his district with the number of persons, distinguishing their sex and condition.

APPENDIX C: TWO LETTERS

A total of 47,359 is thus arrived at for the free native Malay population. Of these 14,875 were males above, and 9,313 below, 16 years of age. The females numbered 14,761 and 8,410.

The number of slaves was returned as 1,670, of whom 775 were males and 895 females. The slave debtors were respectively 728 and 652, giving a total of 1,380; the two servile classes numbering, of both sexes, 3,050. I fear, however, that these numbers do not include all the bond population, as His Highness the Regent and one or two others with extensive claims did not give in returns.

I regret to state that the attempt which, as reported in my letter of the 14th December, was liberally made by the Toh Puan Halimah, chief wife of the ex-Mentri of Perak, to facilitate the manumission of her slaves and debtors by working off the just claims against them on fair terms, was successful only to a very inconsiderable extent. The Malays of Perak are, as a rule, so adverse to and so unaccustomed to steady labor, and can so easily provide for their wants, that they altogether decline, except for short periods, to perform services of any nature even for high wages.

The opinion of those having claims upon the servile classes is now pretty general in favor of manumission upon equitable terms, and although a few old Conservative families in such districts as Kinta would prefer to adhere to the former state of things, I have considered that the time has arrived when a general measure having this end in view may be taken into consideration in the hope of carrying it out completely in the year 1883.

His Excellency the Governor may have observed in the minutes of the March Session of the Council of State that the subject of manumission of slaves and debtors was brought to the notice of His Highness, the Regent by the Resident, and that a meeting of the Council was appointed for the 15th May, for the purpose of considering the terms on which such a measure should be based, and the manner in which it should be carried out.

My own idea is that a commission, consisting of one or two native chiefs and the principal European officer of each district, should be appointed to inquire, under written instructions, into the circumstances of each case, and award, subject to the approval of the Government, such compensation as may seem fair to both parties; that the money necessary to pay the amounts awarded shall be advanced by the Government; that the sum adjudged to be paid for manumission shall remain in whole or in part, as may be determined in Council, a debt from the freedman to the State, which he shall be bound to repay by a deduction of a portion of his wages for labor on the public works of the country, which he must continue until his debt is cleared off, should he be unable or unwilling to raise the money by other means; that male relatives shall take upon them the obligations incurred for the freedom of female relations who may themselves be unable to pay; and that, from the date of the completion of the measure, every person in the State shall be absolutely free, and slavery and bond indebtedness declared to be illegal institutions and forever abolished.

I have formerly stated it as the opinion of the best informed natives that a sum varying from $60,000 to $80,000 would be sufficient to meet the necessary expenditure, but I fear that the larger amount would be insufficient, as it would be advisable to deal with an institution involving so great a change in the habits of, and loss to the people, with a certain measure of liberality. I have, etc.

(Signed) Hugh Low, Resident.
The Hon. the Colonial Secretary, etc., etc., etc.,
Straits Settlements.

ABOUT ISABELLA LUCY BIRD

Early Life & Background

Isabella Lucy Bird entered the world in 1831 as the daughter of a prosperous Yorkshire family. Her childhood did not portend the adventurous life ahead. Instead, Bird suffered from persistent health issues that often left her confined indoors.

As a young girl, she endured debilitating headaches, spinal troubles, nervous disorders and other chronic ailments. While bedridden for long stretches, Isabella passed time and fed her imagination by immersing herself in books that brimmed with tales of travel and cultures beyond England's shores. With the limited mobility she experienced in her early years (due to nervous system disorders), reading was one of the most pleasant things she could do.

When in her early 20s, Isabella's desire for autonomy aligned providentially with her doctor's prescription to travel as a remedy. Having come from wealth, she now had the means to set sail as an unchaperoned woman gaining strength through adventure - a privilege that defied normal Victorian conventions.

Early Travels

In 1854 (at age 23) Isabella embarked on a monumental journey that launched her career as an explorer - setting sail for America and Canada on her first major solo trip. Funded by her family's wealth, Isabella spent nearly four months immersed in the frontier cultures of North America that had so enthralled during her years of convalescence.

About Isabella Lucy Bird

This inaugural voyage nurtured the independence and resilience that defined Bird's adventurous spirit for the next fifty years. No longer confined to her bedroom in Yorkshire, the young woman who had dreamed of distant lands as an invalid now traversed sees and rugged landscapes as an explorer.

Two years later in 1856, Isabella traveled further west to pioneer Mormon settlements in Utah. During her time there, she honed the keen observational eye and literary acumen that allowed her to publish "The Englishwoman in America" - a memoir on transatlantic travels which cemented her fame as an intrepid female explorer and solidified her trailblazing status.

Though much of Isabella's early frailties had limited her mobility early in life, she now pushed forward with record-setting travels only previously accomplished by men.

Later Expeditions

Isabella spent the 1870s voyaging intrepidly across ever more remote corners of the world. From 1873-1875, she embarked on extensive travels exploring the depths of Asia, immersing herself in the vibrant diversity of Japan, China, Vietnam and beyond.

During her journeys across Eastern kingdoms, Isabella relied upon her fluency in language and culture to forge connections with inhabitants from all walks of life. Her vivid depictions of sights and encounters captured timeless insights even as global forces began to erode regional traditions.

When she yearned for further conquests, the Hawaiian archipelago and its towering volcanoes called to Bird's thirst for natural grandeur. Through the 1870s, she spent months traversing Hawaii's rugged wilderness terrain on solitary climbs many native guides dared not attempt. From snow-capped summits over 13,000 feet high, Isabella's pen poured forth lyrical admiration.

ABOUT ISABELLA LUCY BIRD

Her adventuresome spirit only grew with age. In her late 50s from 1889-1890, Bird traversed the Middle East through India's vibrant landscape, then to Kurdistan and Persia's arid mountain kingdoms - amassing still more tales for the Victorian audiences enraptured by her decades of boundary-shattering exploration.

Significant Achievements

Isabella's decades of intrepid global wanderlust cemented her legacy as a female explorer ahead of her time. In recognition of this, the Royal Geographical Society (in 1892) formally inducted her into their group of eminent explorers of her time.

Through over 10 acclaimed books published across her lifetime, Bird transported enraptured audiences on lyrical literary adventures spanning continents. Her prolific travelogues granted pioneering glimpses into remote cultures through a woman's eyes for readers back home.

But Bird's most enduring legacy remains the paths she blazed as a female lone explorer pushing limits across oceans and peaks at a time when prudence confined women close to home. Where prevailing wisdom cautioned that frail constitutions should shelter indoors, Isabella conquered 14,000 feet heights and roamed rugged wilderness for months sans companions at age 60 - living proof of what a determined women could endure.

With her courage and chronicles of the dizzying spaces she carved out for herself, Bird inspired future generations of female explorers and travelers to harbor ambitions beyond what society deemed possible. Though she passed in 1904 after seven decades of restless roaming, her intrepid spirit endures as a beacon to women – and men – with a desire for exploration.

ABOUT ISABELLA LUCY BIRD

Later Life & Death

In her late 50s, Isabella Bird opted to largely settle down in Edinburgh, Scotland - drawn by its thriving literary scene. Yet not even the comforts of home could still the wanderlust that had defined six decades of her life.

Though residing mainly in Edinburgh, Bird occasionally grew restless. When this happened, she once again embarked on another adventure. When not on the road, Bird's prolific pen sustained her as she published book after book recounting her decades of adventures for enraptured readers. Through her 60s and 70s, she produced a steady outpouring of memoirs and travelogues until her death.

To the end, the intrepid explorer stayed fiercely true to the enduring passions of her life – traveling the globe and enthralling audiences by pen as she tirelessly recorded her adventures. She departed the world in 1904 at the age of 72 as she had spent her life - immersed in literary travels still longing for the majestic beyond.

BOOKS BY ISABELLA LUCY BIRD

A Lady's Life in the Rocky Mountains: This book, written in 1879, is a collection of letters addressed to Bird's sister, documenting the incredible journeys of the explorer through the Colorado Rockies. Over six months, Bird traveled on horseback, covering more than 1,000 miles across largely uncharted wilderness. Each day posed uncertainty about where she would rest or spend the night. In her letters, Bird vividly describes the breathtaking beauty of the landscapes—snow-capped peaks, hidden valleys, and imposing canyons. However, the book's focal point lies in her poignant depictions of the enduring difficulties faced by the resilient pioneers she encountered. Bird witnessed firsthand the hardships of settlers making a living in the remote mountain settlements. She recounts scenes of isolated and basic cabins, lawlessness, the constant threat from Native tribes and outlaws, and the unforgiving harshness of winters with plummeting temperatures. Yet, amidst these challenges, Bird also admires the strength and integrity of the close-knit pioneer communities she visited. She forms meaningful connections during her weeks spent in isolated mining camps and ranches, assisting with cattle drives. Overall, this memoir serves as a vivid historical account of both culture and nature in the untouched Rocky Mountain frontier, offering a daring woman's perspective on this era.

Among the Tibetans: Published when Bird was 63 years old, this book recounts her challenging journeys across the high Tibetan Plateaus and the Himalayan mountain regions in the late 19th century. Starting her voyage in 1889, Bird explores lands like Ladakh, a region with a Tibetan culture bordering India. She crosses daunting mountain passes, some towering over 15,000 feet, entering Tibet proper and navigating to cities such as Lhasa and Gyantse. Bird is awestruck by the majestic peaks of the Great Himalayan Range, towering over high-altitude valleys and passes that test her physical endurance. She observes and documents cultures and Buddhist heritage largely unfamiliar to the Western world at that time. With her characteristic poetic style, Bird provides insights into the daily lives of remote Tibetan villages, largely untouched by modern influences. She develops a deep admiration for the principles and resourcefulness ingrained in their ancient traditions, enabling survival in a harsh, unforgiving landscape. As she journeys eastward on her return, Bird explores lesser-known Himalayan regions like Yarkand before heading back to India. Her memoir brought the mystique of enigmatic Tibet and Central Asia to Western audiences through the perspective of a pioneering female explorer traversing one of the world's most challenging terrains.

Chinese Pictures—Notes on Photographs Made in China: This book, first published in 1902, invites readers into the captivating world of China through the camera lens of one of history's most intrepid explorers. This compilation captures Isabella L. Bird's keen observations and vivid descriptions, complementing a series of photographs taken during her extensive travels across China. Through her lens and insightful prose, Bird unveils the essence of China's landscapes, people, and traditions. With each photograph, she weaves a narrative, providing a glimpse into the rich tapestry of Chinese life, from bustling cities to remote villages, picturesque landscapes to vibrant marketplaces. In her characteristic style, Bird delves into the cultural nuances, historical significance, and everyday moments frozen in time through the camera's lens. Her notes on the photographs offer a deeper understanding of the scenes captured, breathing life into the imagery and enhancing the reader's connection to the sights and stories behind each snapshot. 'Chinese Pictures' stands as a testament to Isabella L. Bird's ability to blend visual storytelling with her eloquent prose. This compilation serves as a captivating window into China's diverse landscapes and cultural heritage, painting a vivid portrait of the country through the lens of a pioneering traveler and perceptive observer."

Journeys in Persia and Kurdistan: This book, published when Bird was 59, recounts her bold and perilous travels through the regions of Persia (modern-day Iran) and Kurdistan in 1890. It provides a glimpse into a volatile period just before significant upheavals reshaped the fate of the region. Despite warnings about roaming bandits and tribal conflicts in the rural Ottoman and Persian frontiers, Bird was determined to venture into these areas, far from the usual tourist paths. Her Middle Eastern voyage took her through stunning yet unforgiving landscapes, where ancient ruins and bustling bazaars punctuated her journey. She relied on the hospitality of Kurdish and Persian village leaders while being guarded by armed escorts against desert marauders. With eloquent storytelling, Bird recounts her profound interactions with diverse regional cultures and religions, shedding light on the disdain towards oppressive Turkish rulers and offering glimpses into the practices of slavery and the harem system. Her engaging narrative provided Victorian readers with captivating insights into these distant lands, transporting them into the precarious realms at the fringes of crumbling empires on the verge of modernization sweeping through the Near East."

Korea and Her Neighbors: In this book, Bird chronicles her explorations through Korea and its surrounding regions during the late 19th century. Published at a time when knowledge about East Asian cultures was limited in the West, Bird's book provides an intimate portrayal of Korea and its relationships with neighboring countries. Embarking on her journey, Bird ventures into the heart of Korea, traversing its diverse landscapes and immersing herself in its unique traditions. She delves into the bustling streets of Seoul, experiencing the pulse of the country's dynamic capital. Throughout her travels, she embraces the local customs, witnessing the intricate cultural tapestry woven by the Korean people. Beyond the borders of Korea, Bird extends her exploration to the neighboring regions, unraveling the complex dynamics between Korea and its neighbors. She navigates through borderlands, encountering glimpses of life in China and Japan, and observes the interplay of cultures and influences at these junctions. Bird's vivid descriptions paint a captivating picture of Korea's rich heritage and the interactions between this enigmatic nation and its surrounding countries. Through her keen observations and engaging narrative, she provides readers with a nuanced understanding of the region, bridging the gap between the East and West during a transformative period in history.

Last Travels in West Africa: In this memoir, published just two years before Bird's passing at age 70, she recounts her final journeys to sub-Saharan Africa in the early 1900s, specifically focusing on British colonies like Sierra Leone and Nigeria. Starting in Freetown, Sierra Leone, Bird is captivated by the vibrant Creole communities thriving in trade after the collapse of the Atlantic slave routes. She immerses herself in exploring their bustling streets and also observes the customs of indigenous groups like the Timne people. Traveling by boat to Nigeria, Bird investigates cities such as Lagos and former slaving ports. Her journey takes her upriver to reach northern towns like Nupe. Throughout her travels, she meticulously documents the immense diversity of cultures, religions, livelihoods, and the sometimes controversial aspects of Britain's colonial rule. As an intrepid explorer defying societal expectations of retirement in old age, Bird ventures boldly across the region. Her memoir serves as an ethnographic study, shedding light on the complexity of British West Africa at the turn of the century, offering readers a deeper understanding beyond common stereotypes. Her vivid accounts in this memoir mark the culmination of a six-decade career exploring the world's farthest frontiers as a Victorian woman wanderer. Despite her age, she approached this adventure with the same courage and insight that characterized all her extraordinary exploits since her youth.

Notes on Old Edinburgh: In this book, Bird invites readers on a captivating journey through the historic streets and landmarks of Scotland's iconic capital. In this engaging work, Bird eloquently captures the essence of Old Edinburgh, transporting readers back in time to explore the city's rich history and vibrant character. With meticulous attention to detail, Bird traverses the cobblestone streets, unveiling the layers of history etched into the city's architecture, alleys, and renowned landmarks. Her keen observations breathe life into the nooks and crannies of Edinburgh, reviving the spirit of bygone eras. Through her vivid descriptions and insightful commentary, Bird sheds light on the city's storied past, delving into its medieval roots, royal connections, and cultural heritage. She navigates through the charming corners of Edinburgh, sharing tales of its inhabitants, traditions, and the enduring charm that has captivated visitors for centuries. 'Notes on Old Edinburgh' stands as a testament to Bird's knack for storytelling and historical preservation. Her evocative prose invites readers to stroll alongside her through the winding streets of this ancient city, painting a captivating portrait of Edinburgh's captivating allure and its timeless significance in Scottish history.

Six Months in the Sandwich Islands: In this classic work, published the same year as Bird's renowned 'The Hawaiian Archipelago,' she compiles letters she wrote to her sister Henrietta during her extensive six-month exploration of the Hawaiian Islands in 1873. This work provides a detailed account of her diverse adventures across Hawaii's eight major islands. Starting from Honolulu, Bird explores the volcanic slopes of Maui and Hawaii, the lush valleys of Kauai, and the coral-fringed atoll of Molokai. Throughout her journey, Bird revels in the lush tropical abundance of the islands, vividly capturing the ever-changing landscape shaped by volcanoes and the ocean. She immerses herself in the vibrant indigenous culture of the Native Hawaiians, documenting their traditions, artifacts, folklore, and more. However, the most captivating parts of her narrative recount Bird's daring escapades into Hawaii's rugged wilderness—solo climbs that even native guides hesitated to attempt. She delights in crossing treacherous rivers, ascending steep ravines, and camping in remote forests amidst wild storms. These experiences test her physical limits while fueling her adventurous spirit. Through her letters, readers witness Bird's transformation from an ailing Victorian woman to a fearless horsewoman and mountaineer. Her engaging writing style transports readers into the heart of ancient Hawaii's untamed landscapes and traditional ways of life.

The Aspects of Religion in the United States of America: Published merely three years after her initial American memoir, 'The Aspects of Religion in the United States of America' dives into the religious tapestry Isabella Bird encountered during her travels in the US. It provides an extensive exploration of the major Christian denominations she encountered, shedding light on lesser-known sects and emerging faith groups. From the lively camp meetings of Methodists to the simplicity of Quaker practices and the closely-knit Mormon communities out west, Bird covers a diverse array of religious experiences in this captivating book. She actively participates in and keenly observes various religious services, dissecting doctrines, rituals, clothing, and the architectural spaces tied to different churches. Beyond formal religious practices, the book delves into broader dimensions, such as the pervasive influence of Christian morality on American laws and social norms during the country's formative years. Bird also highlights how churches championed social causes, from temperance movements to anti-slavery activism. This book serves as an anthropological exploration of Christianity's role in everyday 19th-century America through Bird's perceptive lens. It offered unprecedented insights for British readers of her time and continues to captivate modern audiences with its depth and relevance."

BOOKS BY ISABELLA LUCY BIRD

The Englishwoman in America: Written in 1856, 'The Englishwoman in America' is Isabella Bird's memoir chronicling her inaugural overseas journey to the United States and Canada at 23 years old. Lasting nearly four months, her expedition covered vast stretches of the eastern U.S. and Canada. Health improvement motivated Bird, spurred by doctors who believed travel could be therapeutic. Departing from Britain, she landed in Halifax, Nova Scotia, then ventured southward to New York, Philadelphia, and Washington D.C. Her observations, as an outsider, offer keen insights into life in America's emerging frontier towns and cities. Bird paints a vivid picture of cultural nuances—social customs, politics, material culture, and architectural landscapes. She also draws comparisons between American and British ways. Amidst her social commentary, Bird beautifully captures the raw beauty of American wilderness, showcasing landscapes like the Catskill Mountains and Niagara Falls. This initial book, launching over four decades of bold travels and subsequent publications, foretold Isabella's future renown as an explorer and captivating writer. Her travelogues became sought-after windows into distant lands, presented uniquely through a woman's perspective for Victorian audiences."

The Golden Chersonese and the Way Thither: In this book, Bird transports readers on a mesmerizing journey through the exotic and mysterious landscapes of the Malay Peninsula. Written with the allure of an explorer's journal, this book recounts Bird's intrepid travels through the vibrant and enigmatic region. Setting out on her exploration, Bird takes readers along ancient trade routes and uncharted paths, immersing herself in the diverse cultures and breathtaking landscapes of the Malay Peninsula. From bustling ports to remote villages, she captures the essence of the people and places she encounters. Bird's narrative unfolds as a vivid tapestry of the peninsula's history, traditions, and natural wonders. She explores the lush jungles, encountering fascinating flora and fauna, and navigates through the dynamic tapestry of

Malay society, observing the customs and rituals that shape its identity. Throughout her journey, Bird's keen observations and evocative prose offer readers a glimpse into the region's rich past and its present-day allure. 'The Golden Chersonese and the Way Thither' serves as an invaluable window into the captivating allure of the Malay Peninsula, weaving together history, adventure, and cultural immersion in a way that captivates the imagination.

The Hawaiian Archipelago: In this 1875 travel memoir, Isabella Bird recounts her captivating journey through the enchanting Hawaiian Islands in 1873 at the age of 41. The narrative focuses on her daring exploration, particularly her challenging treks up two of the world's tallest volcanoes located on the Big Island: Mauna Loa and Mauna Kea. Starting her journey on Oahu, Bird explores the bustling city of Honolulu and the verdant windward valleys before setting sail for Hawaii's Big Island. There, she is mesmerized by the ever-changing volcanic landscapes shaped by the continuous eruptions of Mauna Loa and Kilauea over the years. Driven by a quest for adventure, Bird embarks on a courageous 13-hour ascent of Mauna Kea, scaling its 14,000-foot icy summit without guides. The solitude and breathtaking views fuel her spirit. Buoyed by this accomplishment, she ventures to conquer Mauna Loa, the largest volcano on Earth. Camping along the way, she reaches the summit ridge at nearly 13,700 feet, gazing over the vast crater Mokuaweoweo. Bird's journey is marked by overcoming steep trails, high altitudes, freezing nights without proper shelter, and physical exhaustion—defying societal expectations for a supposedly delicate Victorian woman. Her poetic descriptions of Hawaii's volcanoes helped introduce their magnificence to the Western world. The allure of the landscape deeply captivated Bird, drawing her back to the islands in later years whenever she yearned for tropical adventures.

The Yangtze Valley and Beyond: Published when Bird was 68, this book recounts her extensive travels through China, Japan, and Korea during the 1890s. The highlight of her journey involves navigating the

Yangtze River Valley aboard a houseboat. This later addition to Bird's collection primarily focuses on her exploration of China, covering both its inland regions and eastern coastline. Traveling along the Yangtze River, Asia's longest river, Bird observes vibrant river commerce that predates Western trade by centuries. She delves into cities like Nanjing and Wuhan, shedding light on China's interior, going beyond the well-known Treaty Ports. Over the following years, Bird ventures northward, exploring Beijing to witness remnants of Imperial dynasties and iconic sites such as the Great Wall. Continuing her offbeat path, she travels through Manchuria by rail to Harbin, witnessing the enduring impacts of Russian imperialism on the northern frontiers. Crossing the Yellow Sea by ship, Bird extends her voyage through Korea and Japan, observing the significant modernization reshaping East Asian nations at the turn of the 20th century. She passes through places like Port Arthur before returning to Scotland, where she compiled her detailed notes into a memoir for eager readers.

Unbeaten Tracks in Japan: This book chronicles Bird's 1878 journey through Japan, focusing on its remote northern and central areas seldom explored by foreigners. She adopts an unconventional writing style, offering a unique narrative of her off-the-beaten-path adventures. Rather than sticking to the bustling cities, Bird ventures deep into Japan's countryside and less-traveled regions. She discovers feudal villages largely untouched by Western influence, witnessing a fascinating blend of ancient customs and the modernization of the Meiji era. A highlight of her expedition is her trek to Hokkaido, Japan's northernmost main island, where she encounters the indigenous Ainu people. She's captivated by their culture while noting the encroaching imperialist influences threatening their traditional way of life. Throughout her travels, Bird vividly portrays picturesque landscapes—mountains, lakes, and rural scenes populated by farmers and artisans harmonizing with nature. With a mix of literary references, historical insights, and poetic language, Bird weaves an eccentric travel saga that mirrors the mystical realm she explored. 'Unbeaten Tracks in Japan' presented the charms of old Japanese culture to Western readers through a distinctive feminine perspective."

www.ingramcontent.com/pod-product-compliance
Lightning Source LLC
Chambersburg PA
CBHW070046080526
44586CB00013B/926